What is happening?

People are getting angry. Ou   Our jobs are at risk. Our savings a   our homes. We fear we won't hav   We're losing confidence in the ability   hools to educate our children and our   protect us. Our public services keep getting cut while our taxes go up.

Yet a small group of politicians, bureaucrats and bankers seem magically immune to the realities that the rest of us wake up to each morning. They take more and more of our money in salaries, bonuses, expenses and pensions. They are constantly rewarded for failure. And they shamelessly spin and lie in order to justify their plundering and pillaging of our hard-earned money.

In *Fleeced!* we expose how we have all become the dupes of the lazy, the grasping, the ambitious and the incompetent who have increasingly taken control of our lives. And we show why and how we need to fight back against our new arrogant, self-serving masters if we are ever to stop the rapid decline in our society and once again start to improve our own and our children's lives.

David Craig has spent most of his career working for some of the world's best and worst management consultancies. He is the author of the controversial bestsellers *Rip-Off! The Scandalous Inside Story of the Consulting Money Machine*, *Plundering the Public Sector* and *Squandered: How Gordon Brown is Wasting Over One Trillion Pounds of Our Money* which won the Hammond Whiteley journalism award. Most recently, he co-wrote *The Great European Rip-Off* with Matthew Elliott.

Matthew Elliott is co-founder and chief executive of the TaxPayers' Alliance, the UK's most high-profile campaign group. He is a Fellow of the Royal Society of Arts and sits on the Advisory Committee of the New Culture Forum. He wrote *The Bumper Book of Government Waste*.

FLEECED!

How we've been betrayed by the politicians,
bureaucrats and bankers . . . and how
much they've cost us

David Craig and Matthew Elliott

Constable • London

Constable & Robinson Ltd
3 The Lanchesters
162 Fulham Palace Road
London W6 9ER
www.constablerobinson.com

First published in the UK by Constable,
an imprint of Constable & Robinson Ltd

A copy of the British Library Cataloguing in Publication Data
is available from the British Library

ISBN: 978-1-84901-2-867

Printed and bound in the EU

CONTENTS

INTRODUCTION: WHY WORRY?

- Under New Labour over £3 trillion of our money has been taken from our pockets

- About half went in an uncontrolled splurge of public spending in the 'boom' and the other half seems to have evaporated in the 'bust'

- That's around £50,000 for every person in Britain

- The money has been squandered by self-serving politicians, wasted by incompetent bureaucrats or destroyed by out-of-control bankers

- Our taxes go up, but our public services decline

- We work ever harder, but our jobs are less secure

- We try to put money aside, but our savings earn almost no interest

- We save for retirement, but our pensions have been savaged

- It will take at least 10 to 20 years for us to pay off all the debts that we have been saddled with by the people in power

- While most of us have become poorer, politicians, bureaucrats and bankers have been busily feathering their own nests with our money

- If we don't fight back, the new ruling elite will continue to take, steal and waste our money and impoverish the country for generations to come

PART I

MAKING US POORER

CHAPTER I

WHERE HAS OUR £3 TRILLION GONE?

BILLIONS, TRILLIONS, GAZILLIONS AND SQUILLIONS

When many of us were children, we played the game where we tried to outdo each other by trying to think of the biggest possible number imaginable, as in 'my dad earns billions and trillions and gazillions and squillions more than your dad, so there', followed by sticking our tongues out. What most of us didn't realize back in our carefree childhood innocence was that when we grew up, the billions and trillions would become real numbers, and real financial problems, rather than just part of a childhood game. When the first *Bumper Book of Government Waste* was published, we revealed that the government had wasted around £82 billion in the year 2005–6. By the time of the second *Bumper Book* this had gone up to £101 billion for 2006–7. With 2008's *Squandered* we looked back over a decade of New Labour's spending of our money and found that probably more than £1 trillion had been wasted. In their own small way these books broke new ground. After all, back then, just over a year ago, many people did not even know what a 'trillion' was. Some of us might have been hard-pushed to say with complete certainty how many zeros there were in a billion. Since then, of course, the economic collapse, ensuing bank bailouts and our government's borrowing binge have made us all depressingly familiar with the idea of billions and trillions.

According to our calculations, at least £3 trillion – that's £3,000,000,000,000 – of our national wealth may have magically disappeared in the 12.5 years since the current government was first elected in 1997. It's difficult to imagine what £3 trillion looks like. If you were to pile it up in £10 notes, you'd have a stack that was bigger than the House of Commons and Big Ben (see Figure 1), provided that our thieving MPs didn't steal most of the money before you had finished. Our working population of about 30 million people would each have to save almost £5,000 a year for 20 years to put this £3 trillion back in the bank. £3 trillion is around £50,000 for every man, woman and child in the country.

Figure I Visualizing £3 trillion

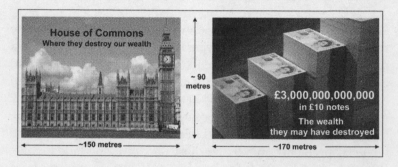

About £1.5 trillion of our cash went on a rush of profligate government spending, fuelled by the boom, and around another £1.5 trillion seems to have mysteriously vanished in the bust. So, when billions and trillions are mentioned by the media and various financial experts, they unfortunately usually refer to what we as a nation have lost or owe rather than anything that we might ever own or earn.

BRITAIN'S BOOMING

Until the recent financial collapse, things were looking pretty rosy for the British economy. Since the recession of 1992, Britain had experienced 15 years of uninterrupted economic growth with low inflation, falling unemployment and rising living standards – what many economists called a 'Goldilocks economy' where growth is believed to be neither too 'hot' (i.e. too fast) or too 'cold' (too slow), but just right. Incredible as it may seem now, Gordon Brown even had a reputation for effective economic management. There was a time when people could keep a straight face when showering Brown with compliments like Tony Blair's in 2007 as he prepared to hand over the keys to 10 Downing Street: 'He is an extraordinary and rare talent and it's a tremendous thing if it's put at the service of the nation as it now can be. He has shown, as perhaps the most successful Chancellor in our country's history, that he's got the strength and the experience and the judgment to make a great Prime Minister.'[1]

More wealth meant higher tax revenues. Quite properly living up to its 1997 election manifesto promises, the government chose to plough much of its increasing tax-take into providing more money for public services like health, education, policing, social services and so on. By the end of the 2009–10 financial year, New Labour will have spent almost £1.7 trillion more in cash terms (about £1.35 trillion when adjusted for inflation) than would have been spent had Gordon Brown and his colleagues kept public spending at the levels inherited from the previous administration (see Figure 2).

Figure 2 Government spending has more than doubled under New Labour

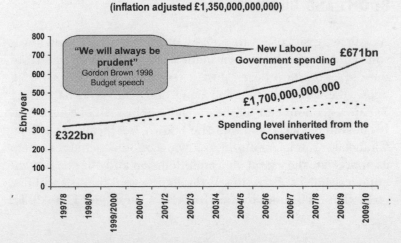

£1,700,000,000,000 more since 1997
(inflation adjusted £1,350,000,000,000)

"We will always be prudent"
Gordon Brown 1998
Budget speech

New Labour
Government spending   £671bn

£1,700,000,000,000

Spending level inherited from the
Conservatives

£322bn

Finance Initiative (PFI) projects and other schemes which the government has kept off its balance sheet through various creative accounting techniques, you're almost up to £2 trillion in cash terms or £1.5 trillion after taking inflation into account.[2] Moreover, now that public spending has shot up to new stratospheric heights, even if we got a government that could trim it by 5 or 10 per cent, it would take years and maybe even decades to bring it back under control. So going forward, we can expect a few trillion more to disappear into New Labour's voracious new public sector.

If you're one of Britain's growing army of over 6 million public-sector workers, you might welcome Figure 2 with joy – the rise in spending is the basis for probably the biggest boom in public-sector employment, rising wages, lavish expenses and inflation-protected pensions in British history. However, if you're one of the rapidly decreasing number of people in the private sector then your feelings may not be quite so positive, as a massive increase in your taxes for the last 12 years and probably for the next 20 to 30 years will be needed to pay for our government's unprecedented generosity to itself, its friends and its own employees.

BOOMS AND BUBBLES

As late as April 2007, our then chancellor Gordon Brown was still repeating his well-worn mantra: 'We will never return to the old boom and bust.'[3] Just a few months later, as we all know, there was a deafening bang and you could hardly see Britain's economy for all the crashing debris, smoke and dust. It's not fair to kick a man while he's down, but recalling our Iron Chancellor's judgements on his own economic genius can help us appreciate the extent of his self-delusion and our consequent impoverishment. Brown used the expression 'boom and bust' more than 100 times in the House of Commons. Thankfully, and for obvious reasons, he tends not to use it anymore. But although Brown will go down in history as the man who said he had abolished Tory boom and bust, he was actually not the only person to make this bold and unlikely claim (see Figure 3).

Figure 3 The end of Tory boom and bust?

Tony Blair "*I want this to be the New Labour Government that ended Tory boom and bust forever*"	**1997**	Gordon Brown "*I am satisfied that the new monetary policy will prevent a return to the cycle of boom and bust*"
Tony Blair "*We have the best chance of ending boom and bust in years*"	**1999**	Ruth Kelly "*The Government have rejected the boom and bust of the Conservative party*"
Alistair Darling "*We have a healthy and stable economy and an end to the boom and bust that characterised the Tory years*"	**2000**	Alan Johnson "*The Government's first priority was to put an end to the damaging cycle of boom and bust*"
Ruth Kelly "*We must avoid a return to the days of boom and bust that manufacturers had to endure under the Conservatives*"	**2002-4**	Yvette Cooper "*We know that they want to turn the clock back, but it would be foolish to turn it back to a policy of boom and bust*"
Douglas Alexander "*We now have the highest level of employment in decades contrary to the position in the boom-bust years of the Conservatives*"	**2005-6**	John Prescott "*Labour economic stability has replaced Tory boom and bust*"
Gordon Brown "*We will not return to the old boom and bust*"	**2007**	Alistair Darling "*Outstanding performance of the economy under this Government in contrast to the boom and bust of the previous Government*"

One of the many other claims that our chancellor turned prime minister made, most of which have subsequently turned out to owe more to fantasy than financial fact, was that he had rescued the economy from the malevolent clutches of the previous, economically incompetent Tory administration: 'because we inherited an economy that was not only in danger of over-heating but where tackling fundamental long-term challenges ... had been neglected for too long'.[4] In reality, Britain had experienced five years of continuous economic growth since the 1992 recession by the time Brown moved into the Treasury in May 1997. So the chancellor was merely mounting a horse that was already racing ahead of the field rather than, as he and his docile Treasury would have us believe, being given a lame no-hoper and courageously spurring it on to a magnificent victory against the background of the thunderous cheers of the crowd's adulation.

During the first ten years' of Brown's stewardship, on paper our national wealth apparently more than doubled from around £3.2 trillion in 1997 to about £7 trillion by 2007. This would count as an incredible achievement for this government and its chancellor if this growth had actually been based on something solid and value-added like raised manufacturing output and increased exports. However, about £3 trillion of the increase came from rising house prices and another £1 trillion or so is due to inflation. Then there were other factors like a rise in population from virtually uncontrolled immigration and the rapid growth of the public sector which also helped create the illusion of economic growth. Once you take these out, you actually find that our real national wealth experienced a decline of close to £1 trillion during the ten years of Brown's supposed economic boom.[5] Chancellor Brown made many claims about how he had increased our wealth and how we could trust him because of his personal integrity – but then so did Bernie Madoff (see Figure 4).

Figure 4 Similar claims from Brown and Madoff

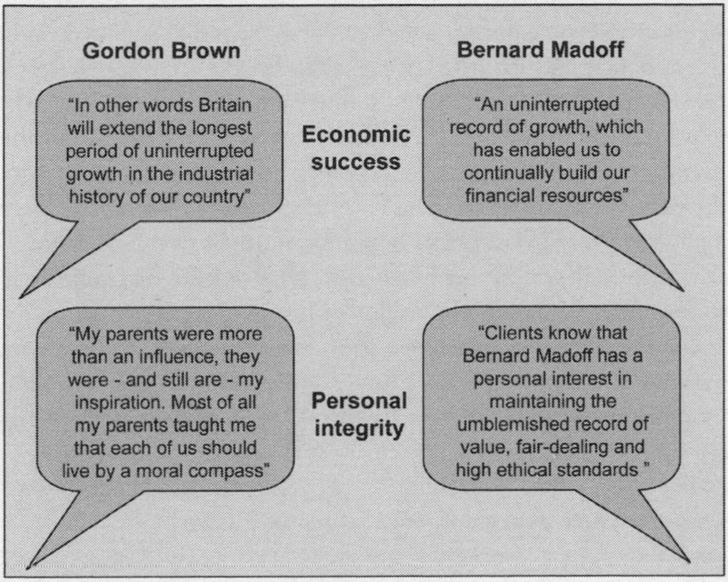

Gordon Brown

"In other words Britain will extend the longest period of uninterrupted growth in the industrial history of our country"

Bernard Madoff

"An uninterrupted record of growth, which has enabled us to continually build our financial resources"

Economic success

"My parents were more than an influence, they were - and still are - my inspiration. Most of all my parents taught me that each of us should live by a moral compass"

"Clients know that Bernard Madoff has a personal interest in maintaining the umblemished record of value, fair-dealing and high ethical standards "

Personal integrity

In a recent book about Bernard Madoff, the author started by asking the question: 'How does one guy lose $50 billion – of other people's money?'[6] *Fleeced!* will try to answer a similar question about Gordon Brown – but sadly for us the sums involved are somewhat larger than the paltry petty-cash of $50 billion which may have disappeared in Madoff's Ponzi scheme.

There were some countries like Germany, Holland, India and China which did actually create real wealth in the 1997–2007 worldwide economic boom. However, in Britain, Spain, Ireland and the USA much, if not all, the supposed growth was unfortunately illusory, based mostly on a housing-price bubble.

Although much of Britain's boom was imaginary, at least there was a huge increase in tax revenues pouring into the government's coffers. When campaigning in 1997, Brown had promised to keep spending at the level proposed by the previous Tory government for the first couple of years of his time as chancellor. Unable to splurge the increasing funds, Brown found that tax revenues exceeded spending and so he almost accidentally managed to reduce Britain's budget deficit and thus the National Debt. By his 1999 budget he was able to claim: 'As a result of sound economic management, debt interest payments next year have been cut by £2.5 billion from their previous forecast.' He seems to have forgotten that it was the previous administration's, rather than his own 'sound economic management', which had provided the cash bonanza. It might well have been this success through continuing his predecessors' policies that contributed to convincing our then chancellor of his own economic genius. By around 2000, once he was freed from the straitjacket of the previous government's financial self-control, Gordon Brown's own financial incontinence kicked in. From then on, even though tax revenues kept on rising and rising thanks to Brown's brilliance in wringing the earning classes dry, incredibly our government managed to spend more every year than it collected in tax (see Figure 5).

Figure 5 Since 2000, even as tax revenues increased,
the government spent more than it collected

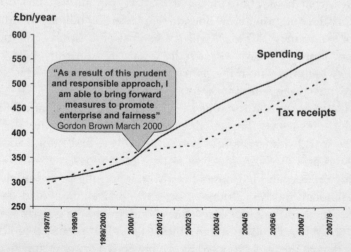

Like so many of his subjects, Chancellor Brown went on a historic spending spree. For us it was three holidays a year, Jimmy Choo shoes, flatscreen TVs, electronic gadgets and drunken nights on the town. For him it was a massive expansion in public services – spending on health shot up from £45 billion a year to over £100 billion, education jumped from £38 billion to about £80 billion and, perhaps surprisingly given that we were supposedly experiencing an economic boom, welfare benefits rose from £90 billion to close to £160 billion. Although it's hardly an original insight, we would be remiss here if we did not remind ourselves of what Charles Dickens' Mr Micawber said about what happens when people spend more than they earn: 'Annual income twenty pounds, annual expenditure nineteen nineteen and six, result happiness. Annual income twenty pounds, annual expenditure twenty pounds ought and six, result misery.'[7] Sadly for us, this well-known piece of financial wisdom applies just as much to countries as to individuals. This naturally meant that our borrowing and debt levels, having gone down for the first couple of years of New Labour, then started to climb inexorably upwards.

Brown and his Treasury liked to claim that HMS *Great Britain* was steaming happily across the calm seas of home-grown economic prosperity when, through absolutely no fault of the captain, the ship hit the iceberg of the US sub-prime economic crisis and then went plunging into the murky depths of a sea of apparently bottomless debt with just enough room in the lifeboats for the passengers with first-class tickets: the politicians, bureaucrats and bankers. In December 2007 Brown told us: 'The global credit problem that started in America is now the most immediate challenge for every economy.'[8] And he kept on repeating the message that he and the government were in no way responsible for anything ever: 'People are worried about the impact of what is a global credit crunch, that people understand started in America and is impacting on Britain.'[9] However, the truth was that due to this government's uncontrolled profligacy, HMS *Great Britain* was already holed below the economic waterline and leaking money rather badly by the time the US sub-prime iceberg came into view. We would eventually have sunk anyway, even in the unlikely event of our captain managing to avoid the iceberg.

BRITAIN'S BUST

We may not have had the boom, but we certainly got the bust. At the moment it's not possible to say exactly how much of our wealth has been destroyed since the crash hit us, but there are indications that it's a fair bit. The value of UK shares, for example, has fallen by around £474 billion since 1997 – this will seriously affect anyone with savings in stocks, unit trusts or a pension fund.

Partly as a result of the government's large expansion of the public sector and the eye-watering pay rises it has given to public-sector managers, and partly due to its cowardice in failing to tackle the public-sector pensions time-bomb, the estimated future costs of public-sector pensions have risen from around £360 billion in 1997 to well over £880 billion today (some estimates put the costs as high as £1.2 trillion). So that's at least another £520 billion we're going to have to find from somewhere.

Then we can add on the cost of the bank bailout. Cautious estimates suggest that of the total £1.227 trillion made available to the banks, taxpayers will lose at least £200 billion. The government and its Treasury will claim that we taxpayers are not really liable for all the banks' losses because each bank will have to bear part of their losses themselves and they will pay interest charges and other fees to the government as part of the taxpayer-funded rescue scheme to help them out of their self-inflicted difficulties. However, there is only one place the banks can go to get the money to pay off their losses, fees and everything else. That place is their customers: us. So, whether the banks siphon off our money directly in the form of massive government handouts or indirectly from charging us more for services and loans and paying us less interest on savings, we will always be the ones to foot the bill for the hundreds of billions in

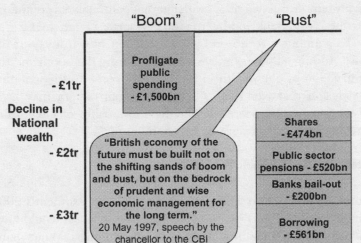

Figure 6 The greatest destruction of national wealth in British history?

toxic loans, credit default swaps, collateral debt obligations and whatever other financial schemes that the short-term, bonus-hungry bankers were only too happy to mistake for money.

However, perhaps the most obvious decimation of our wealth has come from the explosion in government borrowing to make up for the collapse in tax revenues due to the recession. In his last five-year projection as chancellor, Gordon Brown predicted total government borrowing of a mere £142 billion, give or take a few billion. In his successor Alistair Darling's latest far from reliable forecast, borrowing over five years looks like being at least £703 billion. And this is assuming a rapid return to sustained growth of over 3 per cent by 2011, which is far from certain. So the rise in borrowing to £703 billion gives us another £561 billion above Brown's original projections that we're going to have to cough up, long after the main members of the government that got us into this mess have retired to the lavishly expensed comfort of the Lords, to well-paid employment with the banks they saved with our cash or to highly remunerated positions with international financial institutions like the World Bank and International Monetary Fund (IMF).

This amounts to around £1.755 trillion blown away in the bust. Adding all the excessive spending during the boom and the destruction of our wealth in the bust, we come to the irritating conclusion that well over £3 trillion of our wealth may have mysteriously disappeared under the stewardship of Chancellor Brown and his successor (see Figure 6).

THE BUDGET THAT WASN'T

Some commentators and analysts took the government's 2009 budget seriously and tried to calculate what effect it would have on the country's finances and economic prospects. What many experts seem to have failed to understand was that April 2009's exercise in financial futility was not intended to be a budget as we know it. The government was well aware that the country's finances were shot to pieces. It also knew that the only way of beginning to balance the books was by cutting public spending. But that posed a thorny political problem. The government wanted to go into the next election lambasting the Tories as brutal butchers intent on decimating public spending so that children could not go to school, the sick would lie untended in the streets and the elderly would die in poverty and starvation. Therefore, the government could not be seen to be making the slightest change to its own bloated spending plans. Instead, the prime minister and his chancellor made a few populist but economically costly gestures such as raising tax and cutting allowances for higher earners. The Treasury knew that these changes would raise little or no money. Those earning over £150,000 are best placed to avoid any attempts by Her Majesty's Revenue and Customs (HMRC) to take their cash. And even if the wealthy were ready to pay more, the new tax changes would only raise about £5 billion to £7 billion extra per year. That's pretty small beer compared with the government's projected borrowing of £175 billion in 2009–10.

As for the chancellor's projected figures for the British economy that there would be a 3.5 per cent contraction in 2009 and 1.25 per cent growth in 2010, these were contradicted by an IMF report which foresaw two years of economic decline, 4.1 per cent in 2009 and a further 0.4 per cent in 2010. Then a few days after the budget, the Office for National Statistics issued figures showing that the economy had shrunk by 1.9 per cent in the first quarter of 2009 compared with the chancellor's forecast of about 1.6 per cent. But in some ways it seemed that the government hardly cared and its only purpose was self-preservation – to hold on to the privileges and perks of power for as long as possible. Our leaders appeared to have given up on the economy and were just trying to tread water, pocketing their generous salaries and huge expenses while far beneath them HMS *Great Britain* sank, gurgling and spluttering, further down into the dark and dismal depths of an ocean of debt.

How did things get to be this awful?

CHAPTER 2

MONEY MAKES THE WORLD GO ROUND

FINANCE RULES, OK?

Over the last few years there has been an extraordinary rise in global capital flows and in the amount of money tied up in various ever-more complex financial instruments. This mass of money and things that are meant to look like money is now many times greater than the economies of the major developed countries and absolutely dwarf the economies of smaller countries. For example, the total value of the US economy (its GDP) is about $14 trillion, with the 27 EU countries combined at around $15 trillion. Economically powerful countries like Japan, Germany and France all have GDPs somewhere in the $2.5 trillion to $5 trillion range. The UK's GDP is about $2.2 trillion (£1.4 trillion). While most countries' GDPs have risen over the last 10 to 15 years, this increase is insignificant compared with the explosive growth in financial instruments.

There are many indicators showing the massive rise in the power of international finance and the corresponding weakening in individual countries' abilities to be masters of their own destinies. One is the volume of money that is exchanged each day through the Bank for International Settlements. This has risen from around $4 trillion a week in 1992 to over $16 trillion a week in 2008. The value of the positions held by banks in the international market also shot up from about $5.8 trillion in 1992 to over $32 trillion in 2008. Another shock/horror figure is the massive increase in financial products. For example, credit default swaps, which are essentially insurance policies taken out against risky loans, went from about $8 trillion in 2004, close to four times the UK's GDP, to almost $60 trillion by the highest point of 2007, more than 25 times the UK's GDP (see Figure 1).

Figure I Financial activity increased massively compared with economic activity

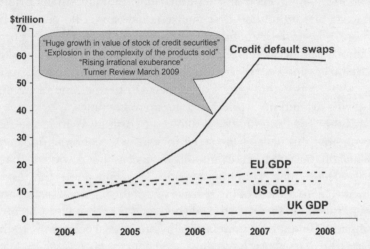

In 2006, while the explosion in financial products was reaching its peak, the International Monetary Fund thought that this new phenomenon reduced the risk of financial instability. In its inappropriately named *Global Financial Stability Report*, it wrote: 'The dispersion of credit risk by banks to a broader and more diverse set of investors, rather than warehousing such risk on their balance sheets, has helped make the banking and overall financial system more resilient.' No doubt whoever came up with that theory got a bonus and a promotion. However, after the whole wobbly house of cards came crashing down, a recent British government report, the *Turner Review*, identified the extent to which the financial markets had become dislocated from the 'real economy': 'The evolution of the securitised credit model was accompanied by a remarkable growth in the relative size of wholesale financial services within the overall economy, with activities internal to the banking system growing far more rapidly than end services to the real economy.'[1]

Compared with this huge and ever-increasing sea of cash and financial instruments sloshing around the world, individual countries' total economic outputs look pitifully small. Britain had its first intimation that international capital flows could be more powerful than individual countries when George Soros famously made $1 billion in a single day when he contributed to Britain crashing out of the European Exchange Rate Mechanism in 1992. Since those days of innocence, the volume of money moving around the world has gone up many times.

If the growth in finance is allowed to drift away from the real economy, this can set the stage for massive economic upheaval when financial markets eventually deflate, as they always do, back to reflect actual economic activity. To again quote the *Turner Review*: 'This growth of the relative size of the financial sector, and in particular of securitised credit activities, increased the potential impact of financial system instability on the real economy.' In the last 100 years there have only been four occasions when stock markets lost over half of their value. The first was during the 1929–31 crash. Then 42 years went by until the next major fall in 1973–4 after the oil price hike. Twenty-six years later there was the 2000–2002 dotcom bubble bursting and then just five years went by before the 2007–9 stock market turmoil. This means that three of the four largest market upheavals have occurred in the last 35 years.

POLITICIANS IN MY POCKET?

Faced with the increasing power of the financial markets, governments need to understand the fundamental changes that are taking place and to produce policies that bring the greatest benefit to their people. But the massive and magically increasing amounts of money flowing around, some of which was made available to politicians who looked leniently upon the goings-on in the world of finance, put our political and bureaucratic leaders in a difficult position and tested their allegiance to those who elected them. In the US, each presidential election seemed to require ever more money. Bill Clinton only raised a modest $50.1 million for his 1992 campaign. His second victory needed $55.8 million. George W. Bush first entered the White House after raising $95.6 million. Second time round, this had gone up to $269.6 million. And Barack Obama managed to draw in almost $750 million in his successful 2008 bid for power. While one innovation of President Obama's campaign was the way he attracted financial support from ordinary voters rather than just a few powerful vested interests, one can only assume that those who made the larger contributions to presidential candidates were expecting something more for their cash than just the warm feeling of having helped someone else into power.

In the 1997 election in Britain, the two major parties both spent more than twice as much as had been used in any previous election. The introduction of the Political Parties, Elections and Referendums Act of 2000 ended the financial 'arms race' by putting a cap on political spending. However, this limit did not reduce political parties' thirst for money. While Labour's local spending dropped from about £37 million in the 1966–70 electoral cycle to just £28 million in the 2001–5 cycle, its central office's spending shot up by a factor of five from £23 million to £118 million over the same period.

Since coming to power in 1997 our government seems to have worked hard to befriend the rich and the powerful, particularly in the City of London. Honours have been given to at least 23 bankers including, of course, the Royal Bank of Scotland's Sir Fred Goodwin, otherwise known as Sir Fred the Shred (see Figure 2).

Figure 2 Labour's bankroll of honour

Knighthoods		Life peerages	
James Crosby	HBOS	Lord Turner	Merrill Lynch
George Mathewson	RBS	Shriti Vadera	UBS
Keith Whitson	HSBC	Lord Leitch	Lloyds TSB
Peter Burt	HBOS	Lord Myners	NM Rothschild
Philip Hampton	Lloyds TSB	Lord Acton	Coutts
John Bond	HSBC	Baroness Cohen	Charterhouse
Fred Goodwin	RBS	Lord Mervyn Davies	Standard Chartered
CBE		**OBE**	
Helen Weir	Lloyds TSB	John White	RBS
Christopher Lendrum	Barclays	Lindsay Tomlinson	Barclays
Susan Rice	Lloyds TSB	Dennis Licence	First Trust Bank
Michael Marks	Merrill Lynch	Michael Ellis	HBOS
Philip Williamson	Nationwide		

It probably won't have escaped many readers' notice that several of the banks listed in Figure 2 have coincidentally been very hungry recipients of taxpayer-funded bailouts. Furthermore, New Labour have brought three bankers into government as ministers and asked another 37 to work on commissions, quangos and advisory bodies. This policy of getting close to people in the City seems to have paid dividends with many City figures becoming major donors to the Labour party, making it less dependent on the trade unions for its money. At one point, just three financiers, with wealth estimated at almost £500 million between them, accounted for close to 40 per cent of donations received by the party.

WHY DID NOBODY SAY ANYTHING?

Since the crash, economists and journalists have been eagerly queuing up to share their wisdom with us by telling us that it was inevitable it would all end in tears. But as we survey the smouldering wreckage of our future economic prospects, the question many people must be asking is why almost nobody said anything at the time.

There was a similar situation before, during and after the 1929 Wall Street Crash. In 1927 the legendary John Maynard Keynes made an unfortunately ill-timed pronouncement: 'We will not have any more crashes in our time.' A year later the president of the New York Stock Exchange denied that: 'we are living in a fool's paradise and that prosperity in this country must necessarily diminish and recede in the near future.' In 1929, as stock prices started to wobble dizzily from apparent vertigo as they hit a peak, the *New York Times* reassured its anxious readers: 'There may be a recession in stock prices, but not anything in the nature of a crash' and one leading economist looked into his crystal ball and predicted: 'I expect to see the stock market a good deal higher within a few months.'

A week or so later, the crash was real, but the head of a major bank opined that there was nothing to worry about: 'This crash is not going to have much effect on business.' And of course there were crowds of market analysts telling their readers it was time to buy, buy, buy! One urged: 'This is the time to buy stocks. Many of the low prices as a result of the hysterical selling are not likely to be reached again in many years.' Another counselled: 'Good stocks are cheap at these prices.' A third derided worriers: 'Some pretty intelligent people are now buying stocks. Unless we have a panic, which no one seriously believes, stocks have hit bottom.' Meanwhile in its 1929 New Year forecast, the US Department of Labour predicted that 1930 would be 'a splendid employment year'. Within 12 months, stocks lost half their value. Within another 12 months they were down to less than a quarter of their 1929 peak, people were jumping off buildings without parachutes and mass unemployment was ravaging the country (see Figure 3).

With the latest financial meltdown, we may have witnessed a similar phenomenon of those in power being reluctant to admit what was going on. Of course, there were a few honourable exceptions. There was Vince Cable, deputy leader of the Liberal Democrats, who famously asked Gordon Brown in November 2003: 'The growth of the British economy is sustained by consumer spending

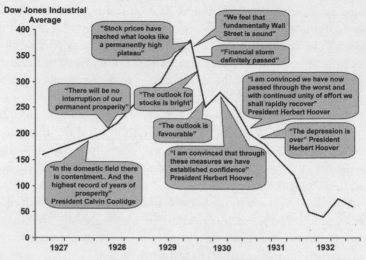

Figure 3 The Politicians, bureaucrats and bankers have
a vested interest in denying reality

pinned against record levels of personal debt, which is secured if at
all, against house prices that the Bank of England describes as well
above equilibrium level. What action will the Chancellor take on the
problem of consumer debt?' Equally famously, Chancellor Brown
replied: 'We have been right about the prospects for growth in the
British economy and the right honourable gentleman has been
wrong'. One stock analyst in October 2005 advised that: 'Investors
should sell all exposure to the American mortgage securities market',
and added, 'Some institutions have been behaving like leveraged
speculators rather than banks . . . The UK economy is heading for
a sharp shock. It just remains to be seen how bad.' And then there
were the founders of websites such as www.stock-market-crash.net
and www.housepricecrash.co.uk. They clearly predicted rough times
ahead. However, the majority of bankers, politicians and regulators
remained remarkably relaxed and uncharacteristically silent as the
economy first heated up and then boiled over (see Figure 4).

Of course, the main problem is that those with power over us
all do very nicely indeed from the economic boom and so are

Figure 4 Our leaders said it could never happen

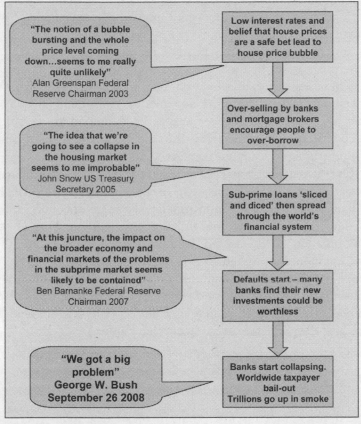

loathe to turn on the lights, switch off the music, stop the party and send everybody home.

SO, WHOSE FAULT WAS IT?

Now that we're well and truly in the financial mire, the people in power have been admirably quick to blame anybody but themselves for the mess. Bankers have accused consumers of over-borrowing, politicians of ignoring the housing-price bubble and regulators of incompetence. Politicians have made the same accusations against consumers and regulators, while falling over each other to attack the bankers for greed and reckless lending. As for the regulators, they claimed nothing was their fault and generously gave themselves record bonuses while the financial system whose health they were charged with protecting collapsed sickeningly around them. Meanwhile, we consumers have been only too willing to finger the bankers for lending to us too easily, the politicians for encouraging us to spend and the regulators for not protecting us from our own greed and recklessness.

Our current problems can be traced back to the extraordinarily benign economic conditions we have enjoyed since the mid 1990s. Falling prices due to the industrial development of countries like China helped maintain low inflation in the West. Due to the way inflation was measured, which excluded house prices, this low inflation contributed to low interest rates. All this led to a set of behaviours from four main groups – financial institutions, consumers, governments and regulators – which in themselves should not have been unmanageable, but which combined to produce the perfect financial storm (see Figure 5).

Financial markets

Faced with low interest rates many financial institutions, investors and pension funds moved into buying riskier investments in order to boost their returns in what has been called 'a ferocious search for yield'.[2] To satisfy the growing demand, ever-more complex financial products were developed. The huge fees which were generated from these products encouraged financiers to keep repackaging and selling on the same basic investments in the form of SIVs, CDOs, CDO2s and an 'alphabet soup' of other even more exotic so-called 'innovations'. But when mortgage defaults started to increase, doubts began to arise about the real value of these products and the market for many of them froze. Under pressure to 'mark to market' (to account for the value of these products at the going market rate which was then at fire-sale prices) some institutions found that they had inadequate capital. Unsure about which banks had sufficient assets, lending froze and the credit crunch kicked in (see Figure 5).

Consumers

Following the losses of the dotcom crash, many consumers turned away from the stock market and put their money into housing. It was seen as a safer bet than shares and, for some people, buying second homes and buy-to-let properties became a substitute for pension savings. More money flowing into housing caused a large increase in house prices. Seeing the value of their homes going ever upwards, people were tempted to borrow more in order to trade up to larger properties. Others decided to withdraw equity from their rising house values to spend on other goods and services. Faced by higher interest rates after housing loan 'honeymoon periods' ended, some borrowers began defaulting. This hit house prices, house-building and spending. With falling house prices and the uncertainties of a general economic slowdown, consumers cut spending, which of course led to further slowing of the economy, house price falls, job losses, more defaults and so on in a self-reinforcing downward spiral (see Figure 5).

Governments

Under pressure from activist groups, the US government had been relaxing credit rules in order to help more people get on to the housing ladder. One crucial step towards releasing credit to lower-income families was the Community Reinvestment Act. This was designed to encourage commercial banks and savings associations to meet the needs of borrowers in all segments of their communities, including low- and moderate-income neighbourhoods. Congress passed the Act in 1977 to reduce discriminatory credit practices, known as 'redlining', against low-income neighbourhoods. The Act required the appropriate federal financial supervisory agencies to encourage regulated financial institutions to meet the credit needs of the local communities in which they were chartered. The Act also stated that this lending should be 'consistent with safe and sound operation'. In the frenzy to earn commissions from selling mortgages, this part of the legislation seems to have been overlooked. Then, when the government-sponsored lending corporations known as Fannie Mae and Freddie Mac took almost half of all sub-prime lending on to their books, this encouraged even more dubious lending which further stoked the mortgage and housing market.

In Britain, too, the government was keen to encourage home-ownership. Also the British government made a fatal error of judgement when it chose the Consumer Price Index (CPI), which excludes housing costs as its key measure of inflation, rather than the Retail Price Index (RPI), which includes housing, to evaluate the economy. This choice meant that the government's view of the economy ignored the rapidly inflating house-price bubble. However, with the good times rolling, politicians were only too keen to enjoy the popularity that came with supposed economic success. When the whole thing first ground to a juddering halt and then went into rapid reverse, our leaders very publicly started shouting abuse at the bankers as if unaware of the part they themselves played in the crash (see Figure 5).

Regulators

With inflation low and the economy booming, regulators in the US and elsewhere believed that a new world of financial stability had arrived and policed the market accordingly. Unfortunately, many of their regulations, which were effective in the good times, backfired spectacularly when the going got tough. The Basel I accords, agreed by central banks across the world in 1988, gave incentives for banks to push lending off their balance sheets, making them appear better capitalized than was the case. Moreover, some of the main regulators had an excessive consumer focus – they spent too much effort regulating the sale of financial products and insufficient focus was given to the stability of the overall financial system.

Once things turned sour, the capital adequacy rules contained in the Basel II accords of 2004 inadvertently managed to turn a drama into a crisis. As the banks' assets declined in value, many were forced by capital adequacy rules to obtain more capital. This led to the dumping of assets and the hoarding of cash. Lending dried up and some banks found themselves unable to get funding. Furthermore, EU rules prevented effective, discreet intervention by the central banks. In 2007 Northern Rock's funding gap, for example, was only about £4.4 billion, but its very public problems and the subsequent run on the bank caused a £15.3 billion decrease in customer accounts. Once one bank had gone under, a crisis of confidence hit the whole banking sector, shares collapsed and we all know what happened next.

The regulators were perhaps even more complicit than the politicians and the bankers in glossing over the economic dangers lurking in the undergrowth. They remembered to turn up for work to collect their generous salaries, they attended lavish meals provided by the financial institutions they were supposed to regulate and they enjoyed all the other perks of a luxury taxpayer-funded lifestyle. They just forgot to look at what the banks were up to. And on the few occasions when they did a bit of war-gaming to stress-test the business models of some of the most vulnerable banks, they were so polite that firms such as Northern Rock and HBOS completely ignored them.

Relying on the ratings

Some people have also started to question the role played by the main credit-rating agencies in the boom and bust. Paid by the larger financial institutions to give ratings to increasingly complex

Figure 5 A simple guide to the financial crisis

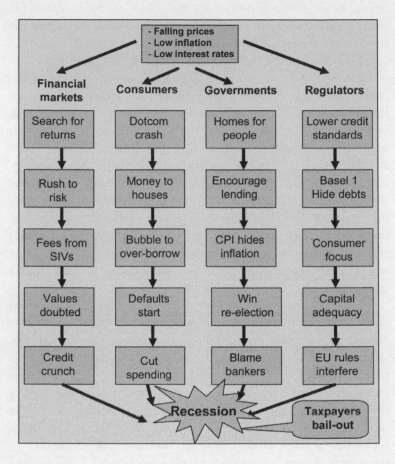

and impenetrable financial products, some rating agencies experienced massive growth in their turnover and profits. For example, the revenue at Moody's whizzed up from $602 million in 2000 to $2,259 million in 2007, while net income rushed from $158.5 million in 2000 to $701.5 million by 2007. Even after the financial meltdown, Moody's described itself as follows: 'Moody's Investors Service is among the world's most respected and widely utilized sources for credit ratings, research and risk analysis. Moody's commitment and expertise contribute to stable, transparent and integrated financial markets, protecting the integrity of credit. Moody's independence and integrity have earned us the trust of capital market participants worldwide.'[3]

Standard and Poor's also seems proud of its services: 'Standard and Poor's is the world's foremost provider of independent credit ratings, indices, risk evaluation, investment research and data. We supply investors with the independent benchmarks they need to feel more confident about their investment and financial decisions.'[4]

Given the post-2007 financial crisis, the doubts cast on the value of many financial products and the fact that some of the banks which had bought them were bailed out with billions and maybe even trillions of taxpayers' money, many commentators have wondered how products which had previously received high credit ratings could be worth so much less than originally thought.

Faced by this institutional chorus about how glorious everything was, how were ordinary people to know that all the money they had carefully entrusted in savings and pensions to long-established and supposedly respectable banks were being squandered on near worthless bits of paper passing from hand to hand in an uncontrolled merry-go-round? Meanwhile, the politicians, bureaucrats and bankers involved all became rich.

CHAPTER 3

SAVING OUR SAVINGS

A FOOL AND HIS MONEY

During the boom years there was a worrying drop in savings rates in the US and Britain as money was sucked into housing and consumer spending. In the US, rates more than halved, falling from 3.65 per cent of earnings in 1997 to just 1.78 per cent by 2008. In Britain the drop was much more dramatic, from 9.6 per cent in 1997 to a mere 2 per cent by 2008. Meanwhile, in Asia's exporting countries like Japan and China total savings shot up.

Now that interest rates have been cut to almost nothing in order to get us out of the financial crisis and spare the profligate from the results of their spendthrift ways, borrowers and spenders must be laughing. Meanwhile, those who have been more cautious and have made the effort to save rather than spend must be crying into their cups as they see the returns on their carefully accumulated nest eggs diminishing by the day and in some unfortunate cases losing their money altogether.

One probable result of the current crisis is that more people will decide to divert money from consumption to saving. However, given historically low interest rates, most of us will be looking around for ways to get better returns on our savings than are being offered by most of our diminishing number of banks and building societies. This will provide a massive business opportunity for those in financial services who are often so pantingly eager to look after our money. But as we contemplate the main savings options – shares, bonds or cash – a key question is whether, following the financial crisis, we can trust those who claim they can help us save and invest, or whether they are mostly in the business of lucratively separating fools from their money.

THE MAGIC OF THE MARKETS

Buyer beware

Amongst all the adverts for unit trusts, bonds and all sorts of other investments in the personal finance sections of our weekend newspapers, frequently there are encouraging articles with helpful charts showing the high returns that can be earned, for example, by investing in shares. In a typical recent example a journalist enticingly claimed that just £1 invested in small value stocks in 1926 would be worth over £72,000 today, only 83 years later. Moreover, according to this journalist, even if you had put your £1 in lower risk, blue-chip large value stocks you'd still walk away with more than £8,000 (see Figure 1).

Figure 1 Newspaper claims of high returns from stocks

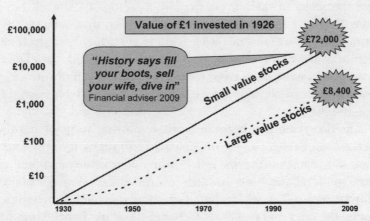

At first glance, judging by this chart, investment decisions become a complete no-brainer. Just look at the way the value of your investment seems to shoot up. Following the logic of this chart would mean that a mere £1,000 invested now would be worth about a mouth-watering £72 million in just over 80 years. You may not be around to collect all the lovely loot, but think about what this would mean to your great-grandchildren and their children. This seems better than winning the lottery and it looks a lot easier: after all, most of us would have no problem finding just one grand to stick in the stock market if it would ensure financial security for our descendants for generations to come. Moreover, even if you sold your investments before the 80-year term, the chart makes it look like you'd still walk away with a huge wedge. No wonder a financial adviser interviewed by a Sunday newspaper about the prospects for the stock market during what might be the dead-cat bounce of spring 2009 enthused: 'History says fill your boots, sell your wife, dive in.'

Before you start telling your grandchildren about the £72 million their children and their children's children will be getting once you've departed, you need to look at this wonderfully seductive chart a little more closely. The first thing to notice is that the scale on the left goes up by a factor of ten each time from £10 to £100 to £1,000, all the way up to £100,000. By crunching the scale in this way, readers get a highly misleading picture of the real rate of growth of their investment. In Figure 2, we produce the same chart for the supposedly rapidly growing investment in small value stocks, but with a normal scale from £1 to £100,000.

The first thing that becomes apparent is that your £1 hardly increases in value at all for the first 10 to 20 years. It's only after about 30 years that the line representing your investment finally starts to lift off and head upwards towards the glorious £72,000. Moreover, we haven't included the lower-growth large-value stocks, the ones that reach £8,400 after 83 years. For the first 40 or so years, the value of these hardly budges.

Figure 2 The investment would hardly grow for the first 30 to 40 years

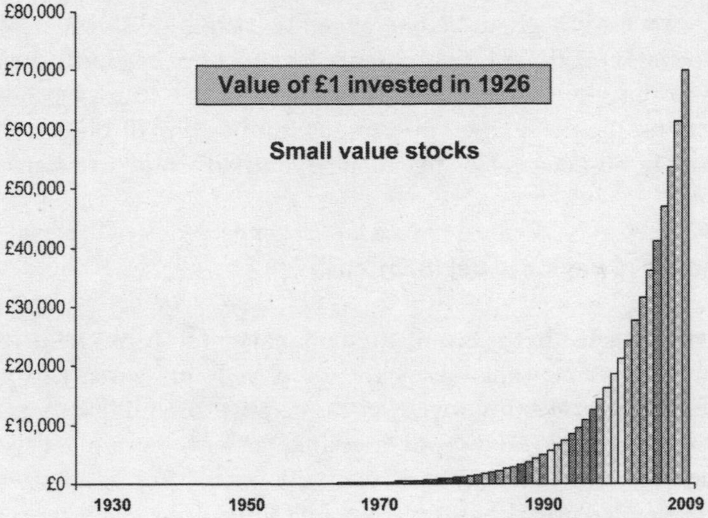

Looking at Figure 1, the chart from the newspaper, you'd be rushing to get as much money into the markets as you could. However, were you to base your investment decisions on Figure 2, you might be a bit more cautious before giving your hard-earned cash to a commission-hungry financial adviser or an ambitious unit-trust manager.

There are a couple of other things to look out for when reading the latest gushingly enthusiastic article about how stock markets will always make you money. Sometimes when showing the rise in stock market indices like the FTSE 100, the FTSE All-Share or the Dow Jones, journalists do not adjust apparently impressive growth lines to take account of the effects of inflation. Once you do this, the stellar increases can sometimes look considerably more modest. Readers can also risk being carried away by the choice of journalists' language. In one Sunday newspaper article, a fund manager used the word 'rich' five times in just a couple of quotes. For example, while warning that returns on stocks were likely to be lower in the future than in the past, he said: 'Today, as we look ahead, while we should expect to enrich ourselves from equities, the process is likely to be one of getting rich more slowly'.[1] This enticing repetition of 'rich' can mask many horrors. Surprisingly, given that the market had just fallen by over a third, he didn't mention the possibility of becoming a lot poorer through losing possibly 30 per cent of the money you had worked so hard to earn.

Shares always outperform cash

We'll stick with the same fund manager for a moment, the one who seems to like using the word 'rich' in its many forms. He also said: 'Equity investors can expect to be more than 40 per cent richer relative to investing in cash over a ten-year horizon, and twice as rich over 20 years.' For many years it's been accepted wisdom that investments in stock markets always outperform cash held in a bank. Actually, you can prove anything depending on which stock market index you use and the starting and end periods you select. But it does seem that in general, unless you are particularly unlucky when you buy and sell your investments, three-quarters of the time you will get considerably better returns from having invested in shares rather than just leaving your money in a bank.

It is worth remembering though that quite a lot of people are unlucky. There have been some periods when falls in stock prices have wiped out any potential gains and it has taken decades for investors to get their money back. The 1929–31 drop was not recovered until 1949, 20 years later. However, more encouragingly the 1973–4 collapse of 73 per cent took only eight years to recover and 1987's 33 per cent drop took just two years. But Japanese stock values have still not yet reached even half the level they achieved in 1989. This is something the experts in the Sunday supplements tend not to mention when they periodically claim that the Far East is the hot new place to put your money.

On the other hand, if you happen to buy just at the start of a bull market, when prices are low compared with the long-term trend, you can make a reasonable amount of money.

If we take UK equities in the 46 years since the start of the FTSE All-Share Index in 1963, these have delivered a nominal return of an average of 11.8 per cent a year. Once you knock off inflation of 6.2 per cent a year, this leaves you with a quite healthy 5.6 per cent return per year.[2] If you had just left your money in cash for the same period, you would have got an 8.5 per cent a year return. Take away inflation and this leaves you with a real annual return of 2.3 per cent. So the benefit of holding shares rather than cash equates to around 3.3 per cent a year. Clearly over a longer period this can amount to quite a difference to the eventual value of your savings. However, if you'd buried money in your garden rather than investing in shares just after this government came to power, you'd have been better off by about 14 per cent, provided you remembered where you'd hidden your cash, and over 30 per cent richer if you'd just left it in a bank.

Leaking pipes and disappearing money

Even if stock market investments do mostly outperform cash, it is only worth investing if you can ensure that you personally are the one who pockets most of the benefits from rising share prices and companies' annual dividend payments. Unfortunately for many investors, much of the value from their forays into stock markets leaks out to other players, leaving them with little to show for their efforts. There are many reasons why value leaks out. These include punters being encouraged into buying at the wrong time; commissions and fees eating up unexpectedly large amounts of people's investments; investors being sold inappropriate products; and market insiders taking the gains from inflating rising markets and then again through shorting falling markets (see Figure 3).

Here we will just quickly look at a few examples of how

Figure 3 Many investors find the value of gains leaks away

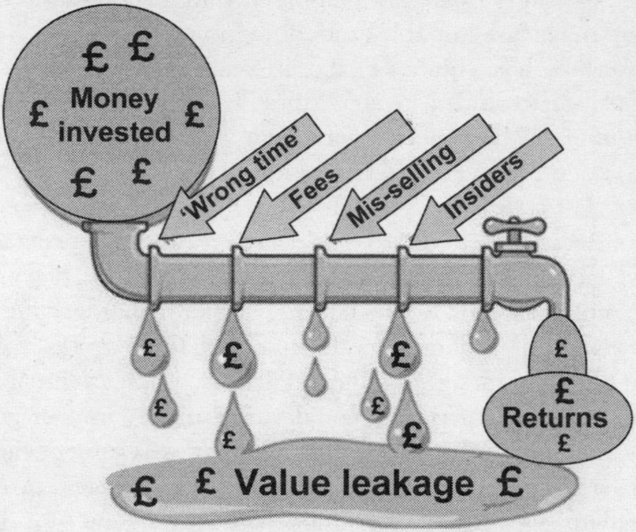

ordinary investors can lose out on their potential stock market investment earnings.

Buy buy baby, baby buy buy

Common sense would say that if a trader or financial adviser was certain a share was going to rise, then they would borrow millions from their bank, buy tons of shares and then retire in luxury, perhaps to a multi-million pound villa in the south of France, near to where Sir Fred Goodwin of the bailed-out Royal Bank of Scotland was recently sighted enjoying his retirement bliss. On the other hand, if a stockbroker or bank investment manager hadn't much of a clue about whether stock values would rise, fall or flatline from here to eternity, but relied on their commissions to make a reasonable living, then they would be pushing you to invest, whatever the market conditions. In fact, listening to most investment experts, it always seems to be the right time to buy stocks (see Figure 4).

Figure 4 It always seems to be the 'right time' to buy stocks

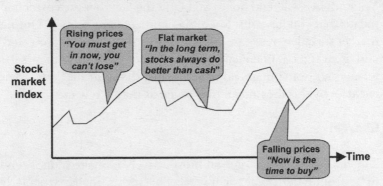

If the market is shooting up, then your adviser will encourage you to join the rush into shares. If stock prices are stagnant, you'll be constantly reassured that in the longer term stocks always outperform cash. And if the market is crashing, you'll be told that prices are cheap according to historical levels and so you'd be stupidly sacrificing your own and your family's future financial well-being if you didn't invest. At the end of the 2008 stock market rout, one analyst said: 'Prospective returns from equities are at the most attractive levels seen for some 20 years in the US and over 25 years in Europe and the UK,' while another warned: 'If you wait for things to get better you'll miss the rally.'[3] Yet experience from the Great Depression indicates that there may be a major fall, followed by a dead-cat bounce (also called a 'suckers rally' or a 'fools rally') and then a further collapse. Perhaps the experts who are constantly encouraging us to jump back into the market really are doing this in order to help their fellow citizens become gloriously rich. Or perhaps their motives are not totally disinterested.

Investment advisers have a wonderful vocabulary to tempt us to give them our money. When the market rises, financial experts are usually keen to talk up the gains to be made and we hear all about 'high yields' and 'double-digit returns'. When prices plummet, we are told this is a 'correction'. This suggests that it is a good thing for prices to be at a supposedly 'correct' level. Your adviser will tend not to highlight the fact that the correction means that you have just lost a big chunk of your money. During market turbulence we are sold all kinds of 'low risk', 'protected' and 'guaranteed' financial products. When discussing their sales techniques, some financial advisers talk about 'grinf**king' their clients – by this they mean they smile as they screw us.

Charge!

The management charges on most actively managed funds tend to be around the 1.5 per cent level. This seems small, particularly if you're convinced you'll be getting returns of 5 to 6 per cent a year. But even if your management fees are modest, once you take account of trading, legal and auditor fees, you can find yourself paying over 3 per cent in what is called the 'total expense ratio' (TER). If you're expecting the real return on shares, which will always carry some risk, to be 3.3 per cent greater than cash, which is what the FTSE has delivered over the last 46 years, a TER of 2 to 2.5 per cent is going to make quite a hole in the benefits you expect by preferring stocks.

Another thing to consider is that seemingly modest charges can soon add up to large amounts of money after a few years. If you have £100,000 invested, you might be paying out £2,500 a year in charges – a not totally insignificant amount of money. And 2.5 per cent a year for ten years suddenly turns into a much healthier (for the fund manager) 25 per cent: £25,000 on a £100,000 investment. Even if your investment does go up by the long-term average of 3.3 per cent a year above what you would get for cash, that's quite a price to pay for being an infinitesimal part of a multi-million pound unit trust fund. Plus, of course, you may have a bid-to-offer gap of around 5 per cent, which further reduces your part of any potential gains. And it's you, not the fund manager, who is taking all the risk.

The traditional model of entrusting money to a fund manager who could pick winning stocks came under attack in the 1970s. Many studies, of which two of the most influential were *Challenge to Judgement* and *The Loser's Game*, suggested that the majority of fund managers underperform the overall market average.[4] In most years just over half of all so-called 'actively managed' funds outperform the market, with about 45 per cent underperforming it. However, in *The Loser's Game* it was reported that over the previous decade 85 per cent of all institutional investors who tried to beat the stock market underperformed the S&P 500 index.

One explanation that has been given for this failure of professionals to beat the market is called the 'efficient market hypothesis' (EMH). This proposes that, with tens of thousands of fund managers and stock analysts and millions of investors constantly searching for securities that may outperform the market, the competition is so effective that any new information about the fortunes of an individual company will rapidly be incorporated into stock prices. Moreover, the advent of computerized market monitoring has probably hugely reduced the chances of someone consistently and repeatedly finding lots of hidden diamonds that nobody else has noticed, as any buying activity or movement in a stock price will almost immediately be picked up by the other market players. There will be occasions when a stock picker can achieve a superior return, but studies suggest that the excess return will seldom exceed the costs of winning it (including salaries, information costs and trading costs). Those few people who have consistently outperformed the markets tend to be those who have a better understanding of macro-economic trends, and so can predict major rises and falls in certain sectors such as technology, natural resources or banking, rather than managers who spend their time hunting for elusive individual bargains.

These studies led to the creation of index-tracker funds. The first was launched in the US in 1976, a year after *The Loser's Game* appeared. These have hugely increased in popularity since the early 1990s. By creating an index fund that mirrors the whole market, the inefficiencies and costs of paying experts to select supposedly winning stocks are avoided. Index funds which just track the market only charge around 0.3 per cent. One calculation which helps illustrate the amounts you are paying for active management, compared with just dumping your cash in an index tracker, goes as follows: if you pay your full annual ISA allowance of £7,200 into a cheap tracker fund for 30 years, you would end up with about £470,000, assuming 5 per cent a year growth. Put the same money into a typical managed fund and you'll have just over £380,000. So you'll have lost almost £90,000 paying for the active management. Even a good fund manager is going to have his or her work cut out achieving sufficiently superior returns year after year to cover the £90,000 that you could potentially miss out on in return for them providing their fund management expertise. Professionally managed funds can outperform the market if there is a clear and dramatic trend, for example a collapse in the value of banking or commodities shares. In this case, a fund manager can get your money out of the worst shares, whereas a tracker must automatically keep a broad spread of shares, including those sectors which are falling.

A recent newspaper article warned savers: 'The already exorbitant costs of looking after your investments is still rising.'[5] In general, when your bank or independent financial adviser says 'charge', you are advised to get your pocket calculator out and assess how long you'll be saving, how much you'll be putting away and what charges they're planning to take out of your money. Once you've crunched the numbers, you may not like what you see.

Suits you perfectly

Every few years there seems to be a new financial products mis-selling scandal. In the 1980s it was from encouraging public-sector workers with safe, guaranteed, inflation-protected, taxpayer-funded pensions to move into high-risk, unprotected stock-market-based pensions. In the late 1980s and early 1990s we were sold about 5 million endowment mortgages, pushed with unrealistically high growth projections, which left a couple of million homeowners with major shortfalls when their mortgages reached maturity. For a few years from 1997 onwards hundreds of thousands of investors were encouraged to put about £7.4 billion in 'high income' bonds, also called 'precipice' bonds. What many of the sellers failed to make clear, when hyping the high annual income paid, was that the original capital was at risk. Sure enough, many of these bonds fell off the precipice. Retired people, who were encouraged to buy these bonds to boost their pension income, were reported to have been particularly badly hit. When the bonds matured and they found their capital had been decimated, they had no way of replacing their losses. In spite of the huge amounts being paid out in compensation, up to about £5 billion of this money may have been lost.

Once we passed the millennium, it seemed to be just more of the same. In the early 2000s it appears that hundreds of thousands of people were mis-sold supposedly 'secure' structured investments. These tended to offer something along the lines of 130 per cent of stock-market growth over a five- or six-year period and guaranteed to repay part or all of investors' capital even if the stock market fell. But the current banking crisis has meant that some of these guarantees will not be met. How many is not yet clear. The companies that sold these products are currently contacting investors to tell them the not-so-good news. Moreover, in the small print of many of these investments, it stated that investors would only receive the benefit of rises in stock market indices and that all the annual dividends paid by companies on their shares would be retained by the financial institutions selling the products. By late 2008, savers were being encouraged into investing in corporate bonds marketed as low-risk investments which would give a higher return than the measly interest rates being offered by savings accounts. In the six months from September 2008 to March 2009 savers took over £2 billion out of deposit accounts and put the money into corporate bond funds. Over the same period the value of many of these funds has fallen by over 16 per cent. The latest product that seems to be doing the rounds is called an Assured Income Plan and is offering an ambitious 10.5 per cent a year for ten years. The sales literature claims 'this is a low risk investment as there is no equity or stock market exposure'. The tempting top rates of return only appear to be available to people who invest within four weeks of receiving the sales pitch.

Our financial memory only seems to last a few years. No sooner has one scandal been uncovered, than the sellers are busily working on the next supposedly innovative product which will invariably earn them attractive commissions, but may not always be as good for our financial health as it suggests in the sales bumf. Unfortunately, each time a new product appears and is gushed over by the Sunday supplement financial journalists, many savers are only too eager to take the 'high returns' bait and end up with severely burnt fingers. Thankfully, there seems to have been a change in some newspapers' policy and there are a few commentators who are now moving away from just reporting financial institutions' PR puffery and are actually looking more critically at the products and services being offered. Some of the headlines in the serious papers in mid 2009 give a feel for the level of concern about the products being marketed and the sales methods being used by many financial institutions. Typical examples included: 'Borrowers ripped off in the flight to fix';[6] 'These sinners are soon back to their old tricks';[7] 'Banks preying on desperate savers';[8] 'Another triumph for the sins of commission';[9] and 'A mis-selling scandal waiting in the wings'. [10]

Your pain, their gain

Another issue investment advisers tend not to mention is that many of the potential gains from stock market movements may be captured by insiders rather than by the ordinary investor.

Insiders have a wide range of techniques for extracting money. We show four of the most common in the chart (see Figure 5).

Figure 5 City insiders have many techniques ensuring they capture the value from rising or falling markets

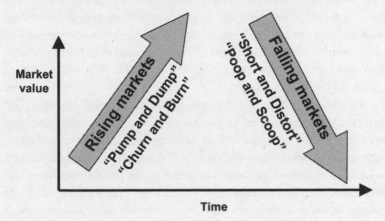

Although the four techniques in Figure 5 can all be used in rising, stable or falling markets, 'pump and dump' and 'churn and burn' are slightly more suited to bull market conditions, while 'poop and scoop' and 'short and distort' work best in bear markets. With 'pump and dump' a trader buys into a share and starts spreading rumours about unrealistically positive prospects for the stock or makes buy recommendations based on misleading or greatly exaggerated information. Then, when others rush in hoping to make a quick buck and the price rises, the pump-and-dumpers sell their holding, making a nice profit. Meanwhile, those who fell for the trick lose a fair bit of money as the share usually settles back down again to its original level and sometimes even overshoots this on the way down. Pump-and-dumpers tend to work on smaller company stocks as these are much easier to manipulate. With 'churn and burn', traders increase their commissions by excessive selling and buying of their clients' portfolios. 'Churn and burn' can also be used by unit trust managers and pension fund managers, sometimes in collusion with brokers, as this enables them to earn higher management fees. Churn rates for stocks (the percentage of stocks sold in a year) have increased from just 30 per cent in 2007 to 50 per cent in 2008 to almost 90 per cent by 2009. This rise in turnover rates may just be indicating that diligent fund managers are working much harder in order to maximize their clients' investments. On the other hand, such a dramatic increase might be telling us that that churning and burning is alive and well and is siphoning off an awful lot of our money.

'Poop and scoop' is the opposite of 'pump and dump'. The poop-and-scooper tries to push down the value of a stock by spreading false information or issuing a 'sell' recommendation. Once the stock falls, they can buy it at a low price and then cash in when their rumours turn out to be unsubstantiated and the stock goes back up to its original level. 'Short and distort' is similar with the difference that the trader actually shorts a stock before spreading stories intended to drive the value down.

Then there are other methods like circular trading, jitney, dividend pumping, double dipping, bucketing, portfolio pumping and dividend selling, all of which give value to insiders and deprive outsiders of potential returns. Traders often refer to these and many other stock manipulation techniques as trading in 'guilt-edged stocks' because they are transactions that make money by possibly unethical means. Culprits supposedly feel guilty having made money in such an unscrupulous way.

Who is taking all the money?

Even if you believe that in the long term shares outperform cash and that you will be able to extract the value for yourself rather than allowing it to go to other people, we may have moved into a new era in which structural changes in the way companies operate could permanently reduce their profit margins and thus their ability to maintain dividend payments and rising stock prices.

One important change is the way that executive remuneration has become disconnected from company results. There have been a series of what have been called 'fatcat failures' – executives awarded massive salary increases, bonuses and share options while demonstrably not performing or else being paid millions to leave. The situation became so serious that in 2003 our government published a consultation document called *Reward for Failure* in an attempt to deal with the problem. However, as the huge payoffs lavished on many of our failed bankers show (see Chapter 12 *The Bank Robbers*), those who are part of the ruling elite will get massive rewards, however well or poorly they perform.

However, perhaps the most serious threat to future stock market returns comes from private- and public-sector pension liabilities. Most companies are trying to reduce their pension commitments by placing all the risk on their employees rather than the company (see Chapter 4 *Protecting Our Pensions*). Nevertheless, some businesses seem to be caught in a vicious spiral. Their pension fund deficits lead to a fall in their share price which increases their deficits. Larger deficits then cause further share price falls and greater deficits and so on. Many leading companies have pension liabilities that are larger than their market values. Reducing these deficits will drain away money that could have been used to make new investments and pay shareholder dividends.

But even if a company is not burdened by large pension liabilities for its own employees, governments have to raise money to pay for their rapidly growing public-sector pension liabilities and the other costs of an ageing population. Governments can only get this money from higher taxes on ordinary taxpayers or businesses. Either way, this will be a burden that may considerably dampen economic performance and companies' profitability in the future. If executives don't siphon off the money made by businesses, we may well find governments doing it instead. So while it is certainly true that in the past shares have significantly outperformed cash, it is not obvious that this will necessarily continue to be the case.

Finding a greater fool

Assuming you manage to avoid market professionals taking some or even most of your potential gains, there is perhaps one final point that is worth making – any investment is only ever worth what someone else will pay for it. According to economic theory, the price of any share should be directly linked to the earnings and future prospects of the company issuing that share. In real life, the value of a share, like the value of a Damien Hirst dead shark or Tracey Emin's bed, is actually only worth what someone else is prepared to give you. You may have lots of shares in an excellent company, but if the market is falling around your ears and nobody is buying, the shares are virtually worthless. This is usually called the 'greater fool' method of valuation: something is only worth what an even greater fool than you is willing to pay for it. This of course means that if you can't find a greater fool to buy your investments for more than you paid for them, then it's you who is the greatest fool.

DON'T BANK ON IT

While some of the situations described above might put people off investing in shares, plonking your cash in a bank is not so rewarding either. Banks are understandably profit-maximizing businesses; they make as much money as they reasonably can. Moreover, our government is being slightly disingenuous, or even dishonest, when it claims that pumping taxpayers' billions into the banks will lead directly to increased lending. At the same time as the government maintains it is putting pressure on the banks to lend, it is also pushing the banks to build up their capital bases to make up for the enormous losses made over the last couple of years. The only way banks can do this is by taking even more of their customers' money, not by lending it to us. Moreover, banks and building societies may have to pay an extra £20 billion into the Financial Services Compensation Scheme to build up its funds in case there are further banking failures. All this amounts to a form of indirect taxation by the government to get us to pay for the banking collapse. Assuming the banks need another £100 billion in capital[11] – nobody seems to know the real figure – with a population of about 46 million adults, this means each of us will have to contribute over £2,000 to the worthy cause of propping up our banks. So, two groups of people – borrowers and savers – are going to find themselves picking up yet another bill for our banks' buccaneering adventures over the last decade or two. Moreover, now that the financial crisis has significantly reduced the number of financial institutions and thus the level of competition between them, we can expect worse conditions for both borrowers and savers in the future.

Borrowers' blues

Borrowers with tracker mortgages have already found that their mortgage rates have failed to fall in line with the Bank of England's reductions in interest rates. For example, after February 2009's 0.5 per cent cut in the Bank of England's base rate, only 31 out of 91 lenders offering standard variable rate mortgages were intending to reduce their rates and of these only 12 committed to passing on the full 0.5 per cent cut.

Overall, interest rates for borrowers seem to have fallen by around half the Bank of England's reduction in interest rates, considerably boosting lenders' profit margins. Borrowers buying fixed-rate mortgages are also seeing quite dramatic increases in the margins they have to pay. In mid 2008, the average mortgage deal for a fixed two-year deal was only 1.4 points higher than the cost of funding. By mid 2009, the banks' margins had risen to around 2.39 points above the cost of funding – a 70 per cent increase. With about 30,000 fixed-rate mortgages sold a month, the lenders will make almost £500 million a year more just from this increase on new mortgages. On many variable rate mortgages margins seem to have risen from around 0.5 percent above the cost of borrowing to over 2.6 per cent. In total, assuming UK mortgage lending of just over £1 trillion, if lenders manage to increase their margins over all this lending by 1 to 2 per cent, and most have achieved even more, this will give them an extra £10 billion to £20 billion of our money a year. In view of this, we can probably anticipate some record profits and bonanza bonuses in the banking sector in the near future.

Savers' sorrow

As for savers, unfortunately for them most of their accounts have energetically kept pace with reductions in interest rates and some have even comfortably exceeded the Bank of England's interest rate cuts. This, of course, widens the margin between what banks are charging borrowers and what they are paying on deposits. For example, the average interest rate from instant access accounts in the UK, including current accounts, stood at 2.77 per cent at the end of January 2008. But a year later this figure had dropped to 0.21 per cent. A month later it was down at 0.16 per cent and at the end of April 2009 it was at 0.10 per cent. By mid 2009, over a quarter of all variable rate savings accounts were paying 0.10 per cent or less.[12] Rates on ISAs have also dropped almost as sharply.

A particularly worrying feature of the historically low interest rates is that savers in search of higher returns will start withdrawing their money from deposit accounts, where they at least get a £50,000 guarantee from the government against losses, and be tempted into riskier financial products where they are not told about, or may not fully understand, the degree of risk and potential for losing money. In February 2009, the British Bankers' Association reported that savers had withdrawn a record £2.3 billion. The previous high was just £1.5 billion in 1997. Some of this money would have been used to pay off

Christmas and credit-card borrowing, but a significant portion would have been taken out by savers looking for a higher return on their cash.

Corporate bond funds paying yields of 5 per cent or more were the most popular choice accounting for two out of every three unit trusts bought. But in the past year many corporate bond funds have lost 10 to 15 per cent of their value. Soon people will realize that corporate bonds were not such a good idea and the money will change direction yet again and move into government bond funds. That makes sense as long as interest rates keep falling. But as soon as the recovery starts and inflation begins rising, interest rates may also go up and this will lead to a drop in government bond prices. As seems to happen so often with supposedly 'high-income' investments, what you get today in increased returns you lose tomorrow in decreasing capital value.

Particularly vulnerable are older people who might be relying on their savings to provide them with much of their income. In mid 2009, there were many shocking stories of pensioners who had lost significant amounts of their savings after being advised by their banks to move them from risk-free deposit accounts into more speculative investments. One 85-year-old woman was reported to have lost over £33,000 of her £75,000 savings in just two years. She claimed she had told her bank Barclays that she was prepared to take a small amount of risk in order to improve her income. In December 2007 her money went into the solid-sounding Aviva Global Balanced Income Fund. Unknown to her, in July 2007 Barclays had reclassified the fund as 'adventurous'. Barclays offered her £50 for her inconvenience, though another Barclays customer, an 89-year-old retired farmer, advised to put half his savings into this fund and half into the Aviva Global Cautious Income, received £193,865 from the bank after a newspaper took up his complaint.[13]

An 83-year-old HSBC customer was reportedly advised to put £137,000 – more than half his savings – into another attractively named product, the Morgan Stanley Growth Protected

Plan.[14] The journalist investigating the case wrote that HSBC had received £4,795 commission for proposing and organizing the investment. On the positive side, the plan was designed to return all the capital invested. The problem was that it had to be held for six years or more and there were large penalties for early withdrawal. While the HSBC adviser could obviously not have predicted when the customer would die, the fact that the average life expectancy for a British man is 85.8 years might have suggested that a six-plus-years investment product was not the most suitable for an 83-year-old customer. About six months after making the investment, the customer died and the investment had to be sold as part of dividing the deceased's estate, leaving the family with a loss of £31,500. An HSBC spokesman said: 'We believe we've acted ethically and properly at all times and only after ensuring that Mr M. understood and was completely comfortable with the recommendations made.' However, the bank was reported to have returned £31,498.39 as 'a goodwill gesture'.

Selling machines

Most of us have now understood that bank staff are no longer careful custodians of our money. Instead, they have become commission-hungry salespeople, constantly pushed by their management to flog us products we may not want or need and many of which may seriously harm our financial health, whilst always improving our banks' economic well-being. It's vitally important that people realize that we seldom if ever get real advice any more. Our banks are just selling machines, so we need to be better prepared to understand what we are being sold and how this might actually be very different indeed from what we think we may be buying.

CHAPTER 4

PROTECTING OUR PENSIONS

NOT A PRETTY PICTURE

If you work in the public sector or are a politician, you and your partner are guaranteed a well-paid, comfortable and carefree retirement at the expense of future British taxpayers. Almost 90 per cent of the 6 million public-sector employees have what are called defined-benefit or final-salary pension arrangements. These guarantee an inflation-protected pension for them and their partners for the rest of their lives based on their final salaries. They often also have the option to take early retirement at any time between 55 and 60. In the private sector, only about 2.5 million people – 11 per cent of employees – are members of final-salary schemes, though many of these are at risk of having their benefits reduced or their schemes closed altogether. A further 8 million people save for their pensions in 'defined-contribution' schemes. Much of this money is invested by pension managers in bonds and shares and there is no guarantee as to the level of pension these will eventually provide – this depends on the performance of the pension funds and annuity rates at the time of retirement. The majority of private-sector workers and the unemployed – about 20 million people – make no pension provisions at all and so are relying on the state pension plus various credits and benefits to tide them through their retirement (see Figure 1).

Figure 1 Most people risk having very little retirement income

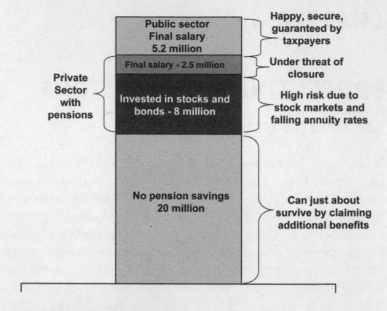

STATE PENSION POVERTY

The state pension Ponzi scheme

Ponzi schemes have been in the news again following the arrest of Bernard Madoff in the mystery of the missing billions. In their definition of a pyramid or Ponzi scheme, the Securities and Exchange Commission explains that: 'Fraudsters simply use money from new recruits to pay off early stage investors. But eventually the pyramid will collapse. At some point the schemes get too big, the promoter cannot raise enough money from new investors to pay earlier investors, and many people lose their money.'

Interestingly, this has many similarities to Britain's state pension scheme. We are using the National Insurance (NI) contributions of people working today to pay current pensioners. But between now and 2050 the number of pensioners will rise by 36 per cent from 11.8 million to over 16 million. Moreover, due to increasing longevity the time these pensioners will live to claim their pensions will rise by almost 20 per cent (four years) by 2050. So we will have more pensioners living for longer. However, the number of people working and paying NI contributions will either be static or even fall. In many ways this is equivalent to a Ponzi scheme needing more and more money because of promises made to earlier entrants and yet there are insufficient new investors to fund the rising cost of payments to earlier entrants to the scheme (see Figure 2).[1]

Figure 2 Who is going to pay for the rising cost of state pensions?

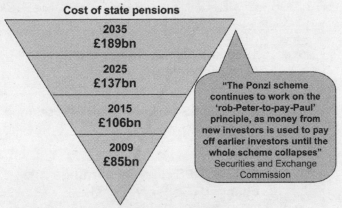

Cost of state pensions

2035
£189bn

2025
£137bn

2015
£106bn

2009
£85bn

"The Ponzi scheme continues to work on the 'rob-Peter-to-pay-Paul' principle, as money from new investors is used to pay off earlier investors until the whole scheme collapses"
Securities and Exchange Commission

Or is this a Ponzi scheme that will eventually collapse?

Promises, promises

At the moment, we pay our NI contributions of about £100 billion a year and about £85 billion goes to today's pensioners, most of whom will have qualified for their state pensions from paying NI throughout their working lives. In return for us paying our contributions now, we expect that the government will provide pensions for us when we retire. Moreover, we are encouraged to make NI payments for as many years as we can up to the total required to qualify for a full pension (now 30 years), as we are told by the government that the amount of pension we will receive depends on the number of qualifying years of NI contributions we have made. However, unlike a public-sector final-salary scheme, there is no formal, written agreement between us and the government detailing how much we will eventually get as state pension income in return for the money we have handed over.

Confronted with the rising cost of state pensions, our leaders seem to be getting cold feet about being able to pay and are finding subtle and not so subtle ways of trying to wriggle out of the unwritten commitments that many of us believe they have made to us.

Figure 3 Most of the changes to the state pension have reduced the benefits paid

1980 link with earnings broken (Conservatives)

1986 SERPS widows' benefits reduced (Conservatives)

1988 SERPS relevant earnings rules changed (Conservatives)

2000 death in service benefits cut (Labour)

2007 Started increasing state pension age to 68 (Labour)

Reduced years of NI contributions to qualify (Labour)

The state pension was started in 1908 when David Lloyd George's Old Age Pensions Act introduced a means-tested pension for the over 70s. In 1946 the Clement Attlee government passed the National Insurance Act which led to a contributory state pension for all – one we all pay into through national insurance rather than being financed out of general taxation. The purpose of the state pension was to provide a minimum standard of living 'below which no-one should be allowed to fall'. But it has been 'reformed' and reneged on many times as governments realize that they increasingly cannot afford it (see Figure 3).

Perhaps the most important change was when the Tories cut the link between the state pension and average earnings, instead linking increases in the pension to changes in the Retail Price Index. One result of this is that the value of the state pension has fallen against average earnings and is now down about 20 per cent compared with its 1950 level. The minimum standard of living 'below which no-one should be allowed to fall' provided by the state pension is now so low that well over half of pensioners rely on additional benefits such as the Pension Credit and housing allowances to survive. The average European state pension is around 57 per cent of average earnings – in Britain it has fallen to about 16 per cent of average earnings and is likely to go even lower in coming years. The government naturally denies that British pensioners are having financial problems or that they are worse off than their European counterparts: 'It's absolute nonsense to suggest this government is not committed to pensioners. Measures such as pension credit and winter fuel payments mean that even the poorest pensioners in the UK are still better off than the poorest pensioners in other countries.'[2]

In the 2007 Pensions Act, the government committed to restore the link between the state pension and average earnings from 2012. However, this is 'subject to affordability and the fiscal position'. Given the economic collapse, the drop in tax revenues and the explosion in national debt, it seems unlikely that this promise will be met.

The state pension is payable to women from the age of 60 and men from 65, but between 2010 and 2020 women's pensionable age will increase from 60 to 65. Then from 2024 to 2046 the age we can all start receiving our state pension will gradually go up for both men and women to 68. Though if money gets really tight, whichever government is in power could decide to bring forward rises in pensionable age. So, just as they have almost got within grasping distance of the pension, for which they believe they have paid for during their working life, many people may see it being pulled further and further away. In August 2009, the pensions regulator mooted the idea that the state pension should be paid from the age of 70 rather than the planned 68, so the state pensionable age is far from being a fixed point on which people can rely.

The one positive change that has been made to the terms and conditions of the state pension was when the Labour government reduced the number of years of NI contributions required to qualify for the full state pension down from over 40 to 30 in order to help provide a better pension for people who might have taken time out from their careers to look after children or relatives requiring care and so hadn't been able to keep up their NI payments. But critics might say that anyone who only has the state pension to live off is already entitled to additional benefits, so it's not obvious that this supposedly generous change will actually result in many people receiving much more money. For example, someone who has made just 35 years of contributions would now have a higher state pension under this new ruling, but this will probably mean they get less money in benefits. Their pension may have gone up, but their overall income will probably have stayed the same.

The government now wants to introduce the National Pensions Savings Scheme (NPSS) to push people to take more responsibility for saving for their retirement. However, like so many other changes made by governments, what looks at first sight to be a worthwhile proposal hardly stands up to more than a couple of minutes scrutiny. The problem is that for lower earners, contributions to the NPSS may turn out to have been almost worthless as they may deprive pensioners of benefits they would have received anyway due to the basic state pension already being far below the poverty level.

As the government finds itself increasingly unable to afford state pensions for all, it will have to further water down the unwritten pension obligations which people feel entitled to from their NI contributions. At the moment all pensioners, rich or poor, receive the state pension. It seems more than probable that governments will begin to argue that pension money should be directed towards the less well off. At first they will probably just let the state pension fall even further below what is required to live above the poverty level, so that payments to pensioners become increasingly made up of means-tested benefits. It's unlikely any government would have the courage to scrap the state pension for people earning over a certain amount. But if the country's finances get much worse, serious conditions may require drastic responses. Then the idea of scrapping the state pension for those with a private pension above a certain minimum level might be considered as an emergency response. If such an emergency measure was implemented, it would save so much money (maybe around £20 billion a year) that most governments would be reluctant to repeal it. However, against this pressure to renege on its pension pledges will be the increasing voting power of a rising number of pensioners. Future governments will struggle between balancing the need to cut pension spending against the power of the growing pensioner lobby.

AN ENDANGERED SPECIES

Killing off private-sector final-salary pensions

Since this government came to power, the number of people in the public sector eligible for a guaranteed, secure, final-salary, inflation-linked joint pension for themselves and their partners has increased from around 4.4 million to 5.2 million – a rise of 18 per cent. Worryingly for future taxpayers, a large number of the extra 800,000 people entitled to these pensions are well-paid managers rather than more modestly paid frontline workers. Moreover, many public-sector managers have seen their salaries more than double over the last 12 years. As government actuaries have reworked their figures to take account of an increase in highly paid public-sector managers, falling interest rates and increasing longevity, this has led to an apparently huge increase in public-sector pension liabilities from about £360 billion in 1997 to at least £880 billion today – a 140 per cent rise. However, some experts believe the government is still deliberately underestimating the real cost and that it has actually reached about £1.02 trillion, while others have gone for the even more impressive £1.2 trillion.[3] At the same time there has been an almost catastrophic fall in the number of people in private-sector final-salary schemes (see Figure 4).

There are currently about 34,000 public-sector pension millionaires – people who have already retired with pensions

Figure 4 Private-sector final-salary schemes have collapsed while public-sector final-salary liabilities have shot up

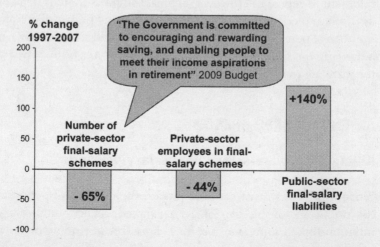

worth more than a million pounds. They will cost taxpayers over £34 billion pounds. Over the next 10 to 20 years, this number will probably double or even triple as all the executives and managers of the well-paid New Labour generation take their (usually early) retirement.

Meanwhile, in the private sector the threats to the retirement welfare of the few remaining people in final-salary schemes are increasing. A survey of 1,000 blue-chip companies found that 96 per cent believed their final salary schemes were unsustainable.[4] Most companies have been trying to cut their pension liabilities by closing their final-salary schemes to new joiners – and this has not been helped by Gordon Brown increasing the tax on company pension schemes. In fact, at the time of writing only about four blue chip firms (Tesco, Cadbury, Shell and Diageo) still had defined-benefit schemes open to new recruits. Moreover, some of these may be what are called 'silver-plated' average-salary schemes, rather than the 'gold-plated' final-salary arrangements enjoyed by almost all public-sector employees.

A new phase in the destruction of private-sector final-salary schemes started in June 2009. Already in 1997 Barclays had closed its final-salary scheme to new members of staff, but by 2009 the scheme had a deficit of over £2 billion and the bank decided to also close it to over 17,000 existing staff. A Barclays spokesman said that 'all benefits for future service would be provided by our more modern schemes' and that the move was 'in the best interests of employees and shareholders'.[5] However, a union representative didn't seem to agree: 'This attack on the pensions of the loyal and hard-working staff at the bank is utterly alarming.' About 24 hours after the Barclays announcement, supermarket chain Morrisons said that it would be doing something similar. Where Barclays and Morrisons have boldly gone, we can now expect many other companies to follow.

Gift horse or Trojan horse?

Another worrying development has been the increase in the number of companies offering their employees cash payments in exchange for giving up their rights to a final-salary scheme. We have been in similar territory before, when pension salespeople lured hundreds of thousands of public-sector workers away from their guaranteed, taxpayer-funded, final-salary pensions into much more risky money-market schemes and ended up paying close to £20 billion in compensation. Many private-sector employees are finding themselves being offered tens of thousands and in some cases hundreds of thousands of pounds cash to give up their final-salary scheme pension benefits. The offers may look attractive, but the only reason employers are proposing these cash payments is because they believe that this is much cheaper than letting employees keep their final-salary pension entitlements. So, logically, what the employers gain, the employees must lose – this is most definitely not a win-win situation from an employee's perspective.

One of the key things to watch out for are employers' actuaries using hugely unrealistic investment growth projections and today's annuity rates of around 6 per cent to 7 per cent when calculating how much they should pay employees to give up their final-salary rights. Falling interest rates on government bonds and some of the changes in the stock market we have described in the previous chapter mean that future investment performance is likely to be lower than previous returns. Moreover, as we are living longer, this will put further downward pressure on annuity rates. So if employees take the cash now, based on historical investment returns and current annuity rates, by the time they come to converting it into a pension, they might get an awful lot less for it than they had been led to believe.

When describing this new trend, some Sunday newspapers have been a little more cautious than they tend to be when covering new developments in pensions and savings. One advised: 'Switching out of final-salary schemes was at the heart of pension mis-selling in the 1980s . . . Most people should stick with their final-salary schemes.' However, a financial products website was a little more direct when it advised: 'Hellish pension buy-out offer you should refuse.'[6]

The only situation in which it would be worth accepting a payoff now would be if a person thought their employer might go bankrupt and be unable to pay their pension. Even then, taking a cheque today would only be attractive if someone was expecting a substantial pension as the state Pension Protection Fund currently guarantees any pension losses from employers' bankruptcy up to a £28,000 per year cap.

Easing employers' pension pains

There are quite a few specialist pension consultancies who advise companies on how to cut the costs of their pension schemes. One explains in its promotional material: 'There has been a massive increase in the number of organizations looking to reduce their pension risks and their cash commitment to pension schemes.'[7] The firm then goes on to explain about its 'simpler, less costly, and more easily understood solutions' which include 'closing schemes to new entrants' and 'severing any link to final "pensionable salary"'. As an example of its success the firm described a situation where it had made these changes for a client and 'less than 0.1 per cent of the affected employees entered a formal grievance over the changes'. We do not know the name of the client or the terms offered to employees to swap their secure, risk-free final-salary schemes for possibly much riskier defined-contribution policies, but one could surmise that once they reach retirement, many might look at how much pension they'll be getting and regret their decision to give up their secure final-salary entitlements.

Buy-out or sell-out?

There is a further trend that could threaten the retirement bliss of those in the private sector blessed with that rare treasure of a final-salary pension. As companies try to unburden themselves of their future pension liabilities, some are moving to sell their schemes to a growing number of specialist pension management companies such as Paternoster, the Pension Corporation and Legal & General. The pensions buyout business went from a turnover of around £2.5 billion in 2007 to over £8 billion in 2008. There were forecasts that it would hit £12 billion in 2009, but the collapse in shares and bond values greatly increased company pension deficits and thus made many funds unsellable for the time being. However, once the economy starts to pick up again, we will probably see a bounce-back in pensions buyouts with anything up to £1.2 trillion in defined-benefit schemes up for grabs.

The main concern with the rise of buyouts is the potential conflict between the interests of pensioners and the need for the buyout firms to make healthy profits from their acquisitions. In 2008, the minister for pensions reform explained: 'I am concerned that some emerging business models might not give the same protection for pension schemes as traditionally provided by a sponsoring employer or insurance capital.'[8] A pessimist could imagine all kinds of worrying scenarios where the opportunity to increase their returns on the huge sums held in pension schemes might prove irresistible to managers and shareholders in buyout firms. One could also imagine that what is good for the buyout firms might not be quite so wonderful for the pensioners. In a report into one such buyout by the Pension Corporation at Telent (the sad remains of the once proud GEC and Marconi industrial empire), the Pensions Regulator was highly critical of Telent for failing to appreciate that there was an 'acute conflict of interest' between its wish to run the pension scheme's investment strategy for the benefit of its investors and the interests of the scheme's members.[9] The report went on: 'Nothing that the Pension Corporation said or did gave the regulator any comfort that the conflicts the regulator had identified were likely to be avoided by the Pension Corporation, or even that they were properly understood.' Extreme care should be the order of the day when your employer starts talking up the fantastic benefits for employees from flogging off your pension scheme to a profit-maximizing buyout firm.

LIVING IN A FOOL'S PARADISE?

The impending virtual extinction of final-salary pensions for private-sector employees means that well over 80 per cent of those saving for a pension will be relying on defined-contribution pensions for their retirement. Here, their future financial security in retirement will depend on the performance of their fund managers' investments and the level of annuity rates when they stop work. Many may well retire wealthy and healthy on their pension savings. One would hope so. But there are several reasons to be cautious about how much they will actually get when the time comes to realize the value of all the pension contributions which they and their employers have made over many years. Some people saving for a private pension may well be headed for pensions paradise, but many others may be living in a fools' paradise if they expect a comfortable, well-funded retirement.

Promising the improbable

When pension providers send out savers' annual statements, they usually provide projections of the eventual size of customers' pension funds by the time they reach 65. The Financial Services Authority (FSA) advises that providers should use three investment growth rates when making these projections: a low rate of 5 per cent, a medium rate of 7 per cent and a high one of 9 per cent. There have been brief periods in the past when pension managers have come near, and sometimes even exceeded, these levels. In the 1990s some funds achieved up to 16 per cent a year. However, some of these have occurred during times of high inflation, so the real rates of return were actually much lower than they first appear to be. Moreover, in the last decade, returns have averaged about 0.9 per cent a year.[10]

Over the last 46 years (since the start of the FTSE All-Share Index in 1963), the overall pensions fund industry averaged real returns of 4 per cent a year above inflation.[11] Even if we knock off the terrible year of 2008 when the pension funds index fell by 17.2 per cent, the 45-year performance ending in 2007 is only about 4.6 per cent a year. While writing this book, we contacted a few actuaries and other pension specialists to see how many thought that pension funds could consistently deliver returns of the FSA's recommended 7 per cent or even 9 per cent in real terms over the long term. We still have not found one who was confident that the FSA's lowest recommended projection rate of 5 per cent was achievable.

Anyone saving for a private pension might be well advised to take the FSA recommended projections with more than a pinch of salt, set up their own spreadsheet and work out how much they will have on retirement assuming a 4 per cent growth rate at most. The difference between 4 per cent and the FSA's lowest proposed rate of 5 per cent may look small at first, but over 20 to 30 years this may make the difference of a couple of hundred thousand pounds between what was projected and what a saver's fund actually ends up being worth when they retire. As for the FSA's suggested 7 per cent and 9 per cent rates – these should be treated with the greatest of care, or better still ignored, otherwise people risk being awfully miffed when they find out what their pension fund manager really achieved for them.

Fees glorious fees

Anyone saving up for a defined-contribution pension would be well advised to investigate exactly how much of their pension savings are going into the pockets of financial intermediaries and their pension management company rather than into their own pension funds. On some pension schemes, advisers can take half the first year's savings and then a percentage for many years after that. Even if a scheme is not so generous to an adviser or some other middleperson, savers may still lose a significant chunk of their money in management fees. Typical management fees may vary between 1.5 per cent and 1.75 per cent. When finding out that they will be paying these annual management charges, most people probably feel that this is a reasonable amount to pay for someone to invest their money. After all, anything under 3 or 4 per cent probably sounds pretty small, but as pension savings grow the seemingly modest management charges can soon mount up to considerable sums.

If a person saves around £3,600 a year with 5 per cent growth a year and 1.5 per cent in annual charges, then they will have almost £190,000 in their pension fund after 30 years. By the time they start approaching retirement, they'll be paying over £2,500 a year in management fees. In all, over the 30 years, they'll have paid almost £36,000 in fees. However, if they had a fund with much more modest fees of say just 0.7 per cent, their pension fund would be worth almost £220,000 – about £30,000 more. Many people will be saving much more than £3,600 a year and by the time they retire will find that they may have paid £100,000 to £150,000 in management fees. That's quite a chunk of cash, equivalent to somewhere from £6,000 to £9,000 a year more on your pension. So a seemingly small, almost negligible difference in fees can have quite a major impact on a person's retirement funds. Some older pensions may even have annual fees that can be as high as 6 per cent, meaning that over a longer period more than half their money could go to the fund managers rather than to them.

Research into the introduction of self-invested personal pensions (Sipps) has also started the alarm bells ringing amongst some financial commentators. One specialist financial magazine estimated that there were 500,000 Sipps plans worth more than £3 billion and warned: 'Investors could lose 35 per cent of returns over ten years as plan providers, fund managers and financial advisers all take their cut, compared with 15 per cent for a stakeholder pension'.[12]

One of the most powerful incentives for pension savings compared with keeping cash in a bank or putting the money into other investments is the tax relief of 20 per cent for lower-rate taxpayers and 40 per cent for higher-rate payers. However, for anyone paying 20 per cent tax, almost all the tax benefit gets eaten up by charges. Re-using the example above, someone saving £3,600 a year will have a pension pot of £190,000 and have paid about £36,000 in fees – this means the fees will be equivalent to around 19 per cent of the final savings, pretty much eating up the tax advantage. Actually, there is also a benefit from the growth gained on the extra 20 per cent received from the tax benefits, so the situation is marginally better than it looks. Moreover, if someone puts their money into an investment like a unit trust instead, they would still be paying high management fees and wouldn't get the tax benefit. So pension savings do make sense. However, savers should watch out as even apparently low fees can knock a fair bit off the money they thought would eventually end up in their pockets.

Missing the highs and hitting the lows

As we saw in the previous chapter, over the longer term, unless someone is unlucky enough to invest at the wrong time, stock markets investments usually outperform cash. Fortunately with pensions, investors will always avoid going in at the 'wrong time' as their money will be trickled into the market each year over many years. However, to get a decent return, their fund has to get the benefit of increases in stock market values and dividend payments. Yet, while overall UK equities clocked up a respectable real return of an average of 5.6 per cent a year since 1963, the pension industry only achieved 4 per cent a year. So the pension industry underperformed the market by almost 30 per cent. Again the 1.6 per cent difference between the market's 5.6 per cent and the pension industry's 4 per cent looks small at first sight, but on an investment of say £5,000 a year for 30 years it will make a difference of almost £100,000 in the value of someone's pension savings – not a sum to be sneezed at.

There are some quite convincing reasons why pension funds may significantly underperform the overall market. For a start, the conservatism of fund managers will often mean that they are slow to move when markets start rising and so will miss out on much of the value to be gained. Similarly, when markets are falling, pension fund managers may be slow to get out of poorly performing stocks and so may bear a disproportionately larger share of losses than many other investors.

A second reason pension funds may give low returns is that they are a prime target for commission-hungry broking houses eager to boost their profits by encouraging funds to keep moving their money from share to share. Analysts issuing recommendations are under intense pressure to be positive about the companies they study. Most research into analysts' recommendations has identified what is politely called 'a bias towards optimism': analysts tend to issue about three to five times as many recommendations that clients should 'buy' than proposals that they should 'hold' or 'sell'. In 2003, ten large US investment banks paid about $1.4 billion in fines when they were found to be pressuring their analysts to take overly positive positions about companies so that the banks could win business from those companies. The recent book *Cityboy* gives an entertaining insight into the environment in which analysts are encouraged towards this 'bias to optimism'.[13]

Thirdly, the average salary for pension fund managers, though fabulous by most people's standards, is less than can be earned by people in more adventurous and even buccaneering activities. This can result in some of the sharpest pencils in the City not being overly enthusiastic about joining the ranks of pension fund management. If this is the case, it does not bode well for those of us relying on consistently excellent pension fund investment performance for our retirement happiness.

Down, down, keep going down

In 1990 a £100,000 pension pot would have bought an income of £15,000 a year. By 2000 this had dropped to £9,000. In 2009, it's about £7,000. Even if interest rates rise, with people living longer it's unlikely that annuity rates will fully follow interest rates upwards. On current projections the average life expectancy will increase by one year every ten years.[14] This should knock at least 0.3 per cent off annuity rates every ten years.

However, this £7,000 a year is for a single pension with no protection against inflation. The rates for a joint, index-linked pension are nearer 3.5 per cent. Given the government's decision to do a bit of quantitative easing, it's likely that inflation will start to rise again, so it would be wise to protect oneself by taking an inflation-indexed pension. To ensure a pension of about the level of the average salary, say £25,000, a couple would need to have pension savings of over £700,000. With a 4 per cent growth rate, they would need to put aside something in the region of £12,000 a year for 30 years to get anywhere near this kind of pension pot. A good rule of thumb is that if you want a reasonable pension for yourself and your partner of somewhere between £30,000–£40,000 a year, then you should at least be aiming at a £1 million pension fund between you by the time you retire – that means you, your partner and your employers jointly putting more than £17,000 a year for 30 years into your pension savings.

A pot of gold at the end of the rainbow

Amidst all this doom and gloom, there is one area of glorious and seemingly unending sunshine – the pensions that will be enjoyed by managers in the public sector. A public-sector middle manager earning £70,000 a year can expect a joint inflation-protected pension of at least £35,000 a year from the youthful age of 60, plus a useful, usually tax-free, payment of two or even three times their pension, £70,000 to £100,000, when they decide to retire. Any private-sector worker would need to save more than £1,100,000 to get a similar sum in retirement. An NHS chief executive on about £150,000 a year can look forward to early retirement on about £75,000 a year plus a couple of hundred thousand in their hand, equivalent to a £2 million pension pot. However, even this pales into insignificance compared with our MPs' pension benefits. While cheating on their expenses and claiming they could not live on their £64,700 a year salaries for eight months' work, our MPs don't mention that we would have to put over £50,000 a year into our pension funds every single year we work to get the same pensions as them. So their salary and pension package is actually worth about £115,000 a year – plus all those expenses.

Now that we've caught them with both hands in the till, our MPs have begun softening us up for their next clever wheeze – a massive rise in their pay and thus pensions. When Harriet Harman says that the expenses scandal must not be used to make entering Parliament financially unattractive to poorer people because 'we don't want to have a millionaires' parliament', she's conveniently overlooking the fact that for the majority of people in this country an MP's basic salary of over £64,700 a year with four months holiday is actually rather attractive. Perhaps what she's really saying is that she believes MPs deserve a huge pay rise to make up for some of the expenses they can no longer steal. The figure being bandied about is another £35,000 or so to take

MPs up to around £100,000 a year. MPs are now considering handing over all decisions on their salaries to a quango, probably the Senior Salaries Review Board (SSRB). MPs know that the SSRB has already been talking of linking MPs' salaries to those of upper mid-range civil servants, GPs or school heads – that would give them the magical £100,000 a year they desire. If they get this, which seems increasingly likely, their salary and pension package would be worth about £170,000 a year. And they'll still have time to do two or three other jobs, while we're paying them so handsomely to represent us in Parliament. Surely we won't get fooled again!

PART 2

THE BUREAUCRATIZATION OF BRITAIN

CHAPTER 5

SELF-SERVICE IN PUBLIC SERVICE

SO HOW MANY CIVIL SERVANTS ARE THERE?

On its website, the main civil service employees union, the Public and Commercial Services Union (PCS), passionately rails against what it calls 'divisive myths about job security, pay and pensions in civil and public services' and derides the notion that the public sector is 'having it easy compared to the private sector'.[1] But then there are probably people who still think the world is flat.

Let's take job security. If civil servants are having just as tough a time as the rest of us, then as people in the private sector lose their jobs, we might expect to see some belt-tightening in the civil service. This does not seem to be the case. When New Labour first came to power in 1997, there were 472,412 civil servants. By 2004 this had gone up by about 11 per cent to 523,580.[2] Then something wonderful started to happen – the government launched an efficiency programme and the number began to go down to 498,960 by 2007 and then to about 496,000 in 2008. There are other figures for numbers of civil servants provided by the Office for National Statistics (ONS). These suggest that there were 516,000 civil servants in 1997, going up to 570,000 in 2004 and 2005 and then beginning to drop again to 522,000 in 2008. Although considerably higher than the figures we are using, they still show a similar trend of civil service numbers rising for six or seven years, levelling off and then beginning to fall. So perhaps we should give the government credit for starting to control civil-service costs and maybe it is a myth that civil servants have job security.

Sadly not. The government claims to have cut civil service numbers, but there is evidence to the contrary. The First Division Association (FDA), which calls itself 'The Union of Choice for Senior Managers and Professionals in Public Service', slightly gives the game away when it admits that there are now around 540,000[3] civil and public servants that 'keep this country running' (see Figure 1). If this number is accurate – which it should be as the senior civil servants' union has privileged access to the real situation – then there would seem to have been a continual rise in the number of civil servants since 1997 in spite of government claims to have reduced its own staff. This does suggest that job security is alive and well in today's civil service.

Figure 1 The government claims 'The number of Civil Servants has fallen in every quarter over the past 4 years and now stands at its lowest level for a decade'

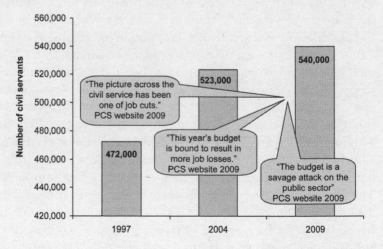

The former trade minister Lord Jones caused a bit of a rumpus in early 2009 when he told a group of MPs that Whitehall could be run with 'half as many' civil servants and that he had been amazed by how many staff 'deserved the sack'. Naturally, the prime minister's spokesman rushed in to deny Lord Jones' allegations: 'I think you will find the civil service is full of honest, decent people who work hard.' When asked about Lord Jones' remarks, the general secretary of the PCS also had a fair bit to say including: 'These are narrow-minded and naive comments which show a complete lack of understanding of what the civil service does.'[4]

The rise and rise of the quangocrats

At the same time as the government claims the number of civil servants is being reduced, there has been a frightening rise in the number of people working for quangos and the amounts we spend on them (see Figure 2). Often their employees do not count as civil servants even though many of them may have been transferred from the civil service.

Figure 2 The increase in quango spending has been extraordinary

Body	Spending £m		Increase
	1998/9	2007/8	
1. Learning and Skills Council*	5,539	11,440	+107%
2. Higher Education Funding Council	3,586	7,360	+105%
3. Housing Corporation	913	2,060	+126%
4. Environment Agency	593	1,103	+86%
5. Engineering and Physical Sciences Research Council	395	757	+92%
6. NHS Litigation Authority	354	3,137	+786%
7. Arts Council England	275	530	+93%
8. Natural Environment Research Council	215	407	+89%
9. Particle Physics and Astronomy Research Council**	214	338	+56%
10. Construction Industry Training Board	100	335	+235%

*first figures from 2001/2   **final figures from 2006/7

It is becoming increasingly difficult to find out the total size of the quango state as the government is deliberately suppressing this information. The Blair regime started with a flurry of openness, but soon it began to fudge the quality and comparability of the data it was publishing, for example by claiming that all 302 Primary Care Trusts in the NHS only counted as one quango 'for statistical consistency'. In 2006, the government closed down the online directory listing quango information and confined publication to an annual booklet called *Public Bodies* which has been getting thinner every year even as more and more quangos are being set up. Finally, when Gordon Brown became prime minister he disbanded the Cabinet Office unit which monitored quango activity. Now, apart from a few summary tables about a restricted list of bodies, no information is released centrally at all.

One authoritative study of quangos suggests that the overall number has actually declined from 692 in 1998 to less than 564. However, the number of employees of these fewer quangos has gone up by 50 per cent from around 1 million to over 1.5 million. Meanwhile, quango spending has leapt from just £49 billion in 1998 to a whopping £130 billion just eight years later.[5]

Yet in spite of the devolving of many powers to the EU, the regions and quangos, there seems to have been no corresponding reduction in the size of government. As a result, there is widespread duplication and overlap of functions so the taxpayer pays for the same service two or even three times. The hugely expensive Regional Development Agencies and English Partnerships share many responsibilities for regeneration; the School Food Trust's campaign to improve school meals is partially duplicated by the one run by the Food Standards Agency; and the Energy Savings Trust and the Carbon Trust both exist to encourage greater energy efficiency. Perhaps nothing quite matches the overlap and duplication at the Department for Communities and Local Government which has created all kinds of bodies to run a plethora of programmes to tackle disadvantage. There's the Supporting People programme (£5 billion); the Working Neighbourhoods Fund (£1.5 billion); the Local Enterprise Growth Initiative (£300 million); the Safer and Stronger Communities Fund (£660 million); the New Deal for Communities (£257 million in just 2007–8); and the New Communities Fund, just to name a few.[6]

Hiding them by the hundreds

We should provide some evidence for our assertion that the government is deliberately concealing thousands of civil servants in order to make it look as if it is managing our public services more effectively than is really the case. As an example, we will look at the department at the heart of the whole civil service: the Cabinet Office. On its website the Cabinet Office explains its critically important role: 'The Cabinet Office is at the centre of government, making government work better.' If the government has been eagerly chopping away at the number of civil servants, we should see some evidence of this in the department that claims to be the nerve centre of Whitehall.

At first sight, the figures for the Cabinet Office's staff reduction efforts look almost astonishingly impressive – in 2005, at the beginning of the government's latest programme to reduce civil service headcount, there were 2,372 staff. The department was given a target of reducing its staff numbers by 150 by the 2007–8 financial year. By March 2008, there were only 1,414 staff left on the department's books – an amazing reduction of 958 people, many times their modest target. No doubt there were congratulations, bonuses and maybe even a few promotions for such an astounding success.

Sadly for us long-suffering taxpayers, the headcount reduction of 958 appears to have been achieved more by embroidering the truth rather than by any semblance of effective managerial action. In 2005–6 the Cabinet Office transferred about 300 civil servants in the Government Car and Despatch Agency to the Department of Transport; it redesignated civil servants in the Government News Network as employees of the Central Office of Information (COI); it transferred the support offices of the Whips to the Privy Council; and it moved the Government Social Research Unit to the Treasury. This enthusiastic redesignation continued into 2006–7: the Media Monitoring Unit was transferred to the COI;

261 civil servants in the National School of Government were redesignated to a new non-ministerial department with its own separate annual report and accounts; responsibility for civil service statistics was moved to the Office of National Statistics; and the Office of Public Sector Information went to the National Archives. Finally in 2007–8, the Better Regulation Executive was moved to the Department of Business, Enterprise and Regulatory Reform; the Prime Minister's Delivery Unit went to the Treasury; and two quangos were established so their staff and costs were not in the Cabinet Office's accounts. Going against the flow, some staff and activities were moved from the Home Office to the Cabinet Office with the establishment of the Office of the Third Sector.

When all these changes are included, the apparent reduction of 958 employees actually becomes an overall increase of 293. This might help explain why taxes and public spending keep going up at the same time as the government claims to be saving tens of billions a year by making the public sector more efficient. If this book-cooking is being repeated across government, which seems depressingly likely, this increase of over 10 per cent in the Cabinet Office might suggest that civil servant numbers may be nearer the FDA's estimate of 540,000 rather than the government's figure of 496,000. It is unusual for a cull to result in an increase in the population of the creatures being culled, but that seems to have been the result of our government's attempts to look like it was trying to reduce the size of the civil service.

PARKINSON'S DISEASE

Nowadays it's easy for us to laugh at Parkinson's Law. This is the adage that 'Work expands so as to fill the time available for its completion', originated by Cyril Northcote Parkinson as the first sentence of a comic essay published in the *Economist* in 1955. Parkinson derived the dictum from his extensive experience in the

British Civil Service and used it to describe the rate at which a bureaucracy grows over time by 5 to 7 per cent a year 'irrespective of any variation in the amount of work (if any) to be done'. He attributed this rise to several causes including officials wanting to increase their subordinates and to staff members making work for one another. One example he used was from the Royal Navy where the number of admiralty officials shot up while the number of ships and sailors was significantly reduced (see Figure 3).

Figure 3 Parkinson taught us that even though frontline staff numbers decrease, bureaucracies still grow

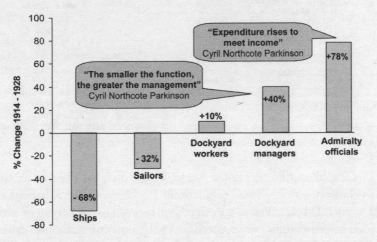

What's slightly worrying for us is that under this government Parkinson's Law seems to have been thriving. In some departments, it's even doing better than Parkinson could have imagined. In the NHS, for example, a 30 per cent decline in the number of hospital beds since 1997 has been accompanied by a doubling in the number of managers necessary to manage the ever-decreasing quantity of beds. There is a similar situation in Westminster. Ten years ago about 60 per cent of our laws were made in Britain with the other 40 per cent coming from Brussels. Now Brussels probably makes over 80 per cent of our legislation with less than 20 per cent coming from our Parliament. However, this two-thirds reduction in the proportion of our laws still made in Britain has been accompanied by a correspondingly impressive two-thirds increase in the amount of money in salaries and expenses our MPs need to do much less work (see Figure 4).

Figure 4 Parkinson's Law may help explain the rise in bureaucracy under this Government

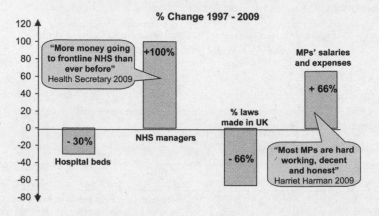

Graphs similar to Figure 4 could be drawn for the police, the probation service, local government and even the Ministry of Defence (MoD). While hundreds of thousands of private-sector jobs have been lost since the start of the current economic crisis, the public sector has proved to be a recession-free zone and is still expanding its workforce by over 30,000 a year.

One reason why some government departments have even exceeded Parkinson's highest estimates for bureaucratic expansion has been this government's creation of a new public-sector managerial class. In 2007–8, for example, the civil service recruited about 40,000 new people. Of these, an extraordinary one-third (14,400) were managers and senior managers with only 25,600 being administrative staff, so one manager was recruited for about every two administrative employees. Many of these managers will spend their time expensively setting and checking targets, ticking boxes, writing reports, spreading best practice, attending endless conferences at comfortable country-house hotels and wasting frontline employees' time with initiatives to make themselves look active while generally achieving nothing of any lasting value except for improving their own financial wellbeing.

The (in)efficiency drive

It would seem fortunate for us hard-pressed taxpayers that our government launched a major efficiency drive to bring down the cost of the public sector and the number of administrative posts. In his spring 2003 budget, Chancellor Gordon Brown announced that he was commissioning a review to find 'new ways of providing departments, their agencies and other parts of the public sector with incentives to exploit opportunities for efficiency savings, and so release resources for front line public service delivery'. Five months went by before Sir Peter Gershon, then head of the deservedly much derided Office of Government Commerce,[7] was asked to start work. He delivered his report *Releasing Resources to the Front Line* in July 2004, over a year after Brown first decided to improve public-sector efficiency. Nobody could accuse the government of rushing into this project too hastily. The Gershon Review concluded that the public sector could save about £21.5 billion. Included in these savings were headcount reductions of somewhere between 70,000 and 80,000 posts.

The government seems quite proud of its success in meeting the Gershon targets. In 2009 a Cabinet Office spokesman claimed: 'With headcount falling for sixteen consecutive quarters and annual efficiency gains worth £26.5 billion, the civil service continues to meet the challenge of doing more with less, becoming leaner while remaining the driving force behind excellent public services that are available to all.'[8] Most government departments now have clear cost-cutting and efficiency targets and each year they proudly announce their success in meeting or even beating the goals set by their political masters. Yet curiously, in spite of all these no doubt noble efforts, public spending keeps on rising each year by more than inflation. Meanwhile, there isn't much obvious evidence that services are improving. Moreover, every couple of years the Office for National Statistics confirms that productivity in the public sector is falling.

A clue as to why government spending keeps on going up, while government departments are supposedly saving billions, can be found in the most recent National Audit Office (NAO) review of our government's Efficiency Programme. Any taxpayer with a weak heart is advised to look away now. The NAO studied just £13.3 billion of what the government claimed were 'annual efficiency gains'. Even the pusillanimous NAO could not help but conclude that £10 billion of the £13.3 billion cuts were 'uncertain'. When NAO employees, always careful not to upset any Whitehall bigwigs, use a word like 'uncertain', most normal people would reach for more forthright words like 'absolute rubbish'.

As for the remaining £3.3 billion, which were supposedly more 'certain' – this wasn't money that could be put in the bank or knocked off our taxes. For example, the Department of Health (DoH) claimed it had saved hundreds of millions 'through patients spending less time in hospital'. Unfortunately, the rate of emergency readmissions had also risen sharply (by over 20 per cent) suggesting that throwing patients out of hospital prematurely was having an adverse effect on their health and costing us more money when an increasing number had to be readmitted, often by emergency ambulance. The DoH also managed to clock up another £300 million savings from altering the baseline period used for measuring improvements in productivity. The MoD proudly announced huge savings by 'decommissioning some of its fast jets ahead of their original decommissioning date'. This might help explain why the number of Britain's military aircraft has gone down by over 40 per cent under this government. Perhaps scrapping quite usable planes was not altogether a good idea considering that Britain was fighting a couple of savage wars at the time and that casualty rates have been rising every year. Meanwhile, MoD bureaucrats reached their targets and got their £48,264,950 or so in annual bonuses, with some employees pocketing around £50,000 each.[9]

Other departments and agencies are also guilty of extremely dubious actions during the efficiency drive. Her Majesty's Revenue and Customs laid claim to having saved us money but unfortunately their savings may have been partly responsible for unclaimed VAT going up from 11 per cent to 14 per cent, costing us taxpayers about £2.4 billion – rather more than the money that was 'saved'. The Rural Payments Agency (RPA) expected to make savings by launching 'a major business modernisation programme of which putting in place the arrangements to make payments to farmers was just one part'. The abject failure of the RPA to make payments to farmers led to British taxpayers having to pay at least £75 million, and possibly much more, in fines to the EU. The Home Office laughably celebrated meeting 90 per cent of its efficiency targets in the same year as it was declared by the Home Secretary as 'not fit for purpose'. Several departments claimed massive savings from putting in new computer systems. For example, the Department for Work and Pensions reported '£300 million of efficiency gains from an initiative to pay benefits electronically'. However, the department didn't mention up to £164 million extra costs and further additional annual running expenses for the new system which probably exceeded their 'efficiency saving'. Meanwhile at the Department of Transport their botched programme to save us £57 million from setting up a shared services unit cost us about £81 million.

Moreover, throughout Whitehall, departments spent hundreds of millions making people redundant at the same time as they were hiring more people. In fact, one result of this government's attempts to cut bureaucracy, while actually increasing it, has been a massive redundancy bonanza for civil servants. Over the years of the Efficiency Programme, the government has given about 15,000 civil servants around £900 million of our money

– an average of £60,000 each – in redundancy payments while at the same time recruiting another 42,020. A further 27,245 temporary and 11,135 agency staff were also employed. Then, of course, there is an army of consultants costing us £2.8 billion a year. Central government alone manages to spend £1.8 billion a year on consultants – costing us £3,300 per civil servant or, to look at it another way, equivalent to an eye-popping £100,000 a year for each of the 18,000 members of the FDA. Given that FDA bosses are continually appearing in the media to tell us how diligent and hard-working their members are, one could wonder why we need to pay so much for consultants to help each of them work out how to do the jobs for which they are already more than handsomely rewarded.

The Department for Work and Pensions is the clear leader in bogus staff reductions, spending £401 million to make 8,479 people redundant while recruiting 16,554 new employees. Some of the most generous departments were the Foreign and Commonwealth Office paying an average of about £140,000 each to 9,372 people and the Home Office dishing out payments averaging £114,000 to 2,094 former members of staff.

When questioned by the Public Accounts Committee (PAC) about why most of the government's efficiency savings were what one committee member called 'an enormous amount of smoke and mirrors in the whole of the public service', the civil service's top bosses were less than convincing. Asked why they didn't take into account costs incurred making efficiency savings, Sir John Oughton, Chief Executive of the Office of Government Commerce at the time, replied: 'The basis on which the current efficiency programme was established, on Sir Peter Gershon's recommendations, was that efficiency savings should be scored regardless of whether investments had been made or needed to be made in order to achieve those efficiencies.' To translate this into normal language, if you had an old car that used a lot of petrol and you spent £15,000 on buying a new car that would save you say £500 a year on petrol for ten years, then according to the way that 'Gershon' savings were calculated, you would have saved £5,000. The unfortunate fact that you would have spent £15,000 to 'save' £5,000 was completely ignored. So the government's way of calculating its savings overlooked the fact that taxpayers would have to pay the costs of making many of the claimed savings, meaning that in many cases we were paying more than was 'saved'.

The PAC reported that by not accounting for the costs incurred in making savings, departments were giving an 'overly-optimistic picture of what has actually been achieved and of the true benefit of the initiative to the taxpayer'.[10] This is a rather mild reading of the facts, which point to widespread buffoonery in the Alice in Wonderland world of today's supposedly increasingly efficient civil service. In fact, the ludicrous answers and evasive responses from senior officials when appearing before the PAC to explain their efficiency savings were so outrageous that the PAC Chairman commented that some of the answers 'should really have figured in an episode of "Yes, Minister"'.[11] In gratitude for the work done during his career, Sir John Oughton was able to take early retirement at 54 with a £612,000 leaving present and a sizeable pension to be paid for by us, the invariably fleeced taxpayers.

THE (PUBLIC-SECTOR) RICH GET MUCH RICHER

Poor civil servants

One of the myths that the PCS tries to debunk on its website is: 'Some people think that civil and public servants are well paid and have enjoyed better pay rises than the private sector.'[12] The PCS claims 'civil servants' average earnings growth has lagged behind other sectors for ten years.' It's not clear where the union got its figures, but every respected analysis comparing private-sector and public-sector pay has concluded that since this government came to power, pay in the public sector has increased by substantially more than in the private sector. Both the Annual Survey of Hours and Earnings and the Labour Force Survey concluded that, between 1997 and 2006, rises in public-sector earnings far outstripped those in the private sector.[13] This trend continued into 2007. Then in 2008, as private-sector earnings stagnated, public-sector salary increases raced ahead. The union goes on to state: 'nearly half of the civil service or approximately 250,000 people earn less than £20,000 a year.' This is probably true, because pay for useful frontline staff and many lower grade administrative staff doing necessary tasks such as issuing driving licences and passports has been kept reasonably under control. However, at the top of the civil service, what's called the senior civil service (SCS), there's been an unprecedented pay, pensions and bonus boom.

The FDA seems a little more circumspect when pleading poverty for its members. Not daring to claim that their pay is falling behind the private sector, it instead maintains: 'Because civil service pay is being squeezed in this way, basic awards in the civil service are often lower than those in other key groups in the public sector.' Yet the facts seem to suggest that the FDA's members are not quite on the breadline yet. Just in the one year 2007–8, the number of staff in the SCS went up by 3.4 per cent, but the number in the top pay band of £102,100 to £209,300 went up by a shocking 14.7 per cent. Overall, the number of people in the SCS has gone up by over 35 per cent since 2000. Moreover, in spite of the government ostensibly controlling civil service headcount, SCS numbers have increased in every single year that the New Labour government has been in power. The government's explanation for the rise in SCS numbers is that: 'Developments in information technology and online services lead to a saving of clerical and administrative posts. At the same time an increase in the amount of policy work has necessitated an increase in the number of senior posts.'[14] But if this is true, why is the civil service still recruiting about 25,000 administrative and clerical staff every year?

The top ten most highly paid civil servants all earn comfortably above £200,000 a year (see Figure 5). Since these figures were published in a report covering 2007–8[15] the salaries for most of the people in the top ten will have increased and some of them may have moved on to other, often better paid, positions.

Figure 5 The top ten civil servants all earn over £200,000 a year

Organisation	Person	Position	Remuneration
1. HM Revenue & customs	Stuart Cruickshank	Director General	£285,125
2. Cabinet Office	Sir Gus O'Donnell	Cabinet Secretary	£285,000
3. Dept for Work & Pensions	Joe Harley	Chief Information Officer	£264,000
4. Dept. of Health	David Nicholson	Chief Executive	£252,000
5. HM Revenue	Steve Lamey	Director General	£245,000
6. Cabinet Office	Sir Richard Mottram GCB	Permanent Secretary	£237,300
7. Cabinet Office	Stephen Laws	Permanent Sec.	£225,000
8. Dept. for Work & Pensions	John Codling	Finance Director	£211,000
9. Ministry of Defence	Sir Bill Jeffrey	Permanent Sec.	£209,700
10. Dept. for Work & Pensions	Leigh Lewis	Head of Dept.	£202,000

If a member of the SCS pockets £200,000 a year, it is likely that they will be able to retire at 60 with a £100,000 a year inflation-linked pension and a one-off tax-free payment of three years' pension. The rest of us would have to put about £3 million in our pension funds to get a similar amount. To put it another way, each year a member of the SCS works they're getting the equivalent of close to £60,000 in pension benefits. This is pretty impressive, but even this hugely underestimates the benefits of a SCS pension. The government has now introduced a Lifetime Earnings Limit (LEL) for people in the private sector of £1.8 million in pension savings. Income from anything above the LEL is subject to tax at 55 per cent. This LEL, of course, doesn't apply to members of the SCS. Once you take our LEL into account, any of us would have to save over £4 million in our pensions to get a pension similar to one of the SCS supremos, equivalent to putting around £75,000 a year into our pension funds for 30 years assuming annual growth of about 4 per cent.

Recently the FDA, the SCS's union, bemoaned that fact that the Senior Salaries Review Board had only recommended pay increases for their members of about 2 per cent: 'Unfortunately, civil servants are often the losers in public sector pay.' But for a top SCS employee, a 2 per cent pay rise can mean another £4,000 a year in salary and an increase of £2,000 a year in their pension. Anyone in the private sector would have to shove another £60,000 into their pension savings to get this £2,000 a year pension increase from the age of 60. It might be worth bearing this in mind next time we hear top civil servants bleating that they're hard done by and that they should be given even more of our money.

Quids in for the quangocrats

Although top civil servants' pay and pension packages might look eye-wateringly generous to the taxpayers who have to pay for them, one cannot help feeling a little sorry for the SCS muckamucks as they perhaps enviously contemplate the massive amounts of money being showered on the government's favourite quangocrats. These must make our £200,000-a-year civil servants feel very poor indeed. In 2007–8 the top ten quango bosses' remuneration packages were all well north of £700,000 (see Figure 6).[16]

Figure 6 The top ten civil servants might envy the pay of the top ten quangocrats

Organisation	Person	Position	Remuneration
1. Network Rail	Iain Coucher	Chief Executive	£1,244,000
2. Royal Mail	Adam Crozier	Group Chief Exec.	£1,242,000
3. Channel 4	Andy Duncan	Chief Executive	£1,211,000
4. British Nuclear Fuels	Lawrie Haynes	Chief Executive	£1,138,000
5. Network Rail	Peter Henderson	Infrastructure Dir	£917,000
6. Channel 4	Kevin Lygo	Director of TV	£888,000
7. Financial Services Authority	Clive Briault	Managing Director Retail Markets	£883,000
8. Network Rail	Ron Henderson	Group Finance Dir.	£873,000
9. BBC	Mark Thompson	Director General	£816,000
10. British Nuclear Fuels	Mike Parker	Group Chief Exec.	£762,000

In fact, there are over 60 quangocrats who earn more than the highest paid member of the SCS and at least 169 quangocrats who earn more than the prime minister. Ludicrously, at the little-known British Waterways Board (BWB) no fewer than four executives receive a higher salary than our country's prime minister. One enigmatically explained their monster pay packages: 'We don't just run the canals, we have to earn the money to run the canals.'[17] If the economic life of our nation depended on goods being transported by canal, as happens in Holland, one might have understood BWB executives being given shed-loads of cash. However, as British canals are pretty much an economic irrelevancy, it's hard to see why their bosses should be paid so much. Still, at least the BWB employs over 1,950 people. The UK Film Council only has a very small staff of around 90 yet the chief executive gets around £230,000 a year and four other executives are picking up about £150,000 each. In fact there are many thousands of quango jobs where you can earn a six-figure salary, have lavish expenses and get a generous pension working on the periphery of government. But, of course, you have to know the right people in the New Labour sycophantocracy to get yourself a lucrative quango sinecure.

Bonanza for the bosses at the Beeb

The BBC is just one of many public-sector organizations which exemplify how public service seems to have turned into self-service. In early 2009 the Conservatives proposed to freeze the TV licence fee for a year on the basis that as the country's economic problems worsened, public bodies should learn to live within their means rather than expecting continually increasing budgets. As the shadow culture secretary explained: 'When times are tough, you don't just pocket the money allocated to you in happier times – you listen to people's concerns and you respond to the very changed economic circumstances of 2009.'[18] The BBC, of course, opposed what most people would probably feel was a quite reasonable suggestion. BBC Trust chairman Sir Michael Lyons dramatically called the proposal a 'recipe for curbing the BBC's editorial independence'.[19] Andy Burnham, the culture secretary, backed up the BBC top brass when he claimed, again with perhaps more histrionics than were appropriate, that 'ripping up the licence fee settlement' would 'undermine' its work and 'take away its creativity and stability'. Most of our MPs agreed that the BBC should be given more of our money and in May 2009 Parliament voted by a margin of two to one against the Tories' modest better-housekeeping proposal. Yet looking at the way BBC executives' pay, bonus and benefits packages have shot up over the last couple of years, one does not get the impression that the organization is particularly strapped for cash (see Figure 7).[20]

Figure 7 While fighting for an increase in the licence fee, the BBC seems to have been quite generous to its own senior management

Person	Position	Remuneration*		Increase
		2006/7	2007/8	
1. Mark Thompson	Director General	£788,000	£816,000	+3.6%
2. Jana Bennett	Director of Vision	£433,000	£536,000	+23.8%
3. Mark Byford	Deputy Dir. General	£437,000	£513,000	+17.4%
4. John Smith	Chief Executive BBC Worldwide Ltd.	£460,000	£486,000	+5.7%
5. Ashley Highfield	Director of Future Media and Technology	£359,000	£466,000	+29.8%
6. Caroline Thompson	Chief Operating Officer	£361,000	£440,000	+21.9%
7. Zarin Patel	Group Finance Director	£386,000	£440,000	+14%
8. Jenny Abramsky	Director of Audio & Music	£329,000	£419,000	+27.3%
	Total	£3,553,000	£4,116,000	+15.8%

*Cost to the licence fee payer

There are about 47 BBC executives earning either the same as or more than the prime minister. Moreover, there are at least five BBC executives with pension pots worth between £1.3 million and £3 million – these include John Smith whose pension value shot up from £3.167 million in 2008 to £3.673 million by 2009, Mark Byford who had an increase from £2.763 million to £3.406 million, and Caroline Thomson with a much more modest rise from £1.308 million to £1.475 million. As all three are in their early fifties, and assuming they all manage to get an increase in their salaries of 10 to 20 per cent by the time they retire, they will end up with pension pots in the £5 million to £7 million range.[21] At least 50 other BBC executives will have pension entitlements worth over £1 million each.

By early 2009, the BBC did seem to be aware that the age of lavish spending might be over and the director general proposed 'a budget which includes a further £400 million of painful cuts and reductions in expenditure, from freezing senior management pay and withdrawing discretionary bonuses to the amount we pay top talent'.[22] In 2008–9 several of the top bosses' packages did go down a little, but that of the director general Mark Thompson continued its upwards trajectory jumping to £834,000, giving him £46,000 a year more than he took home just two years earlier while the BBC chairman's remuneration also increased, going up £35,000 in just one year from £642,000 in 2007–8 to £677,000 in 2008–9. The director general denied that the BBC was especially profligate: 'The picture of a BBC swimming with cash and people and able to make additional savings at the drop of a hat is simply out of date.' But anybody looking at Figure 7 and admiring BBC bosses' salaries and pensions might come to a quite different conclusion.

There have also been a number of incidents which have possibly created the impression of an organization that is congenitally profligate with the money it takes from us. In 2008, for example, the BBC bid about £200 million for the rights to screen Formula One. This was £50 million more than the previous contract held by ITV, yet it is not clear that there were any other bidders. One ITV insider was reported to have said: 'This is about a 30 per cent increase in what ITV is paying. I can't tell you why the BBC is paying this much for it. I don't know how Bernie Ecclestone pulled it off.'[23] Also in 2008, the BBC sent 437 staff to the Beijing Olympics. This cost us around £3 million and was 124 more people than the 313 athletes that made up Team GB. Perhaps the BBC was trying to win a medal for the largest, most expensive media team at the event. In 2009, the BBC repeated this sort of extravagance when it sent around 400 staff to the Glastonbury Festival – no doubt they had lots of fun junketing at the public's expense.

However, the greatest cause of the BBC's financial incontinence comes from it apparently forgetting its whole purpose. There has been much comment in the press in recent months about the huge pay packets that the BBC has given to its 'big names'. We've been told that Jonathan Ross has a £6 million deal (£18 million over three years), Graham Norton £2.5 million, Jeremy Paxman £1 million, Chris Moyles £630,000 and Fiona Bruce £500,000. We do not know the figures for certain, because the BBC has spent about £250,000 of our money paying lawyers to find ways to avoid responding to Freedom of Information questions. The BBC's charter is very explicit: 'The BBC exists to serve the public interest.' Only by sticking to this public service obligation does it deserve the £3.6 billion or so a year it takes from us. If there are expensive stars who can attract huge audiences, then the BBC should allow them to be snapped up by commercial companies who are always keen to find talent to boost their viewing figures and thus advertising revenues, although one wonders if they really would be willing to pay the equivalent salaries to talent such as Jonathan Ross and Graham Norton.

We may not know exactly how much each of the stars costs the BBC, but there are intriguing clues that the corporation might be overpaying. For example a 2009 NAO study of costs at the BBC's radio stations showed that 'for most breakfast and "drivetime" slots, the BBC's costs are significantly higher than commercial stations, largely because of payments to presenters.' The report also stated: 'The BBC has been increasing its hourly rates for top presenters when commercial radio has been reducing its hourly rates for presenters.' These findings seemed to contradict a 2008 report produced for the BBC by the BBC which unsurprisingly concluded: 'The BBC was not paying more than the market price for talent and, indeed, that it may well be paying less.'[24] The report did let slip that the total bill for talent is about £750 million a year – over 20 per cent of the BBC's budget. Reviewing the NAO report, the PAC concluded: 'The BBC has not convinced us that it needs to pay so much more than the commercial sector to some of its presenters, who can owe their fame to their jobs at the BBC.'

As a public service, the BBC is charged with providing broadcasting services that commercial broadcasters would not normally supply. It is not meant to compete with commercial broadcasting; it is intended to supplement it. Too often the BBC seems to forget its public-service role and gets dragged into pointless bidding wars for sporting events and talent that just inflate prices and waste hundreds of millions of pounds of our money. Sometimes, as with Formula One, the BBC even manages to push up prices when there apparently aren't any other bidders. Whilst pleading poverty, the BBC never seems to question whether it really needs to pay so much for buying talent for which there might not be any market elsewhere. Nor does it question whether it really needs to provide so many TV channels and so many programmes, some of which like *Cash In The Celebrity Attic*, *Snog, Marry, Avoid?* and *Young, Dumb and Living Off Mum* may have negligible public-service content and may be more suited to a commercial channel.

In June 2009, there were some interesting goings-on at the Beeb. Faced by the collapse of Channel Four's advertising revenues and cost pressures at ITV's regional news, the government made a suggestion that just £100 million or so of the BBC's licence fee could go to supporting other media. Quite rightly seeing this as potentially being the end of the era of the BBC's monopoly over TV licencepayers' money, the BBC's panjandrums howled in protest and searched around for ways to justify keeping all our cash, or at least to prevent anyone else getting their hands on it. Having ignored the public's wishes for decades while pushing the licence fee ever higher, BBC bosses suddenly came up with the original idea of asking the public if they would rather any leftovers from the licence fee were returned to licence fee payers or handed over to commercial stations. Oddly, the BBC supremos have never before suggested giving us any of our money back.

CHAPTER 6

THE WASTERS AND THE WRECKERS

JUDGING BY RESULTS

As the economy comes crashing down around our ears, we might not resent the well-paid, over-pensioned and privileged public-sector elite if they were capable of delivering some reasonably good public services at an acceptable cost. Unfortunately, in department after department, the performance of the prosperous public-sectorcrats has generally been dismal and in some cases catastrophic. One way to understand the success or otherwise of this government's attempts to improve our public services is to look at how much we pay in taxes and the quality of our public services compared with other countries.

According to Organisation for Economic Co-operation and Development (OECD) figures Britain is the world's fifth richest country in terms of its total GDP. Things may have changed a bit in the last year or so, but we're still up with the big boys. In 1997, we were number 17 in a ranking of countries according to the percentage of their GDP paid in tax. Since then, thanks to our government's many tax increases we had risen to number 11 by 2007 and now are probably at about number 9, if not even higher. Yet although we have moved effortlessly ever upwards on the league table in the level of taxes we pay compared with other countries, it is far from obvious that our public services have been improving in line with our rising taxes. Depending on which statistics and reports you choose, you can prove just about anything, but there does seem to be an overwhelming body of evidence that our main services like health, education, skills training, policing and pensions are performing pretty dreadfully.

One international study put Britain in 13th position on the quality of healthcare provided, even though we spent much more on our health service than some of the countries above us in the rankings.[1] The government naturally rejected the findings. The health secretary at the time, Alan Johnson, said: 'The European Health Consumer Index report is not anchored in any reputable academic or international organization.' However, on a much more statistically grounded comparison of survival rates from common serious main conditions like cancer and strokes, what is called 'mortality amenable to healthcare', we have managed to crawl up from 18th to 16th place (see Figure 1).[2]

Figure 1 Britain is wealthy and our taxes are rising, but healthcare has hardly improved and in education we're falling behind

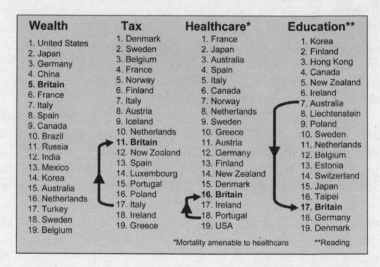

Wealth	Tax	Healthcare*	Education**
1. United States	1. Denmark	1. France	1. Korea
2. Japan	2. Sweden	2. Japan	2. Finland
3. Germany	3. Belgium	3. Australia	3. Hong Kong
4. China	4. France	4. Spain	4. Canada
5. Britain	5. Norway	5. Italy	5. New Zealand
6. France	6. Finland	6. Canada	6. Ireland
7. Italy	7. Italy	7. Norway	7. Australia
8. Spain	8. Austria	8. Netherlands	8. Liechtenstein
9. Canada	9. Iceland	9. Sweden	9. Poland
10. Brazil	10. Netherlands	10. Greece	10. Sweden
11. Russia	**11. Britain**	11. Austria	11. Netherlands
12. India	12. New Zealand	12. Germany	12. Belgium
13. Mexico	13. Spain	13. Finland	13. Estonia
14. Korea	14. Luxembourg	14. New Zealand	14. Switzerland
15. Australia	15. Portugal	15. Denmark	15. Japan
16. Netherlands	16. Poland	**16. Britain**	16. Taipei
17. Turkey	17. Italy	17. Ireland	**17. Britain**
18. Sweden	18. Ireland	18. Portugal	18. Germany
19. Belgium	19. Greece	19. USA	19. Denmark

*Mortality amenable to healthcare   **Reading

In education, the picture is more worrying. Here we're actually falling behind compared with other countries. Every three years the OECD conducts an international study called the Programme for International Student Assessment (PISA). About 400,000 students in 57 countries take tests in reading, mathematics and science. While there will be questions about how valid rankings are due to different countries' educational curricula, nevertheless by following trends over time PISA does give a good idea of how countries are progressing (or in Britain's case regressing) against their international competitors. In the 2000 study Britain was 4th in science, 7th in reading and 8th in mathematics. Commenting on the results, the then education secretary, Estelle Morris, claimed the PISA results showed British schools were 'world-beaters'. The 2000 study would have been measuring our children's performance before this government started to throw money at our schools as part of its education-education-education policies. Six years later, after tens of billions had been spent on improving our schools and paying our teachers more, the PISA results told us that in science we slipped from 4th to 14th, in reading we went from 7th to 17th and in maths we plunged from 8th to 24th (see Figure 1).

Given that Estelle Morris had apparently endorsed the 2000 PISA results, it was now slightly difficult for our government to rubbish results that it didn't like by dismissing PISA as meaningless, so education secretary Ed Balls had to admit: 'The scale of these falls is less significant than the direction of change – we have gone backwards.'[3]

In fact, the only areas where we're near the top of international tables are in negative performance indicators like our high crime rates and in the large proportion of the labour force that is unskilled. All this doesn't look too impressive. However, Prime Minister Gordon Brown seemed to have a different view of the situation when he said in mid 2008: 'This Government is making strong progress in tackling the issues that people really care about, from cutting crime and increasing opportunities for young people to creating a fairer, more responsive NHS.'[4] So, has this government delivered on its pledges to radically improve public services as Gordon Brown seems to be claiming or should we believe international comparisons suggesting this government has been an abject managerial failure?

Spending or investing?

The government now spends about twice as much each year on our public services as it did in 1997. There are two possible ways of looking at what can be expected from increasing spending on public services. One is the Law of Diminishing Returns which proposes that for every additional £10 million you spend, you will get fewer results than you did for the previous £10 million. However, there is an alternative view. The government claims to be 'investing' in public services and not just spending our money. If you invest properly you can set in train a series of events which will generate a return that can be many times the original investment.

To give an example: suppose a business is selling £100 million of a certain product and it decides to spend £50 million on developing and making another product that should also generate £100 million of sales. One way of viewing this investment is using what we call 'binary' or 'simplistic' thinking. According to this, an investment of just £50 million has given sales of £100 million, so you've got a very nice two-to-one return. However, if we use what is often referred to by the rather clumsy expression 'systems thinking' we can see a different picture. In this scenario, a £50 million investment gives the extra £100 million in sales, but it also broadens the range of people who use the company's products, leads to more power with retailers and allows greater economies of scale for advertising and distribution and so on. Also, because the company becomes known for innovative products, it attracts better, more innovative staff and this leads to even more innovation and further new products. Thus a £50 million investment has given the company much more than just some extra sales. Instead, it has set it off on a positive self-reinforcing upwards spiral that leads to yet more products, more sales, more market share and greater success. You can also call this the multiplier effect or self-reinforcing positive feedback.

We should see a similar effect with investment in public services, providing that it is accompanied by public-sector reform. Suppose you double the amount spent on education per child, as this government has done. Assuming the money is used effectively, we will have hundreds of thousands of children becoming much more qualified than would have happened without the doubling of investment. A better-educated workforce should make our businesses more competitive and therefore more successful in export markets. This will produce more wealth and so more tax revenue which can then be reinvested in even better education. Moreover, improved education will tend to lead to higher employment, less social deprivation, falling crime, a smaller prison population, less money spent on benefits and so on. This in turn should lead to better-functioning communities, more stable families and further reductions in social disorder. And that, of course, should make policing easier and cheaper. Also more people in successful jobs will mean much lower social costs and so taxes can be lowered which should further stimulate investment and economic activity.

You can do the same exercise for investments in health, policing, social policy or whatever. In theory, if a government did invest successfully in areas like education, health and social advancement and if a government managed to set off these kinds of self-reinforcing positive spirals, after maybe five or ten years, it could create conditions where public spending could actually be cut as the more prosperous and cohesive society became, the less need there would be for expensive government interventions.

So, with this in mind, let us see whether more than 12 years of hugely increased investment by this government have actually set this country off on a self-reinforcing positive spiral where advances in one area have knock-on beneficial effects throughout the whole of society or whether spending without reform has meant that the money has mostly been frittered away.

COULD DO BETTER

In education, the extraordinary way our children's exam results have improved every year has allowed the government to claim that doubling the amount of taxpayers' money it spends on each child has led to an impressive rise in Britain's educational standards. In 2009 a stunning 97.5 per cent of A-level entries passed, up from 97.2 per cent the previous year. Some of us may remember that when we were younger there actually was a genuine risk of people failing A-levels. When the 2008 A-level results were announced, the Schools Minister stated: 'They also show a good return on a decade of record investment and policies which have encouraged more young people to continue and achieve in education.'[5] Critics, on the other hand, have argued that exams have become increasingly dumbed down with easier questions, more use of multiple choice and the removal of more complex and theoretical content. A review by Ofqual, the exam regulator, of the new single science GCSE, which was intended to make the subject more relevant for teenagers, 'raised significant cause for concerns about standards'. The regulator found that many of the multiple choice questions were too easy as some of the possible options were 'too obviously incorrect' and that there were too many 'short-answer questions that were fairly limited in their requirements or in the scientific content they address'.[6]

A key task of education is to equip our children with a reasonable level of reading, writing, mathematics and science. Some recent statistics suggest that after 11 years of state education and at a cost of over £75,000 per child this is far from being achieved (see Figure 2).

By looking at some typical questions from recent GCSE papers, exams that children will typically sit at the age of 15 or 16, some light can be thrown on the argument about whether our children's education is improving or whether our examination standards have been reduced to allow more children to succeed.

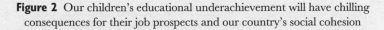

Figure 2 Our children's educational underachievement will have chilling consequences for their job prospects and our country's social cohesion

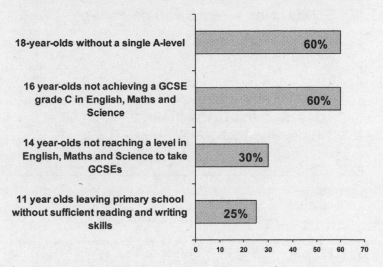

Figure 3 shows an essay question from an English paper. Helpfully the examiners give examinees some hints about what to cover in their answers. Somehow this seems less complex than having to comment on the quality of characterization or importance of the landscape in a Thomas Hardy novel, the role of the sub-plot or the nature of tragedy in a Shakespearian play or the imagery used in First World War poetry.

Those of us who still don't understand Ohm's Law or how to calculate the effect of different forces on a moving object might think that some of the questions from the physics paper don't seem to require a particularly deep knowledge of the subject (see Figure 4).

Figure 3 English GCSE November 2008

5. Describe a place you do not like.

Remember to:

- choose the place carefully
- describe the place in detail
- make clear why you do not like it

Figure 4 Physics GCSE March 2008

Question 3

Generating electricity causes problems for the environment

Match words, **A, B, C,** and **D** with the numbers **1-4** in the sentences

A   acid rain
B   global warming
C   noise pollution
D   radioactive waste

Nuclear power stations produce...**1**.......

Wind farms produce....**2**...........

Coal-fired power stations produce sulphur dioxide which causes...**3**....

All fossil-fuel power stations produce carbon dioxide which causes...**4**..

The Human Physiology and Health GSCE doesn't appear to be especially stretching either – being able to count from 0.1 to 10 is probably sufficient to answer this question (see Figure 5).

Figure 5 Human Physiology and Health GCSE June 2008

Table 1 shows the mass of nutrients in 100g of some fruits

	Apple	Fig	Guava	Lemon	Mango	Orange	Papaya	Pear	Pineapple
Protein (g)	0.2	1.3	0.9	1.0	0.6	0.7	0.6	0.6	0.4
Fibre (g)	0.3	2.2	5.2	1.7	0.7	0.3	0.8	1.0	0.5

2   (i)   Which fruit contains least protein?

....

(ii)   Which fruit contains most fibre?

....

Figure 6 Mathematics GCSE November 2008

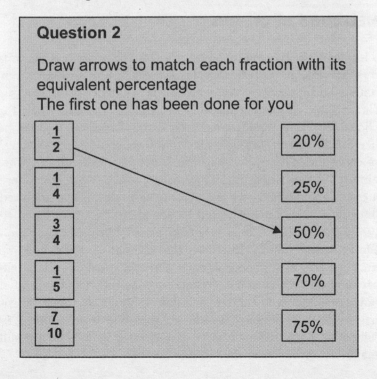

Question 2

Draw arrows to match each fraction with its equivalent percentage
The first one has been done for you

$\frac{1}{2}$ 20%

$\frac{1}{4}$ 25%

$\frac{3}{4}$ 50%

$\frac{1}{5}$ 70%

$\frac{7}{10}$ 75%

In mathematics, there's apparently no need to battle through the rigours of calculus. Instead, the examiners helpfully start to give part of the solution to an extraordinarily simple question, thus reducing the already limited possibility of students answering incorrectly (see Figure 6).

There are, of course, more difficult questions in all these exam papers. Moreover, the mathematics, physics and chemistry A-levels look almost as horrific as they always did. However, the above examples do suggest that there has been a deliberate attempt to lower the bar so that many more pupils can almost accidentally stumble over it rather than increasing children's academic capabilities so more of them can jump over a bar at a similar height to the one their parents would have faced.

MELTDOWN IN THE NHS

This government's failure to improve public services is perhaps most obvious in its recidivist, bungling attempts to reform our national health service. When looking for evidence of our leaders' catastrophic mismanagement of the NHS, you are spoilt for choice. A recent report comparing survival rates for conditions like cancer and strokes estimated that if we could reach the level of comparable European countries, over 17,000 deaths a year – almost 50 every single day of the year – could be avoided.[7] There are also about 6,000 people a year dying from hospital-acquired infections – the number would be just about 120 if we matched the performance of some other advanced European countries. On its website, the NHS admits that around 34,000 people die unnecessarily in our hospitals each year and an additional 25,000 are unnecessarily disabled.[8] Whatever your choice of figures, the only conclusion you can reach is that although this government has more than doubled healthcare spending from about £45 billion to £105 billion a year, death rates in Britain are still massively above where they should be.

One striking feature of this government's approach to reforming the NHS has been the extraordinary amounts of money that have been squandered on building a new managerial class, most of whom have absolutely no healthcare training. The number of managers and senior managers in the NHS has shot up from around 20,000 in 1997 to about 40,000 today. We now have 5,000 more managers than we have medical consultants (34,900). Just in the year 2008, when the recession had already started, the number of managers in the NHS went up by around 10 per cent while the number of medical staff only increased by about 2 per cent. There are various reasons for this almost obscene spawning of bureaucrats. These include the government's obsession with poorly thought through target-setting, reports, form-filling and box-ticking and the fact that many managers are often uncomfortable dealing with highly trained medical staff, so they surround themselves with other managers and live in their own little world, all holding important meetings with each other where they can speak management gobbledegook and think up new and exciting initiatives. In most hospitals today you'll find directors of strategy, of communication, of planning and development, and even marketing directors. Naturally, they all feel they need fully staffed offices undertaking tasks which could be deemed superfluous to improving the quality of care delivered by the NHS.

Not only have the numbers of managers shot up, so have their salaries compared with most frontline medical staff like nurses and midwives. The average salary of an NHS trust chief executive is now over £158,000 a year, more than double the 1997 level. Moreover, with this salary comes early retirement with a tax-free lump sum of up to £240,000 and an inflation-linked pension of over £70,000 a year. All the plethora of finance directors, marketing directors, strategy directors and communication directors will be getting similar enviably large pay and benefits packages. The increased cost to the NHS of these extra 20,000 managers is over £3 billion a year. If we could just get back to the level of management of 1997, the NHS would have an extra £10 million every single day to spend on medicines and patient care.

Yet while the managerial population is growing, the number of hospital beds the increasing army of managers have to manage has been falling – from about 250,000 in 1997 to less than 180,000 now. Where we once had 12.5 beds per manager, we now have 4.5, and the number keeps on falling. Then, of course, we should not forget the £600 million a year or so being spent by the NHS on management consultants, a cool £15,000 per manager, to show all these managers how to do their jobs.

Of course, it's not all bad news. If we are to believe the government's figures, then waiting times for many operations have fallen. The government also claims that no patient now has to wait more than four hours in Accident and Emergency (A&E). However, stories of hospitals fiddling their figures to meet the target, of patients being wheeled around hospitals to avoid breaking the four-hour goal and of patients dying because ambulances are being forced to hold patients until there is room in A&E might suggest that in some cases the government's supposed achievements are doing more harm than good. We also have many new hospital wards, car parks, other buildings and whole new hospitals. However, we have hardly started paying for most of these yet – there are about 100 new NHS construction projects being done under the government's inordinately expensive and failing Private Finance Initiative (PFI), costing over £10 billion which we will have to pay back over the next 30 years.

Shameless

Perhaps the most serious change in the NHS under this government has been a cultural change where the public-service ethic for which the NHS was once so respected has been replaced by the kind of corporate cover-up culture that gave us the Bhopal and Exxon Valdez disasters, but which public pressure and legislation have largely eliminated from the private sector.

In this new environment, the NHS, its lawyers and our many healthcare regulators seem to do all they can to conceal appalling standards of care, to deny any mistakes are ever made and to give the run-around to any families who dare question whether their loved ones were properly looked after. In her book *Who Cares?*, Midlands housewife Amanda Steane described her years battling with the NHS to try to discover why her husband was horrifically disabled after a series of unforgivable blunders. She only found out the truth when a nurse at one hospital, in defiance of her management, anonymously sent Amanda copies of incriminating blood test results which the NHS said did not exist. Even then, the NHS, its lawyers and the main regulators tried every trick they could think of to protect the doctors, nurses and managers involved and to avoid ever admitting anyone was at fault.

This new managerial cover-up culture can perhaps best be seen by comparing the fates of two people – whistle-blowing nurse Margaret Haywood at the Royal Sussex Hospital and Martin Yeates, formerly chief executive of the Mid Staffordshire NHS Trust.

Many people will have been amazed by the decision of the Nursing and Midwifery Council (NMC) to strike off Margaret Haywood in April 2009. Her 'crime' was to have cared too much about the appalling treatment given to elderly patients at the Royal Sussex Hospital in Brighton. When her warnings to management were repeatedly ignored, she felt she had no other choice than to take part in a 'Panorama' documentary exposing the scandalous failure to provide basic care to vulnerable patients. After the programme went out, the Sussex University Hospitals NHS Trust issued a public apology admitting 'serious lapses in the quality of care'. Nevertheless, rather than praising Margaret Haywood's dedication in fighting for her patients and exposing the scandalous care they received, the NMC's fitness to practise panel decided to strike her off for supposedly betraying patient confidentiality.

Chief executive Martin Yeates' story could hardly have been more different. Just a few weeks after Margaret Haywood was struck off and thus probably lost her means of earning a living, he resigned from his job secure in the knowledge that we taxpayers would be paying for his considerable financial comfort for the rest of his life. In 2008, Mr Yeates received a pay rise of about £40,000 to a reported £169,000 a year when the Mid Staffordshire NHS Trust was granted foundation status. Just this would probably increase his pension by up to £20,000 a year. A report by the Healthcare Commission into anywhere between 400 and 1,200 unnecessary deaths at the hospital for which he was responsible found standards of care 'shocking' and 'appalling' and concluded that 'hundreds of patients died because the trust's board was more interested in meeting government targets and attaining elite foundation status than in patient care'.[9]

Martin Yeates was suspended on full salary while the report was published. Then instead of being fired, he was allowed by his peers to resign with his pension intact in true Fred Goodwin style without any disciplinary action being taken against him. One newspaper reported that Yeates was likely to receive more than £110,000 in salary payments during his notice and suspension period as well as a tax-free lump sum of up to £350,000 plus a pension of around £65,000 a year.[10] If true, all this would be worth over £2 million.

After Amanda Steane's story was noticed by some journalists, she was approached to see if any of the nurses who had helped her against hospital management, would be willing to conduct covert filming for a TV documentary about poor patient care in their local hospital, a hospital with consistently one of the highest mortality rates in Britain. All the nurses refused as they said they were too afraid of what would happen to them. From looking at how Margaret Haywood was dealt with, it seems that they were right to fear the reaction of their management were they to expose shortcomings in patient care leading to unnecessary injuries and deaths.

The problem with these and many other similar cases is that they send out a clear signal to all NHS staff that if you dare break the rules when you see failings in patient care, you're likely to have your career in healthcare destroyed even if you're saving patients' lives by acting. However, if you're a member of the new privileged managerial class, it may seem that, almost no matter how many patients have been harmed, you'll probably be well looked after by the taxpayer for the rest of your days.

MOST OF US HAVE NEVER MANAGED ANYTHING

One of the reasons that this government, like so many governments before it, has failed to deliver decent public services is that ever fewer of our politicians have ever had any working experience in running an organization of any size. You actually do need some specific skills and understanding of organizational behaviour to successfully run a large government department. Yet our politicians can go from being lawyers, lecturers, union representatives or political advisers to suddenly being responsible for hundreds of thousands of employees. To expect this massive transition to be successful truly must be one of the most extreme cases of the triumph of hope over experience. Moreover, it can sometimes help if a person has at least a smidgen of experience in the area for which they are responsible. Most of us would not dream of trying to run a large pharmaceutical, oil or consumer goods company unless we had a reasonable working knowledge of what such companies did. Yet most British politicians taking over the great departments of state have no working knowledge of their departments' activities. For example, heads of the Department of Health have included: Frank Dobson, who worked at the Central Electricity Generating Board as an administrative officer and then for the office of the Local Ombudsman; Alan Milburn, who owned a bookshop for a while and then was a councillor; John Reid, who worked mainly for the Labour party; Patricia Hewitt, who was press officer for Age Concern then worked at the National Council for Civil Liberties;

Alan Johnson, who came from the Post Office unions; though Andy Burnham, who worked in politics first as a parliamentary researcher and then as an adviser, has had some political, rather than practical, experience of the NHS as he did work for the NHS Confederation as its parliamentary officer, served for two years on the Health Select Committee and was a Minister of State at the DoH for a further year.

There has been a similar situation in education: David Blunkett went straight into politics after graduation, has lectured in politics and industrial relations and was a city councillor in Sheffield; Estelle Morris was actually a teacher, so full marks there; Charles Clarke worked for Hackney Borough Council and Neil Kinnock, though he has spent time at a public affairs consultancy; Ruth Kelly was with the *Guardian* and the Bank of England; Alan Johnson, as mentioned, was from the Royal Mail; and Ed Balls was a journalist at the *Financial Times* and then an adviser to Gordon Brown. We see the same worrying picture in pretty much all the other key government positions. Moreover, even when they have worked, very few senior politicians have ever been in a business which actually had to earn money by providing a useful product or service and so almost none have experienced the unfortunate reality that money has to be earned before it can be spent. Instead, most have been in organizations which have fed off a seemingly unending flow of taxpayers' cash. Throughout their working lives, if they wanted more money for a project or to hire more staff, they could just take it from us.

IT'S TRANSFORMATION TIME

One theme we keep hearing from this government concerns how it is supposedly transforming our public services. Blair was forever using the words 'transform' and 'transformation', promising a 'transformation' of the NHS, a 'transformation' of secondary education, 'transformations' of all our public services and he even had a meeting with top civil servants where he explained the 'Seven Keys to Transformation' which would lead to a 'transformed civil service'.[11] Alistair Campbell said history would judge Blair as a 'great transforming Prime Minister'. Blair's successor also seems to have inherited the word – Gordon Brown has used it many times, for example in 2009: 'When we give people knowledge about their public services, we give them power over them; power to shape and even transform them.'[12] In fact, it's quite a fashionable word throughout government. For the last three years the government has even produced a chunky report called *The Transformational Government Annual Report* in which it details the many successes of its Transformational Government programme, the aim of which is: 'Delivering better, more efficient services for everyone.'[13] And the programme seems to be central to this government's ambitions for improving public services: 'Government is committed to a range of citizen-focused activities designed to optimise service design and delivery, and is proud that the United Kingdom is held up as providing some world-class examples of Transformational Government.'

Sadly, there aren't too many private-sector jobs advertised in the appointments sections of the Sunday newspapers at the moment. However, if you want a career in the public sector then there's definitely a job for you if you're able to spout management gobbledegook like 'stakeholders', 'catalyst', 'drive for continuous improvement', 'customer service delivery' and if you're good at using the word 'transform' in all its many variations (see Figure 7).

Some public-sector recruiters love the word 'transform' so much that they use it two or even three times in the same recruitment ad. Others have set up special websites for interested would-be transformers such as www.mertontransformations.co.uk and www.transformingwarrington.co.uk. The examples in Figure 7 are just taken from a few public-sector job ads on just one Sunday. The mind boggles to think how many times transform, transforming and transformation are used and abused by the public sector in a year.

If you're really lucky, you could even land yourself a job as a Director of Transformation – no well-dressed council nowadays

Figure 7 If you can say 'transform' and 'transformation' while keeping a straight face, there are lots of jobs for you

"Assist us in championing our transformational journey to outstanding"
Warrington Council

"We're about to embark on an exciting period of transformation and change"
Warrington Council

"You will have led a large scale business transformation"
HM Revenue and Customs (HMRC)

"Create and implement a forward thinking blended learning strategy that transforms the direction of development activities" **HMRC**

"We've been planning our transformation for a while now"
Merton Council

"Truly exciting and long term transformation project"
Merton Council

"HMIC has just entered a new period of transformational change"
HM Inspector of Constabulary

"Excellent experience of transformational change will be important"
HM Inspector of Constabulary

"Part of a wide-ranging transformation programme"
Qualifications and Curriculum Authority (QCA)

"Contributor to a number of key reforms to transform the education and skills landscape"
QCA

"There is a transformation underway at City of York Council"
City of York Council

"Help deliver transformational change"
Trafford Council

Appointments section Sunday Times 31 May 2009

seems to be without one. The pay is usually great (typically over £80,000 a year) and, of course, you don't have to do very much as nobody really knows what you're meant to be doing anyway. As long as you organise a few out-of-the-box, blue-sky-thinking, brainstorming workshops and set out a strategic vision to help people reinvent themselves in a customer- and stakeholder-focused learning environment using continuous-improvement methodologies resulting in world-class partnerships – well, you can't really go wrong.

In their excellent book *The Gods that Failed*, Larry Elliott and Dan Atkinson write about New Labour's claims to be introducing a new kind of 'transformational government'. The authors inform us: 'The origins of this phrase are not easy to discern but it has been ascribed (plausibly enough) to Tony Blair'.[14] In fact the government seems to have inherited its enthusiasm for transformation from its friends in management consulting. In the 1990s many of the major consultancies were selling large 'transformation' projects to their clients. One consultancy, David Craig's former employer Gemini Consulting which was part of the Capgemini group, a major supplier of computer systems and consultancy services to our government, even worked on a book called *Transforming the Organization*.[15] Reviewing the book at the time, the respected magazine *The Economist* questioned the value of transformation projects and wrote that a true transformation 'would employ an army of consultants for a century – and cause endless disruption'.[16]

However, our government seems to have enthusiastically embraced the idea of transformation and large numbers of transformation projects have been launched in both central and local government. Capgemini have been particularly successful in supporting the public sector's transformation journey and amongst the many public-sector contracts they have won, have supported 'transformation' projects at Dorset County Council, Derbyshire County Council, Croydon Council and Gloucestershire County Council to name just a few. The jewel in Capgemini's transformation crown is probably the massive Aspire deal: 'a strategic partnership between Capgemini and Her Majesty's Revenue and Customs (HMRC)'.[17] At the time this was won, Capgemini announced that it was 'one of the world's largest outsourcing deals' and 'Capgemini is the prime contractor and has overall responsibility for the transformation and delivery of IT services to HMRC.'

SO HOW MUCH HAS BEEN WASTED?

There are several different ways of trying to assess how much of our money our government has actually wasted. In the two versions of the *Bumper Book of Government Waste* we calculated in detail that about £100 billion a year, around 17 per cent of government spending, was easily identifiable waste. This matches quite well with an international study which compared public-sector productivity in different countries.[18] The conclusion was that if the British public sector was as efficient as the public sectors in countries like the US, Japan, Switzerland, Luxembourg, Ireland or Australia, then we could have the same level of public services that we have for about 15 per cent less money. This 15 per cent of the current £671 billion 2009–10 budget gives about £100 billion wasted each year. Using this approach on the £6.1 trillion that the government has spent since coming to power in 1997, almost £1 trillion will have been wasted. Then you have to take account of the disappointing fact that now public spending will soon reach the giddy heights of over £700 billion a year, it may take a decade or more to bring it back under control, if this ever can actually be done. So, assuming a wastage level of £100 billion a year for the next ten years, there is still another £1 trillion to be flushed away.

However, one could take the view that the gargantuan increase in spending should have put this country on a positive self-reinforcing spiral leading to greater economic success and a falling tax burden. Instead we got the opposite – a self-reinforcing negative spiral of wasted money, rising social breakdown, millions of unskilled people who have never worked, exploding benefits costs, increasing taxes, reduced competitiveness, falling wealth, greater borrowing, higher taxes, further burdens on households and businesses and so on. In this scenario the real costs of the squandered opportunities are almost unimaginable. Trillions more will go up in smoke before we can ever bring public spending and tax revenues back into balance with each other and begin to boost real economic growth. Sadly, this government has spent freely, but it has seldom invested.

CHAPTER 7

THE TRIUMPH
OF INCOMPETENCE

WELCOME TO DOMENOMICS

Domenomics may not be a familiar word, as we have just invented it, but we are all too familiar with the branch of economics it describes: the public sector taking and wasting huge amounts of our money on big projects that nearly always turn out to be catastrophically expensive failures. Domenomics is named after that great triumph of public-sector profligacy, the Millennium Dome. The Dome should have cost us about £399 million, but we ended up with a bill of close to £800 million. Back in 1997, when it became clear that the project was spinning out of control, the government did consider abandoning it. However, Deputy Prime Minister John Prescott was one of those who argued vociferously that the build should continue. 'If we can't make this work, we're not much of a government,' he famously commented as he urged the Cabinet not to ditch the monster. It's not often that we agree with Prescott, but in this case he seems to have perfectly summed up the government's managerial incompetence which has been so magnificently and repeatedly demonstrated since the heady, hopeful days of New Labour's accession to power.

In the private sector, unless you're a banker, when you spend a few hundred million pounds or even a few billion on a project, you're expected to get some kind of return on the investment. Moreover, if your costs start shooting stratospherically over your original budget, you would normally be hauled before your boss to explain why you're eating your way through so much money. Unfortunately for us taxpayers, this is not how things work in the public sector.

Each public-sector project will be slightly different and the excuses for overspending and managerial failure can be both varied and creative. However, in spite of their differences, many will follow a similar sad and predictable four-step trajectory.

Step One: The three Ps – personal vanity, politics and profiteering

Firstly, many large public-sector investment projects are political decisions based largely on the personal vanity of ministers or the greed of their associates and sponsors rather than being justified by any semblance of economic or social necessity. For example, a prime minister wants to celebrate the millennium in style with his hangers-on, showbiz mates and other cronies; or a minister wants to be seen opening a shiny new hospital; or a minister has been fooled by fee-hungry consultants into believing that an all-singing, all-dancing new billion-pound computer system with lots of flashing lights will magically 'transform' the performance of his or her department.

Step Two: The big 'little cost' lie

In order to get a project both approved by the Cabinet and accepted by the public, ministers will collude with career-focused civil servants to massively underestimate the likely costs. Usually they will be helped by profit-seeking private contractors all eager for their lucrative bit of the action should the project get the go-ahead. In polite terms this tendency to downplay the real potential cost is called an 'optimism bias', because ministers are said to be 'optimistic' about the eventual costs. At a conference of suppliers to the public sector, one very senior executive had the audience cracked up with laughter when he explained that his company always pitched their public-sector projects at a price they knew would be accepted, because once they had got the deal, they could increase the cost as much as they wanted and none of the politicians or civil servants involved would ever complain.

Step Three: Spend, spend, spend

Once a project has started, it doesn't seem to matter how much is spent. Politicians will never stop a project because this would mean losing face and possibly harm their political advancement. Likewise, a civil servant will never call time on a minister's pet project however much of our money is being haemorrhaged. If a senior civil servant dared to criticize a minister's showpiece scheme or was seen to actually be involved in scrapping some disaster or other, then they could risk damaging their promotion prospects and even their chances of their OBE or knighthood. Wasting public money never affected a civil servant's career, but acting to prevent waste can be hugely detrimental. Anyway, many large projects last several years, so with an average of two to three years in each post, most senior civil servants will have been promoted out of trouble by the time a project's real costs have become apparent. So why rock the boat? On the other hand, if you've inherited a disaster from someone else, you just carry on spending as you can blame your predecessor for any problems.

Step Four: Bluff the PAC-man

With some of the worst projects, usually when it's far too late to do anything, the politically subservient watchpoodle, the National Audit Office, will make a half-hearted attempt to find out what went wrong and where all our money has gone. Its report will be watered down by the department which has wasted hundreds of millions or even billions and then presented to the Public Accounts Committee (PAC). The MPs on the PAC will then summon a couple of the senior civil servants involved, try to question those who should have been responsible about why things went so horribly wrong and huff and puff in histrionic outrage at the amounts of our money that have vanished. Knowing they only have to face the PAC for an hour or so, the civil servants will expertly duck and weave, usually denying any responsibility for anything and inventing an extraordinary number of new excuses to absolve themselves of any blame. If things really get tough, and they seldom do, the top civil servants will sometimes go as far as admitting that 'important lessons have been learnt'. The PAC chairman will then conclude that whatever project they are reviewing is the 'worst example' of incompetent management the PAC has ever seen.

The Child Support Agency IT system was branded one of the 'worst public administration scandals in modern times' and we were told 'the facts beggar belief'; the Department of Transport's shared services project was implemented with 'stupendous incompetence' and was 'one of the worst cases of project management seen by this committee'; the Libra IT system for magistrates courts was called 'one of the worst PFI deals we have seen'; Building Schools for the Future was 'perhaps the worst case of using consultants'; and the latest Ministry of Justice C-Nomis project to track offenders was 'one of the worst reports I have read'. This is just to name a few; there are many more similar disasters which the PAC has described using various negative superlatives usually including the word 'worst'. Once this process is over, everybody will nod sagely and agree that 'this must never happen again', but exactly the same procedure will be repeated on future projects.

At the start of one meeting in 2009, the PAC chairman finally seemed to understand the utter futility of the whole exercise when he said to a senior civil servant:

> You will come with the classic defence line, that of course you were not there, it is all in hand now, you have learned the lessons, in the sort of school that permanent secretaries

learn when they come to this committee. However, I have had all this before and I just do not know whether there is any point really carrying on, frankly.

But they did carry on with the farce. At the end of the meeting, the chairman summed up: 'Clearly this project was handled badly, it achieved poor value for money, many of the causes of delays and cost overruns could have been avoided. I could make some grand eloquent statement about how we never expect to see this happen again in the Civil Service, but I suspect I would be wasting my breath.'[1]

DOMENOMICS IN ACTION

Ten of the biggest projects run by this government should have cost about £20 billion and will actually set us taxpayers back by over £46 billion – a waste of £26 billion by a government which claims it would be impossible to cut public spending without harming hospitals, care for the elderly and schools. While the Dome is a highly visible symbol of this government's self-delusion, managerial incompetence and profligacy, there are quite a few projects which have managed to waste even more money (see Figure 1).

Figure 1 There are several projects which have wasted much more money than the Dome

Project name	Budget* £m	Actual cost £m	Over-run £m
1. 2012 Olympics	2,400	14,000	11,600
2. NHS IT system	2,300	12,400	10,100
3. Astute class submarine	2,578	3,806	1,228
4. Type 45 Destroyer	5,475	6,464	989
5. Skynet 5 Sat. comms.	2,775	3,660	885
6. Nimrod MRA4	2,813	3,602	789
7. Leicester Hospital	286	711	425
8. Barts Hospital	620	1,000	380
9. Millenium Dome	**399**	**766**	**367**

* Cost to taxpayers

Squandering our money should be an Olympic sport

The greatest and most wasteful of all this government's efforts will probably turn out to be the 2012 Olympic Games in London. Originally we were told that we taxpayers would have to pay only around £2.4 billion of the total £4 billion necessary to stage this spectacle. Now those responsible for the event claim that they will stick to a new commitment of a mere £9.3 billion, almost all of which will now be covered by taxpayers. But recent problems with financing the Olympic Village, land prices, some disturbing building issues and the rapid evaporation of a large part of the £2.7 billion contingency fund with three years still to go before the event suggest that £14 billion may be more likely. There is unfortunately a possibility that the final bill for taxpayers may be even higher once all those riding the Olympics gravy train have been awarded bonuses for spending an Olympian amount of our money. A former Olympics boss foresaw a final total in the region of £20 billion.

It is unclear whether the probable rise in the bill for taxpayers of £11.6 billion above the original £2.4 billion bid is mostly due to the organizers' gross underestimation of the true cost, whether honestly or deliberately, in order to win the public's support, the IOC's approval and fantastically well-paid jobs for themselves; whether much of the over-run is a result of breathtakingly stupendous arrogance and incompetence by those organizing the event; whether the people at fault are greedy suppliers who have inflated costs; or whether the gargantuan over-run is just a bit of bad luck as the whole thing is being run by Britain's best project managers and most dedicated public servants who are all straining every sinew to ensure they deliver value for taxpayers' money. Still, whatever their qualities or otherwise, our olympocrats certainly seem to be well rewarded for their efforts with at least ten of them earning comfortably more than the prime minister (see Figure 2).[2]

Figure 2 Winning Olympic gold

Person	Position	Remuneration 2007/8
1. David Higgins	Chief Executive ODA	£624,000
2. Paul Deighton	Chief Executive LOGOC	£557,440
3. Dennis Hone	Director of Finance ODA	£358,000
4. Howard Shiplee	Director of Construction ODA	£357,000
5. Ralph Luck	Director of Property ODA	£297,000
6. Alison Nimmo	Director Design & Regeneration ODA	£290,000
7. Simon Wright	Director Infrastructure & Utilities OCA	£290,000
8. Lord Coe	Chairman LOGOC	£285,000
9. Hugh Sumner	Director of Transport ODA	£285,000
10. Neil Wood	Chief Financial Officer LOGOC	£260,000

As we are in an economic downturn, up to £14 billion being splashed out on just a few weeks of minority-interest sports (some of which aren't even real sports) may not be the best use of taxpayers' cash. However, instead of venturing into the legally dangerous yet entertaining territory of discussing who was irresponsible for what, we will restrict ourselves to suggesting how the Games could have been run much less expensively had the organizers been a little less ambitious on our, or at least on their own, behalf.

The Olympics stadium was due to cost around £274 million. Unfortunately, somebody got their sums wrong when designing the roof and now we'll be paying around £550 million. This in itself is a scandal, but worse will come after the Games are over. Once the athletes, the press and the gravy-training Olympics officials have packed their bags, most of the seats in the 80,000 seat stadium will be ripped out, leaving just a modest 25,000-seat athletics site, at a price of around £22,000 a seat. While eagerly pouring our money into this expensive white elephant, perhaps the new lords of the rings should have considered using the perfectly adequate facilities at Wembley or Twickenham for the main opening and closing ceremonies and larger events and thus avoided wasting most of this £550 million in the first place.

The swimming pool was originally budgeted at an already massive £75 million. However, while professing that they were keeping costs under control, our olympocrats hired a suitably expensive architect whose supposedly iconic design managed to push the pool's price up to an incredible £300 million. Unfortunately, there are no other suitable pools in the London area – the Crystal Palace pool is not up to date and not big enough – but there are alternative facilities at the Sunderland Aquatic Centre or at the Sheffield Ponds Forge International Sports Centre.

Around another £30 million will be used to build an artificial white-water river in Hertfordshire for canoeists – costing several hundred thousand pounds for each of the lucky canoeists who will use it. No mention has been made by our high-flying Olympics bosses of cutting costs by using the perfectly functional white-water course just outside Nottingham nor of putting the canoeists up in rooms in the nearby university campus, which will be largely empty for the summer holidays at the time of the 2012 Games. Apparently, we also need a velodrome where our cyclists can win lots of medals. There's one in Manchester which could do the job. But rather than using that, our masters want to build an expensive new one as part of a £80 million velo-park in Stratford.

We must also provide suitable working space for the 20,000 journalists who may be attending the event. Spending £355 million of our money on a media centre for them – over £17,000 per journalist for just a few weeks work – does seem out of place in view of the economic difficulties facing this country. We taxpayers may be moving into an Age of Austerity, but our Olympics bosses don't seem to be coming with us, because they have been given almost unlimited access to our money and clearly intend to spend as much of it as they can.

Of the more than £1.3 billion that will be spent building the basic facilities, about half could have been saved with greater management effort. As for the other £12.7 billion the olympocrats are planning to spend – who knows where that's going and how much of that will turn out to be completely unnecessary waste.

The worst computer system in the world

Coming a close second to the 2012 Olympics in terms of flushing huge quantities of our cash down the toilet is the NHS's great new computer system. This was originally called the National Programme for IT (NPfIT), but as with so many other things under this government, the spin doctors invented a sexy new name, Connecting for Health (CfH), presumably in the hope that this street-cred rebranding would divert us from the fact that the whole thing is a badly planned, badly bought, badly implemented mega-disaster. In *Plundering the Public Sector* in 2006 we explained in possibly painful detail exactly what was wrong with the whole project; why it would cost billions more than budgeted; why it would be at least ten years late; why it would never work; and why it wasn't ever necessary in the first place.[3] At the time, co-author David Craig was summoned to a meeting with the then head of the National Audit Office (NAO), Sir John Bourne, and an assorted selection of his sidekicks as the NAO was just about to publish a highly positive report on CfH which one MP on the Public Accounts Committee described as 'gushing' in its praise of the project and its management – a rather different conclusion from the one reached by David Craig in his assessment. In spite of the NAO's laudatory whitewashing of the impending calamity, there was one member of the PAC who wasn't completely taken in by the establishment cover-up and who tried to find out from the project's then boss, Richard Granger, how much the whole thing would cost us:

Q142 Mr Bacon: How much has been committed irrevocably to the programme so far?

Mr Granger: I do not have the exact figure right now.

Q143 Mr Bacon: You do not know? You do not know? We have been told that this programme is going to cost

£2.3 billion, we have been told it is going to cost £6.2 billion, we have been told it is going to cost £6.8 billion and we have been told it is going to cost £12.4 billion or £12.6 billion. Lord Warner, the Minister said only three weeks ago on 30 May that it was going to cost £20 billion and you still cannot tell this committee how much has actually been committed to it.[4]

Since then, of course, the whole thing has predictably gone down the pan and the NAO's 'gushing' report has proved to have been garbage. The project boss has gone – apparently he went to Australia, about as far away from the dreadful mess as he could get without leaving the planet. Two of the four main suppliers have walked out, leaving behind the opportunity of earning billions. One can only assume that no amount of money could tempt them to continue down the highway to hell that the project had taken. Meanwhile, back in the smoking remnants of the programme, it still doesn't work and there has been something approaching chaos in the few hospitals that have tried to use it. Many hospitals are refusing to have anything to do with it, there are endless delays and billions continue to be spent without any clear sign that anything of any value is being achieved. By mid 2009, the latest set of CfH bosses were admitting that it would be 'a huge challenge' to get the systems working by 2013, ten years after the start of the project and seven years after the whole thing should have been completed. As usual, nobody has the courage to pull the plug after billions having already been spent and almost no value achieved. The official attitude seems to be 'we've started, therefore we'll finish', regardless of whether it will ever work and, of course, regardless of the cost.

The government keeps attacking its opponents by claiming that cutting spending on the NHS would mean fewer nurses and fewer doctors. However, scrapping this catastrophic, terminally ill computer system would pay for an awful lot of nurses and doctors. But that might mean the government would lose face.

So CfH, which should have been dead and buried long ago, still stumbles on like a blundering, blinded mummy, spreading organizational chaos, administrative misery and busted budgets wherever it goes.

Still defending the indefensible

The third great sinner in spectacularly overspending its budgets is the Ministry of Defence (MoD), which has no fewer than three projects on the above list of big overspenders. In the MoD's defence, one could say that it is inevitable it will feature in such a list as it tends to run larger, more technically complex projects than other government departments. On the other hand, it could be argued that with so much experience of running major projects, the MoD bureaucrats should know what they're doing by now.

Each year the NAO publishes a report on the MoD's 20 largest projects and then some of the MoD chiefs appear before the PAC to explain their invariably dismal results. In 2004, the PAC was none too impressed by the MoD bosses: 'This report once again records the woeful performance of the Department in procuring defence equipment.' In 2005, the MoD's performance was the worst the PAC had seen up to that point. In 2006 the results were even worse. Unfortunately 2007 wasn't a good year either. Then in 2008, the main projects suffered some of the worst delays and cost increases in many years. One project even managed to be delayed by 27 months in just one year and the total delay for the 20 largest projects is now about 40 years. The PAC lamented the ongoing nightmare of the MoD's incompetence: 'This is a disappointing set of results, particularly because the problems are being caused by previously identified failures such as poor project management.' The MoD worthies have spent hundreds of millions of pounds on accountants and consultants to improve their management systems and to introduce what they call 'Smart Acquisition' and every year they assure the PAC that enormous progress is being made. But reviewing the previous year's results in 2009, the PAC seemed unconvinced:

> The Department repeatedly tells us that many of the projects suffering delays and cost increases pre-date the Smart Acquisition reforms it introduced in 2001 and so do not provide a fair reflection of progress it has made. We were, therefore, particularly unimpressed to note that the three projects reporting the biggest in-year delays were all approved after that date. This suggests that these reforms have been ineffective.[5]

Criticisms made by the PAC were that the MoD was 'failing to act as an intelligent customer' and had 'a lack of grip' on the main projects. Almost in sorrow rather than anger, the PAC concluded: 'The Department has been attempting to improve its processes for nearly ten years and, even on long-running defence projects, we would expect to see signs of progress by now.' As they do every year, the defence bosses agreed that 'there were lessons to be learnt', yet no doubt we'll see the whole miserable charade repeated again next year and the year after that. Meanwhile, our troops lack the equipment they need and lives are being lost unnecessarily. However, every year the MoD bureaucrats in their newly refurbished £2.3 billion Central London offices get their performance bonuses.

ARISE, SIR JOHN!

No description of the public sector's failure to deliver what it is paid to deliver would be complete without a mention of Sir John Gieve. We're not for a moment implying that Sir John has ever been or is in any way incompetent. Sir John is generally described as affable, friendly, likeable and honourable. But he does seem to have had the misfortune to have occasionally been in the wrong place at the wrong time. Sir John was the Permanent Secretary at the Home Office from 2001 to December 2005 – the time when some of the most worrying events took place, including about a million immigrants entering the UK without the Home Office, which is responsible for our borders, apparently noticing they were there. There was also the foreign prisoners cock-up, where more than a thousand criminals who should have been deported were allowed to stay in Britain to carry on robbing, raping and murdering us. A key responsibility of the top civil servant in each government department is to produce a reliable set of accounts so we all know how our money is being spent. The Home Office accounts for 2004–5 were such a mess that the Auditor General refused to approve them and Sir John was personally criticized 'for failing in his duty to Parliament to produce auditable statements for 2004–5'.[6] The PAC report stated: 'This failure reflects a lack of high-level attention to accounting requirements and a poor sense of the corporate importance.'

On the personal recommendation of the then chancellor, Gordon Brown, Sir John Gieve was promoted to Deputy Governor of the Bank of England in charge of financial stability in the banking system. A member of the Public Accounts Committee remarked: 'In any parish council or cricket club the person responsible would have been out on his ear. What actually happened was that Sir John was promoted to become Deputy Governor of the Bank of England in charge of financial stability in the banking system. You might reasonably expect to see this in a Gilbert and Sullivan opera, but not in real life.'[7] Shortly after Sir John's departure to the sunnier climes of the Bank of England, the new home secretary, John Reid, famously declared the Home Office 'not fit for purpose'.

In those balmy days of 2006, long before the financial crisis devastated our economic prospects, as Sir John moved into his new job one newspaper described him as: 'one of those permanent secretaries who's risen through one disaster after another like an angel'.[8] In his new position at the venerable Bank of England, Sir John seems to have surpassed even his dubious successes at the Home Office. He may have been in charge of financial stability, but as some readers might have noticed, that's not quite what he delivered. Unfortunately, while Sir John was on duty at the Bank of England we experienced probably the biggest financial meltdown in British history. The most withering criticism of Sir John's performance in his new role came from a member of the House of Commons Treasury Select Committee who described Sir John during the Northern Rock crisis as being: 'asleep in the back shop while there was a mugging out front'.[9] It perhaps didn't help Sir John's case that when he first learnt of the problems at Northern Rock he reportedly went away for two weeks, first for a funeral and then a week's holiday in France.

In 2008, Sir John stood down early, presumably with a very healthy retirement package for which we will pay for many years to come, and he has since become the chairman of a private company. Reporting Sir John's new appointment, one commentator wrote: 'Sir John's career is proof – if any were needed – that failure in the top levels of the public sector is not something that need end a career. Quite the reverse, in fact; it serves to keep it varied and interesting.'[10]

CHAPTER 8

THE TIMID AND
THE TOOTHLESS

'In the last twelve months our staff have done a very good
job in extremely tough circumstances.' Hector Sants, Chief
Executive of the Financial Services Authority, explaining
why his staff were being given substantial bonuses as the
financial system went up in flames.[1]

A GROWTH INDUSTRY OF WHICH TO BE PROUD

Our manufacturing sector has declined by about 15 per cent
since this government came to power. However, there is one
industry which has seen massive and continual growth over the
last 12 years – the regulation industry. Whatever the problem,
this government's automatic response seems to be to appoint
an 'independent' committee or set up yet another so-called
'watchdog'. There have been so many new watchdogs formed
that it is difficult to keep track of them all.

In 2008, ten of the larger regulators cost us almost £1 billion,
either directly in taxes or indirectly in fees levied on businesses.
Eight of these regulators have been set up by this government (see
Figure 1).

Figure 1 Most of the largest regulators were set up by this government

Regulator	Year	Budget	Staff
1. Financial Services Authority (FSA)	1997	£269m	2,659
2. Commission for Social Care Inspection*	2004	£164m	2,335
3. Qualifications and Curriculum Authority**	1997	£155m	565
4. Office of Communications (Ofcom)	2003	£125m	789
5. Medicines and Healthcare Products Regulatory Authority	2003	£80m	831
6. Office of Fair Trading	1973	£75m	683
7. Office of Gas and Electricity Markets (Ofgem)	1999	£39m	306
8. The Pensions Regulator	2004	£32m	325
9. Office for Rail Regulation	2004	£29m	379
10. Office of Water Services (Ofwat)	1989	£12m	188

*now part of the Care Quality Commission   **now split and reorganised, part into Ofqual

However, even though the growth in their population has been dramatic, it hasn't perhaps been as phenomenal as the increases in their budgets, in the number of people they employ and in the salaries of their bosses. The FSA's budget shot up from about £21 million in 1997 to over £300 million by 2009; Ofcom's budget leapt from £57 million in 2004 to above £125 million now; the Medicines and Healthcare Products Regulatory Authority increased in five years from £47 million to £80 million; and even the humble Office of Fair Trading jumped from £33 million in 2001 to £75 million by 2008. Being the boss of one of these rapidly growing regulators can be rather lucrative. At the FSA, you'll pick up over £880,000 a year, at Ofcom it's more than £410,000, at Ofwat it's £260,000 and at Ofgem it's £245,000.

Wherever one looks, our regulators seem to be failing us. On Ofcom's watch, we've had repeated TV phone-in scandals with little to no action taken by the regulator. In utilities like electricity, gas and water, Ofwat and Ofgem have been pitifully ineffective in protecting British consumers. Water companies keep on pushing up our bills, supposedly to fund investments, while making record profits. Yet in some areas about a quarter of our water is lost due to leakages, and in London it's around a third. When energy prices go up, our energy prices seem to go even higher. But when energy prices drop, our bills fail to follow, earning massive profits for energy suppliers. Ofgem's and Ofwat's failure to protect us can be most clearly seen in the fact that foreign-owned energy and water companies operating in Britain are able to earn four to five times the levels of profit that they could earn in their properly regulated home markets. As for the Qualifications and Curriculum Authority (QCA), part of which became Ofqual, it happily spent over £1 billion of our money on itself while our exams system came close to collapse and some of our exam results became so discredited that university admissions departments no longer recognize them as valid and useful qualifications.

One useful concept to bear in mind as one surveys the disappointing results of most of our regulators is the idea of 'regulatory capture'. This is a term used to refer to situations in which a government regulatory agency, created to act in the public interest, instead acts in favour of the commercial or special interests that dominate the industry or sector it is charged with regulating. In the past, people tended to be concerned about regulatory capture by big business – pharmaceutical, oil, tobacco and nuclear power companies, for example. However, now that the public sector accounts for almost half of our GDP, it is becoming increasingly common to also find public-sector bodies worryingly overfriendly with the regulators which are meant to regulate them. It is also easy to find evidence that our regulators are somewhat dismissive of those in whose interests they are paid to regulate.

Two areas where regulators have seen the greatest growth in their own size, but have still demonstrably failed to regulate, are in healthcare and financial services.

BREEDING LIKE RABBITS

Healthcare has probably seen the most impressive regulatory population explosion. One of the few healthcare regulators that actually predates New Labour is the General Medical Council (GMC). It was founded in 1858 and its motto is the very fine-sounding 'protecting patients, guiding doctors'. As rates of unnecessary deaths in our hospitals have continued to be much higher than in most other developed countries, the GMC's budget has more than tripled – the GMC's costs shot up from just over £20 million in 1997 to £75 million by 2009. Yet the high levels of unnecessary deaths in our hospitals suggest it is not obvious that this eye-watering increase in bureaucracy has benefited anyone apart from the employees of the GMC. The GMC's budget increases have been so staggering that even some doctors, who have to fund it through their registration fees, are questioning why this bureaucratic monster seems to be afflicted by such morbid obesity.

In 2001 the government established the National Patient Safety Agency (NPSA) to 'improve patient safety in the NHS' and by 2009 the NPSA had amassed 292 staff and an annual budget of almost £30 million. Unfortunately by 2006, after spending well over £100 million of our money on paperwork and administration, the NPSA still had no real idea of the number of unnecessary deaths in hospitals each year. One independent study even suggested that the NPSA was only picking up about 5 per cent of incidents where avoidable harm was done to patients. The situation was so bad that in 2006 the Public Accounts Committee denounced the NPSA as being 'dysfunctional' and 'not value for money' because it didn't know how many patients were harmed as a result of medical errors. In spite of management changes following the PAC report, it is not obvious that things have got any better.

In 2002, the Nursing and Midwifery Council (NMC) was set up in order 'to protect the public by ensuring that nurses and midwives provide high standards of care'. Its motto is inspiring: 'Protecting the public through professional standards'. The NMC has been also been quite generous to itself. It has increased its budget from about £14.9 million to £34 million in the first seven years of its existence and it now employs about 220 staff, all paid for by our nurses' registration fees. Perhaps a little worrying for people in hospital is the fact that the NMC takes no disciplinary action against nurses in around 90 per cent of the complaints it receives – most are rejected as 'trivial'. Margaret Haywood's case (described in Chapter 6 *The Wasters and Wreckers*) seems to have been one of the very few instances where the NMC actually did anything. Perhaps we shouldn't find the NMC's desultory results surprising. The dentists' regulator, the General Dental Council, managed to increase its spending on bureaucracy by over 40 per cent in just the last three years, yet still takes on average two years to investigate complaints and similarly rejects almost 90 per cent of them.

In 2002 we were also given the NHS Confederation. It calls itself 'The voice of NHS Leadership' and its aim is to 'help members improve health and patient care'. Although this is not really a regulator as it focuses more on the managerial rather than medical aspects of running the NHS, it still spends our money in order to supposedly improve our healthcare and has been a true leader in the way it has increased its own budget. This rose by a factor of five from a tiny £5.3 million in its first year of operation to a much more impressive £29 million by 2009. Some of its mountains of reports, including *Managing Excellence in the NHS* and *Bringing Leaders into the NHS*, may be useful, but others, like *Why We Need Fewer Hospital Beds*, might seem a little disturbing to those of us who worry that we have less hospital beds per thousand of the population than most other advanced countries and who know that hospital over-crowding is one of the major causes of hospital-acquired infections.

In 2003 we got the Health Protection Agency (HPA) to look after our well-being. Its aim is 'to provide an integrated approach to protecting UK public health'. The HPA has certainly been effective at spending taxpayers' money. Its total costs increased by 50 per cent from £180 million in 2004 to £270 million by 2009 and the number of staff went up from 2,518 to 3,160. The HPA produces a vast amount of presumably valuable literature about almost any medical topic you could think of, including lots of guidance about reducing hospital-acquired infections such as MRSA and C Diff (Clostridium difficile). In the meantime, these infections have claimed over 30,000 British lives. The death toll would have been less than 600 had these victims been living in countries like Holland, Denmark or Sweden.

In the same year, we also were given the Medicines and Healthcare Products Regulatory Agency. It has 80 staff and an £80 million annual budget, yet EU regulations should mean that medicines tested and approved in one member state should be available throughout the whole EU without any need for further approvals in Britain.

The following year, 2004, was a bit of a bumper year for new healthcare regulators with no fewer than three being established. In January 2004, we were blessed by the appearance of Monitor. Its mission is 'To operate a transparent and effective regulatory framework that incentivises NHS foundation trusts to be professionally managed and financially strong and capable of delivering innovative services that respond to patients and commissioners'. Its chairman earned over £215,000 in 2008–9 (almost £20,000 more than the prime minister) and it spends about £12.5 million of our money a year supposedly regulating NHS foundation trusts so they provide better healthcare to us. Yet recent events at the Mid Staffordshire NHS Trust, which was granted trust status in spite of the unnecessary deaths of possibly more than 1,000 patients, might make people wonder what Monitor is up to. At the time of the Mid Staffordshire scandal, the head of health at Unison commented: 'It seems unbelievable now that despite a history of clinical and staffing problems and failures at Mid Staffordshire, the trust was awarded foundation status in February last year. It is time Monitor the regulator was held to account.'[2] Moreover, there are so many other examples of other hospitals being given trust status despite serious concerns about their standards of care that Monitor seems to be a case-book example of regulatory capture as the regulator is possibly being driven by political pressure to increase the number of NHS trusts rather than any real concern for patient care. To quote the head of health at Unison again: 'Hospitals need to get out of the cycle of trying to win foundation status and the regulator needs to be more rigorous in granting that status to failing trusts.'

The year 2004 also gave us the Healthcare Commission (HC). The HC's motto is 'Inspecting, improving, informing' and it has a lofty mission statement for its staff of over 500: 'The Healthcare Commission is committed to driving improvement in the quality of both the NHS and independent healthcare services and to making sure that patients are at the centre of everything we do.' The HC has been slightly more prudent than the HPA: it only increased its spending of our money by about 30 per cent between 2004 and 2009 to £70 million. One of the key focuses of the HC's work since its inception has been getting to grips with hospital-acquired infections, whose incidence and mortality rates have hugely and relentlessly increased since the HC started producing documents about how to go about tackling them. MRSA and C Diff have now started to go down, but they only constitute a small proportion of the hospital-acquired infections which ravage the NHS, so we can expect many more reports and guides to be produced at our expense.

Then in the same year, perhaps to score a hat-trick, the government dreamt up the Commission for Social Care Inspection which by 2008 grew to 2,335 staff and a budget of £164 million. This new organization only lasted about four years as it was rolled into the Care Quality Commission by 2009. This is the mother of all healthcare regulators, combining several existing regulators such as the Healthcare Commission, the Mental Health Act Commission and the Commission for Social Care Inspection. Its aim is: 'To make sure better care is provided for everyone, whether that's in hospital, in care homes, in people's own homes, or elsewhere.' Had any of the other bureaucracies done their job properly, this new regulator would not have been necessary. Moreover, there is only one certainty with today's new generation of expensive, self-serving, regulatory-captured regulators: this new body is likely to be as expensive and ineffectual as all the others.

In its 1997 election manifesto New Labour promised to reduce administrative costs in the NHS: 'The key is to root out unnecessary administrative cost and to spend money on the right things – frontline care.' As we now pay over £450 million a year more for regulators than we did 12 years ago, it is far from obvious that the government has delivered on its pre-election promise.

A FINANCIAL FARCE

The greatest regulatory failure for which this government is exclusively responsible is, of course, the abject dereliction of duty by our financial regulators. Shortly after moving into the Treasury, Gordon Brown set up a tripartite system of regulation in which the Bank of England was made responsible for managing inflation within a situation of financial stability, the Financial Services Authority was given responsibility for supervising financial markets and the Treasury was to design the overall structure of regulation. For ten years, while benign economic conditions meant it didn't have to do anything, this arrangement, which cost us over £500 million a year, seemed to work reasonably well.

It's easy to be wise in hindsight, but this tripartite regulatory model broke so many of the most fundamental rules of management that its eventual failure at a time of stress was reasonably predictable. For a start, the Bank of England was given the wrong target. It was told to monitor the Consumer Price Index rather than the Retail Price Index. The problem was that the CPI does not include housing costs, whereas the RPI does. So year after year the Bank could merrily report that inflation was bumping along around the 2 per cent target while, in fact, there was a massive, unsustainable bubble in house prices, which none of the regulators apparently noticed.

A second concern was that in a crisis you need what we call a 'single line of command' – one person or body must have clear control and accountability. Generally, you shouldn't run a war by committee. Yet by spreading responsibility between three quite different organizations in an unclear way, the government was designing a three-legged camel.

But perhaps the most fundamental error was to give what was essentially a consumer services regulator, the FSA, responsibility for macroeconomic management. The whole ethos, background and skill-set of the FSA was based on regulating the selling of financial products – pensions, savings, investments, unit trusts, mortgages, Ponzi schemes and so on. As mis-selling scandal has followed mis-selling scandal with depressing regularity, it seems clear that the FSA is not even up to this job. Worse still, it simply didn't have the knowledge or experience to be given overall responsibility for regulation of financial markets. To try to draw a parallel: suppose you employ two builders to construct a house. Builder A is used to doing the structure – foundations, walls, roof and so on. That's the Bank of England. Builder B has always worked on the finishing – doors, windows, plastering, painting – although he's never been particularly good at it, so you're always having to call him back to fix his shoddy workmanship. That's the FSA. You would generally not give Builder B responsibility for the basic structure as this would be beyond the builder's experience. Plus Builder B was never very good at his own job in the first place. Yet this is what Gordon Brown chose to do by making the FSA responsible for the overall stability of the main players in the financial markets.

Probably one of the funniest episodes of the regulatory failure concerned Sir John Gieve, whose career we touched upon at the end of the previous chapter. While Deputy Governor at the Bank of England, he was supposedly responsible for the stability of the financial system and, when questioned by the House of Commons Treasury Select Committee, he claimed that he had been 'alert to the dangers in the financial markets' but that it was not his role to scrutinize individual banks.[3] This, of course, was an accurate answer as it was the FSA's role to oversee individual financial institutions. But Sir John's answer does expose the absurdity of a structure where the organization responsible for financial stability wasn't responsible for looking at the institutions that could make or break that stability. It was a bit like making someone responsible for car safety and then telling them they were not able to look at the safety of any individual car models. One expert commented: 'Is it reasonable to have the Bank of England which is responsible for supervising the system but not the companies that make up that system?'[4]

Under pressure to strengthen financial regulation, our government's response has been the usual one of employing more bureaucrats and spending more of our money without any attempt to sort out the obvious coordination problems of the three-legged beast that caused the regulatory breakdown in the first place. At the Bank of England, a new committee has been set up – the Financial Stability Committee. Its job is to manage the Bank's response to future crises and it has 'powers to overhaul banks which come close to collapse'. However, it still won't have the responsibility of monitoring banks to see if they are coming close to collapse. Another change at the Bank is that the Court of the Bank of England is being reduced from 19 to 12 members and it will meet fewer times a year. However, pay for members of the Court will jump from about £16,000 to around £30,000 a year.

As for the regulation of individual banks, that will stay with the FSA. Despite the FSA's betrayal of the people whose interests it is meant to safeguard, it pays some of the highest salaries of any regulator (see Figure 2). Around 174 staff at the FSA receive six-figure salaries.

Figure 2 The FSA rewarded its executives well in spite of its dismal performance

Person	2008/9 Remuneration
David Kenmir*	£800,359
Hector Sants	£623,170
Sally Dewar	£435,179
John Pain**	£312,289

* Resigned March 2009 **appointed September 2008

When the economic crisis broke and the regulators actually had some real work to do, they decided they deserved record bonuses. In the latest bonus round at the FSA, bonuses reached £19.7 million – a 40 per cent increase on the previous year. One FSA mover and shaker got a £90,000 bonus with ten others pocketing more than £50,000 each. In spite of the financial crash which the FSA was tasked with preventing, on average the top 174 managers received bonuses of over £22,000 each and only three of them failed to get a bonus. In fact, almost all the FSA's 2,500 or so staff were awarded bonuses. One insider commented: 'Just about everyone in the building got a bonus. The targets were not exactly challenging. You had to be incompetent not to get an award.'[5]

Moreover, the FSA has been munificently rewarded by the government despite having been utterly delinquent in its role of monitoring the financial health of our banks and having failed so badly to regulate the selling of a depressingly long series of dubious financial products that it generated headlines like 'Failed by FSA apathy' and 'Toothless FSA has left us all at the mercy of the banks'.[6] The government is allowing the FSA to recruit about 280 more bureaucrats and is giving it lots more of our money, taking its budget from around £300 million a year to £415 million a year. Revealing his plans to recruit more staff at higher salaries than in the past, the FSA's head explained: 'We will pay more than necessary to attract the correct quality of people from outside.'[7] It's a pity that it's our money, rather than his own, that he is using when he decided to 'pay more than necessary'.

Poachers and gamekeepers

Following the financial collapse, there have been numerous demands for much tighter regulation of the financial system. This was very similar to the situation after the Wall Street Crash and ensuing Great Depression.

In 2005, Chancellor Gordon Brown extolled the virtues of light regulation: 'No inspection without justification, no form filling without justification, and no information requirements without justification, not just light touch but a limited touch.' This was the same Gordon Brown who claimed in 2008: 'Almost exactly ten years ago in a speech at Harvard University I made detailed proposals to reshape the international financial system for the new world, but then found it hard to persuade other countries.'[8] When he was a 'light regulation' man, Brown was backed up by the former chief economic adviser to the Treasury, Ed Balls, who as City Minister called for: 'a light touch approach at the global and EU level'. He, too, seems to have been converted by 2008 when he said those who had advocated 'light touch regulation' had been 'routed'.[9] Anyway, we all can learn from our mistakes.

The government has now ceded to popular anger by asking various financial services experts and committees to write reports and make recommendations about how to avoid financial collapses in the future. One of the difficulties with this eminently sensible approach is that the experts advising the government often have very close connections with the financial institutions who could be accused of causing the crisis in the first place. These connections could prompt the usual cynics to question the impartiality of their advice.

This possible perception problem was highlighted recently by the excellent Prem Sikka, Professor of Accounting at Essex University and a campaigner for improved ethics in business. He drew attention to the influence exerted by the two former leading financiers on the government's regulatory approach to financial services. One of the experts is Lord Turner, chairman of the FSA. Amongst his many notable roles, Lord Turner was vice chairman of Merrill Lynch Europe from 2000 to 2006. In 1999, just before Lord Turner's arrival, Merrill Lynch was fined £6.5 million by the London Metal Exchange because of alleged involvement in the Sumitomo copper trading sandal.[10] In the US, Merrill Lynch has had several brushes with the authorities. In 2002, it paid $100 million following allegations that its analysts misled investors into buying shares in companies that the investment bank was targeting for selling investment banking services.[11] In 2003, it handed over $80 million in disgorgement, penalties and interest, though without any admission of liability, after the Securities and Exchange Commission (SEC) accused it of aiding and abetting some of the Enron frauds.[12] In 2005 it was fined $14 million by the US Financial Industry Regulatory Authority for problems relating to the sale of shares and there was a further $10 million fine because of poor supervision of its advisors 'whose market timing siphoned short-term profits out of mutual funds and harmed long-term investors'.[13] Then in 2008, a US Senate report concluded: 'Merrill Lynch developed, marketed and implemented a variety of abusive dividend tax transactions to enable its non-U.S. clients to dodge payment of U.S. taxes on U.S. stock dividends.'[14]

Another report about reforming financial regulation was jointly produced by Chancellor Alistair Darling and a former chairman of Citigroup Europe, Sir Winfried Bischoff.[15] Citigroup Europe seems to have a clean record; however, in the US the company had numerous unfortunate skirmishes with regulators. In 2003, Citigroup paid $120 million to settle SEC allegations that it helped Enron and Dynergy with frauds.[16] In 2005 Citigroup Global Markets Limited, the bank's European investment banking arm, was fined £13.9 million for failing to conduct its business with due skill, care and diligence.[17] In 2008, Citigroup agreed to buy back $7 billion in securities when it faced US regulatory charges that it 'misled investors regarding the liquidity risks associated with auction rate securities'.[18] Also in 2008, a US Senate report stated that the group knowingly crafted transactions 'to enable its offshore clients to dodge US taxes on their stock dividends'.[19] Incidentally, both Citigroup and Merrill Lynch benefited from US taxpayers' money as part of the American government's rescue of the banking system.[20]

While both Lord Turner and Sir Winfried Bischoff were working in Europe and would not have been involved in the problems in the US, nevertheless when someone is viewed by many people as having been a key player in the poacher fraternity, there is always a risk that the suspicious public could doubt their loyalties if they were suddenly employed as head gamekeeper.

B is for Bank, C is for Casino

The changes in regulation proposed by the FSA are worrying many people. In their defence, it is likely that they will probably reduce the risk of future financial collapses by amongst other things imposing higher capital adequacy rules. However, some critics of the policies put forward by the government and its experts have expressed concern that the proposals only consider some technical changes and do not deal with the widespread speculative and often unethical culture which caused the banking collapse. Some extreme sceptics might even view the results as protecting the financial services industry rather than ordinary taxpayers who have been so thoroughly fleeced in order to pay for losses incurred by the bankers. For example the Financial Services Global Competitiveness Group report, led by Bischoff and Darling, recommends that the 'government and the industry should collaborate in order to maintain and expand the UK's central role as a finance portal for the rest of Europe and the world'.[21] It also stresses that the 'existing principles, rules and practices should only be replaced with proper justification'.[22] This doesn't sound, look or smell like the advent of a tough, robust, new regulatory framework.

Following the 1929 Wall Street Crash and ensuing Great Depression, the US introduced the 1932–3 Glass-Steagall Act. One of the features of this Act was the separation of commercial (also called 'retail' or 'utility') banking (taking deposits and lending money) from investment banking (trading in sometimes complex financial instruments). The reason for this separation was that investment banking was seen as inherently more risky and possibly leading to enormous losses. Without the separation, these losses could threaten ordinary people's deposits and thus put huge pressure on governments to use taxpayers' money to protect deposits by bailing out failing financial institutions. Basically, the Act split high-street banking from what has been caricatured as 'casino' banking.

Over the years, under pressure from the financial services industry, the Glass-Steagall Act was gradually weakened and then in 1999 it was repealed by the Gramm-Leach-Bliley Act. The repeal of Glass-Steagall could be seen as a contributor towards tempting institutions with solid-sounding names like Northern Rock and Bradford & Bingley, that depositors thought were old-fashioned, low-risk banks, into the more exotic financial engineering which brought about their downfall. However, defenders of the repeal of Glass-Steagall have argued: 'The financial firms that failed in the crisis, like Lehman, are the least diversified and the ones that survived, like J.P. Morgan, were the most diversified.'

One of the conclusions of both the FSA's recommendations and the Darling/Bischoff review was to reject a Tory suggestion that there should be a partial return to the principles of the Glass-Steagall separation of retail and investment banking.[23] This refusal to consider such a separation is disturbing as the government is failing to tackle the big issue at the heart of many of our financial problems – the merging of banking and betting. Perhaps taxpayers' interests would be better protected by separating the hopefully boring business of banking from the more rollercoaster world of complex financial speculation. Supporters of separation believe that banking needs to return to being a relatively safe business where banks take deposits from risk-averse people and use this money to lend to businesses and home buyers, whilst maintaining a reasonable level of real, not make-believe, capital. Further, they propose that there should be other financial institutions that specialize in taking money from risk-seeking investors and leveraging this enormously in the search for high returns. By failing to separate these two types of banking, the government and regulators may be sending an unwritten message to the financial services industry that as long as they stick to the new rules, the taxpayer will bail them out if things go wrong again as they will be too big to be allowed to fail. This is a bit like saying to a bunch of recidivist gamblers that they have to stick to slightly tighter new rules, but that they can carry on gambling with other people's money. Then every time they win, they can keep a big chunk of the winnings for themselves, but if they lose everything, the government will bail them out by giving them yet more money to fuel their gambling habit. To quote the governor of the Bank of England: 'Executives are earning vast sums, beyond the dreams of ordinary people, for a job which it's very hard to say justifies that kind of bonus. It's a form of compensation which rewards gamblers if they win – but with no loss if they lose.'[24]

At the time of writing there seems to be more than a small difference of opinion emerging between the chancellor and the governor of the Bank of England. The chancellor appears keen to retain the still reasonably relaxed regulatory tripartite regime outlined in his report, while the governor has been expressing concern that it will still be difficult for the Bank to regulate anything at all as it doesn't really have much power to assess individual financial institutions. Moreover, while the governor of the Bank of England has been quite outspoken in criticizing the government's spendthrift habits and levels of unsustainable debt, the head of the FSA has been more supportive of government policies. This might lead to a suspicion that by making the FSA the main regulatory body, the chancellor is really just settling a few old scores by taking power away from the Bank of England, rather than acting in the interests of ordinary people.

PART 3

THE UNTOUCHABLE ELITES

CHAPTER 9

LOCAL MISGOVERNMENT

PAYING MORE FOR LESS

Despite council tax doubling since this government came to power, local authorities are continuously complaining that they are short of money. This, they lament, only leaves them with two painful options – they have to either increase council tax still further or else reduce frontline services. Many councils are already aggressively doing both, pushing up taxes yet cutting services such as rubbish collection and care for the elderly.

Given many councils' claims of penury, it might be worth looking briefly at how they use and abuse our money.

Fatcat fiesta

Three years ago, there were at least 645 people in our 469 local authorities earning £100,000 or above. A year later this had risen to 818 and in 2007–8 there were 1,021 – a rise of a staggering 58 per cent in just two years – and this at a time when the economic downturn was starting to devastate the job prospects and limit the pay rises of people foolish enough to work in the private sector. According to the information that the TaxPayers' Alliance was able to obtain, the ten people with the highest salaries in local authorities all seemed to receive more than the prime minister in 2007–8 (see Figure 1).[1]

Figure 1 The top ten council bosses all get more than the prime minister

Council	Person	Remuneration
1. Kent	Peter Gilroy	£255,000
2. Kensington & Chelsea	Derek Myers	£225,000
3. Lambeth	Derrick Anderson	£218,870
4. Bedfordshire	Andrea Hill	£208,767
5. Westminster	Peter Rogers	£205,000
6. Hertfordshire	Caroline Tapster	£202,503
7. Manchester	Sir Howard Bernstein	£199,056
8. Surrey	Dr. Richard Shaw	£199,000
9. Buckinghamshire	Chris Williams	£198,865
10. Staffordshire	Ron Hilton	£198,359
	Prime Minister	**£194,250**

Councils claim they need to pay such high salary packages because council panjandrums manage huge multi-million pound budgets and have large numbers of employees. The chief executive of the Local Government Association, which represents councils in England and Wales, explained: 'Many councils have bigger budgets than FTSE 100 companies and to get the brightest people they need to pay a competitive wage.'[2] Yet a counterargument could be that the prime minister manages an even bigger budget and has even more employees, so why should council bosses be paid so much?

While many local government employees were restricted to a 2 per cent pay rise in the 2006–7 to 2007–8 financial years, the average increase for the top officials was 6 per cent, three times as much. Six per cent may not sound like an excessive amount of money, but the average salary of the highest paid 1,021 council bosses is about £122,140 so the increase gives them another £7,328 a year. As we saw with top civil servants in Chapter 5, the taxpayers really get hit by the increases in pensions resulting from rising salaries. Assuming a council boss gets a pension of half their final salary, then the £7,328 pay increase will give a rise in their pension of £3,664 a year. For any person in the private sector to get a pension of this £3,664 a year, they would have to have pension savings of around £100,000, assuming an annuity rate of 3.6 per cent for a joint inflation-linked pension. This is worth bearing in mind when council chiefs try to play down their 6 per cent pay increases as being justified by the great responsibilities of their jobs.

The table of top ten council salaries in Figure 1 is not complete because councils do not publish details of their top executives' salaries. To get this information the TaxPayers' Alliance had to submit Freedom of Information (FoI) requests to all the councils. Most do answer these, but each year about 20 to 30 councils refuse to respond. The majority of refuseniks justify their secrecy citing 'data protection'. Others just refuse without giving any reasons which is in breach of the FoI Act 2000. And some think up ingenious excuses. For example, one year Hampshire wrote back: 'The County Council estimates that the cost of complying with your request would exceed the sum of £450' and then goes on to claim: 'Your request is vexatious.' The suggestion it would cost more than £450 to get information that the director of human resources should be able to supply in about two to three minutes at most is ludicrous. Edinburgh City Council took a similar line to Hampshire, seemingly suggesting that the council had no idea how much it paid its top bosses: 'There is no aggregate corporate statistical information in existence that would meet your requirement.' Of course, this meant that, like Hampshire, the council could claim it would cost too much to compile the information that the council should have had available anyway: 'The cost of finding, extracting, calculating and checking the information would significantly exceed the prescribed amount and I am therefore unable to supply the additional information.' It probably took the council almost as much time to discuss and draft their refusal letter as it would have taken to supply the information. Some councils were even more creative in avoiding their FoI responsibilities. Harrow council enigmatically replied:

'Disclosure is incompatible with the purposes for which we hold the information.'

An Audit Commission report in 2008 showed that top managerial salaries in local authorities increased by 34 per cent in the previous four years compared with a more restrained 16 per cent for private company chief executives.[3] One possible reason why council chiefs' salaries keep rushing ever upwards is that many councils pay a recruitment company, wholly owned by the Society of Local Authority Chief Executives and Senior Managers, fees of up to £20,000 a shot to headhunt council chief executives and to recommend salary levels. A cynic could suppose that such a headhunting company might err on the side of generosity when proposing how much of taxpayers' money should be given to people who will probably become members of the organization owning the recruitment company.

Bulging in the middle

The huge salaries pocketed by council chief executives make great headlines but the really worrying local authority obesity epidemic seems to be at the level of middle management – all those earning over £50,000 a year. When this government came to power, there were about 3,300 council staff earning more than £50,000. By 2009, this had rocketed to about 38,000. This meant that the number of council staff earning more than £50,000 increased by over eleven times, yet the number of people in the economy as a whole earning over £50,000 went up by only just over three times. Figure 2 lists the councils where the number of people earning over £50,000 has gone up by 15, 20 or more than 30 times since the government came to power. Wages should increase above the rate of inflation in a growing economy, but these increases have been phenomenal. Now that the economy is no longer growing and is in recession, this rate of middle management expansion seems worse than inappropriate. If your council is named, and hopefully shamed, for its profligacy in increasing the number of its middle managers and giving them over-generous salary raises, you might want to consider whether the improvements in services you receive from your council reflect the mind-boggling rise in the number of council employees taking home over fifty grand of your money a year.

Figure 2 Councils with the greatest increase in staff earning over £50,000 (1997–2008)

15 times	20 times	30+ times
Barking	Birmingham	Barnet
Birmingham	Blackpool	Herts.
Bradford	Camden	Lincs.
Cheshire	Doncaster	Salford
Derbyshire	Ealing	
Greenwich	Essex	
Hampshire	Gloucs	
M Keynes	Haringey	
Newcastle u/T	Kingston o/T	
North Lincs	Lambeth	"Councils are working
North Yorks	Manchester	hard to keep council tax
Portsmouth	Norfolk	down"
Southwark	Notts	Chairman, Local Government
Telford	Oxford	Association March 2009
	South Gloucs	
	Tameside	
	Wigan	

In 1997, middle and senior managers in local authorities cost us taxpayers around £207 million in wages alone. When you take account of their offices, secretaries, assistants, expenses and pensions, you could probably reckon on about £400 million. By 2007–8 the salary costs of these managers had soared to almost £2.5 billion. Once again, adding in all the other costs of this multitude of managers, you won't have much change left out of £4 billion. We pay about £24 billion a year in council tax. If the middle manager level in local councils had grown by only a factor of five since 1997, rather than by a factor of eleven times, we could immediately cut council tax by close to 10 per cent. This might be worth bearing in mind next time your council tells you about the 'difficult' choice it's going to have to make between raising council tax and cutting frontline services.

All aboard! All aboard!

Much of the public may be unaware of the vast pay and perks bonanza, fuelled by our money, which has been underway in most of our local authorities for the last decade or so. However, this inviting gravy train certainly hasn't escaped the attention of our tens of thousands of councillors. The purpose of a councillor is to represent the people of a local ward in the council. They are elected to bring their expertise and experience to address the specific needs of their local community. These duties are meant to be separate from their private and professional lives outside the council and their position should be voluntary. The allowances they receive are intended to compensate them for the time they give and for incidental expenses incurred in fulfilling their duties in local government such as the use of their phones, transportation and office expenses. As these payments are described as allowances and expenses reimbursement, they are clearly not meant to be seen as salaries.

Year after year, allowances for councillors have been shooting up by five to ten times the rate of inflation. In 386 English councils which provided information, an amazing almost 20,000 councillors are pocketing about £200 million of our money each year, lending a whole new meaning to the word 'voluntary'. That's an average of about £10,000 a year each. However, while some councillors seem content to take home £2,000 to £3,000 a year, about 3,000 of them are creaming off between £15,000 and £25,000 a year. But councillors' largesse to themselves with our money doesn't stop with their extraordinarily generous allowances. Once they are elected as councillors, some are appointed as members of police authorities and fire authorities.

Being a member of a police authority will add another £10,000 to £15,000 to a councillor's allowances, while being a fire authority member can easily add £5,000 to £10,000 a year. Some councillors are members of both police and fire authorities as well as their local council. Such dedication to serving the public can be quite lucrative: for example, a Birmingham councillor who was also on the West Midlands police and fire authorities would pick up over £40,000 a year, making councillors look an awful like another huge and expensive level of taxpayer-funded bureaucrats in addition to the tens of thousands of local authority executives and managers.

In 2009, co-author David Craig emailed the Leader of the North Somerset council to ask why councillors there had received large increases in their allowances. The Leader of the Council replied: 'In my case I am responsible for a Council that provides a wide range of critical services to local people with expenditure of over £400m a year – to be paid expenses only. For myself and my executive colleagues this is a virtually full-time job.'[4] This answer might be confusing to the North Somerset council-taxpayers as the council seems to be richly endowed with well-paid, fulltime staff, including at least four council executives earning over £100,000 each. Moreover, the number of North Somerset council employees earning more than £50,000 a year went up by almost ten times between 1997 and 2007–8, putting the cost of management in the council at about 45 per cent above the national average.

This impression of councillors starting to treat themselves as salaried employees, rather than elected representatives, is reinforced by the speed with which more than 3,500 of them have joined their Local Government Pension Scheme (LGPS). This suggests that thousands of councillors are treating their allowances and reimbursements as salary on which they can earn pension benefits. It is obvious why they would want to join the pension scheme. According to the LGPS website, the many benefits of membership include:

A secure pension – the benefits you get when you retire are based on your membership in the scheme and on your final year's pay. After you retire your pension keeps up with cost of living increases.

Employer contribution – your employer or council pays whatever amount is necessary to make sure the cost of your benefits is fully funded.

Peace of mind – your family enjoys financial security, with immediate life cover and a pension for your husband, wife, civil partner or nominated co-habiting partner and children in the event of your death.

Early retirement – you can choose to retire from age 60 and receive your benefits immediately, although they may be reduced for early payment. It's also possible to retire from age 55 and receive your benefits immediately.[5]

With so many councillors sitting so comfortably in the LGPS carriage of the council gravy train, this does suggest that it is us taxpayers who are once again being taken for an enormously expensive ride. While we don't have room here to list the number of councillors per authority with their snouts in the LGPS trough, here is a list of the top sinners (see Figure 3).[6]

GUARDIANISTAS APPLY HERE

Every week, the *Guardian* website lists hundreds of public-sector jobs. Usually there are about 500–600 at any one time. On the day this was written there were 604 public-sector jobs, with about 450 of these being in local government. Although many of the posts advertised do appear to involve doing real work – caring for children, helping dysfunctional families, accountancy and so

Figure 3 Councils with the most councillors enrolled in the LGPS

Council	Number of councillors
1. Durham County	63
2. Bradford	56
3. Highland	52
4. North Lanarkshire	50
5. Carmarthenshire	50
6. Surrey	48
7. Fife	44
8. City of Edinburgh	44
9. Birmingham	44
10. Powys	42
11. Nottinghamshire	41
12. Aberdeenshire	41
13. Glasgow City	39
14. Aberdeen City	36
15. Hampshire	36
16. Wandsworth	35
17. Hackney	35
18. Kirklees	35
19. Hertfordshire	34
20. Newcastle upon Tyne	33

on – some look rather superfluous and are advertised using lists of buzzwords which you might find in a dictionary of management-speak, but would not be used by any normal person.

A typical example is provided by Merton's advertisement for a Consultation and Community Engagement Officer for about £40,000 a year plus pension and other benefits. You might be wondering what this valuable person will be doing in these straitened times, but unfortunately the advert may not enlighten you:

> There couldn't be a more exciting time to join Merton, as we embark on a major transformation programme that will help us deliver even better services to the borough... We're committed to involving local people in the decisions that affect them, making this a key role in our drive for improvement. You'll develop innovative, sustainable policies and programmes for consultation and engagement and provide expert advice to managers, councillors and partners in this specialized area. High on your list of priorities will be ensuring we meet the requirements of the Duty to Involve and capitalizing on the opportunities presented by new neighbourhood governance arrangements. We'll look to you to promote cultural change, disseminate best practice and respond to changes in legislation and Government policy.

The ad has a goodly sprinkling of in-words – 'sustainable' is very popular at the moment. 'Partners' is also a must, while 'consultation' and 'engagement' show how responsive Merton is to the views of its stakeholders. Moreover, you couldn't play a game of Buzzword Bingo without 'cultural change' and 'best practice'.

If you don't fancy being part of Merton's exciting transformation, Manchester is also transforming and needs not one but two big transformation honchos. There's a programme Director Head of Business Transformation for £70,000 and there's a Head of Transformation to work in the council's Transformation Directorate for £66,000. The advertisement for the latter tells us:

> Manchester is an exciting place to be. Its shape, look and function are being transformed every hour of every day. New businesses, new ventures and new places to live are helping to reinvigorate the city. As Head of Transformation, you'll be required to work closely with the Strategic Director in order to drive the changes that Manchester City Council need to make in order to achieve the objectives of its community strategy. You'll also work alongside Heads of Service overseeing the implementation of the transformation programmes and service area improvement plans as well as ensuring strategic projects are managed to time and budget.
> BE SURPRISED. BE CHALLENGED. BE PART OF MANCHESTER.

But if you find the idea of an 'exciting' town like Merton or Manchester a bit too stressful, why not head for rural Wiltshire where you can become a dynamic Director of Vision helping Salisbury with its transformation for over £50,000 a year?

> Wiltshire Council Where everybody matters. To transform Salisbury Wiltshire Council is seeking a dynamic and strategic Vision Director who will be able to facilitate and manage high quality development in the key city of Salisbury. Salisbury faces a challenge. Times are hard, investment is scarce, businesses are wary. Have you got what it takes to get past that? To drive forward large scale projects in retail, commercial, residential, leisure and education? Then this role offers huge scope for personal development and a fresh challenge for motivated individuals. We need people with great skills, experience and a genuine can-do approach.

WELCOME TO THE WASTE MIDLANDS

To give an idea of the scale of waste in local government, we propose to cover just a few of the many incidents that were reported in the West Midlands during the past year or so.

June 2008 – Twenty Birmingham delegates head to Chicago

A 20-strong delegation at Birmingham City Council is dispatched to Chicago, a month after they visited Cannes in the South of France. Our representatives are jetting across the Atlantic to promote the city at the Chicago Sister Cities International Festival. The Birmingham stand is expecting around 10,000 visitors per day, and those lucky enough to stumble across it will also be greeted by a juggler in Shakespearean costume, two characters dressed in Aston Villa and Birmingham City Football shirts and an actor dressed as a policeman.

July 2008 – Coventry staff cash in on carbon cutting

Coventry council has launched a 'carbon hotline' for the exclusive use of local authority staff. The 17,000 employees will be encouraged to call the line with their 'carbon cutting suggestions', and if a member of staff does suggest a decent carbon cutting measure they will get a hard cash award. So taxpayers pay for the hotline, they pay for the environmental consultants and the climate change councillors that already exist within the council, they pay for the general staff anyway, and if one of these people actually contributes something that makes a carbon saving, they'll give them some more cash from the public purse.

August 2008 – Sandwell Chief Exec jets off to US on public cash

Sandwell council will soon be doing a considerable amount of jet-setting at the expense of their residents. Not only will six councillors and officers be travelling to Amsterdam on a 'fact-finding' mission to find out how the city de-clutters its streets, but the council's chief executive will be flying off to Florida for a 'self-awareness' training course. The course promises all participants a journey of self-exploration and consequently Sandwell's chief executive will:

- Be more likeable and able to like herself more.
- Be more real and authentic.
- Learn to protect herself against the abrasions of the world.
- Gain a connection with the undefined self.
- Obtain the keys to successfully operate in the world.

The chief executive has already completed stage one of the course in Germany. Far from staying in some squalid kibbutz-style set-up in order to fortify herself from worldly abrasions, she'll be put up at the International Drive resort, billed as one of the most 'dynamic vacation destinations'.

September 2008 – Motivating Sandwell Council costs £14,000

Sandwell Council continues to splurge on unnecessary frills as it spends £14,000 on a motivational speaker who will lead a two-day seminar for its managers. The presenter will talk about stress management and 'whole brain training'. At this price, Sandwell ratepayers should reasonably expect a dramatic turn-around in the efficiency of the authority.

October 2008 – Public outcry causes Stoke teachers' Marbella trip to be pulled

At a time when many people are having to forsake family holidays and trips abroad, Edensor Technology College in Stoke-on-Trent saw no problem with booking to send up to 80 of their teaching staff on a four-day trip to Marbella in Spain. Apparently the purpose of the conference (which was cancelled due to the outrage it incited) was to discuss the new curriculum and the matter of turning the college into an academy. The head teacher of the college was obliged to deny that this trip was a staff jolly, arguing that it's 'cheaper' to gather in Spain than in local conference spaces.

November 2008 – Birmingham City Council doesn't clean up

Birmingham City Council has just spent £20,000 organizing a clean streets campaign. Only 68 £60 penalties were issued at a cost to taxpayers of £300 per penalty and of these about half those who received a penalty notice are refusing to pay.

December 2008 – Stoke bus stops cost almost £37,000 each

No less than £147,000 has been spent on just four 'luxury modern bus stops' for Burslem in Stoke in a move to regenerate the area with central Government funding. The bus stops, which were unveiled at the Christmas lights switch-on this Saturday, will have LCD screens and CCTV but won't be fully functional until the summer. A regular bus user aged 73 commented: 'The council told me there would be new luxury bus stops but there was nothing wrong with the old ones. They just needed seats and everyone would have been happy.' The LCD screens will give expected arrival times for buses and information on delays, though these services won't be up and running until the technology is available for all buses so it looks like there's more expense to come.

January 2008 – Profligacy at The Public

The directors of The Public art gallery in West Bromwich have now spent around £63 million on their venture despite it still being closed six months after July 2008's non-launch.

February 2009 – Birmingham City Council spends £67m on consultants

Despite increasing their middle-management spend by over £11 million in just one year (alongside the raft of six-figure salary directors on their payroll) it was revealed today that Birmingham City Council will spend no less than £67 million on consultants and advisers this year. This completely flies in the face of the advice of the Audit Commission who criticised the council for being over-reliant on consultants.

March 2009 – £23m on new control centre while i54 site still empty across the road

While the West Midlands Fire Service are busy fitting out a new £23 million base for their control centre staff, literally just across the road from the ill-fated i54 technology park – a 220 acre regeneration project run by Wolverhampton City Council – which lies vacant without a single tenant having signed up.

April 2009 – Blackberries for 72 Dudley councillors to cost £18,000

Dudley councillors are already hoping for a 20 per cent rise in their allowances and now it's looking as though they'll be further draining the public purse as 72 of them are in line to receive expensive Blackberry phones at a cost of £18,000. The council claim that equipping elected representatives with these devices will improve their efficiency and they recently spent a hefty £16,000 on Blackberries for housing managers.

May 2009 – Warwickshire 'Go Green' boss submits £8,500 in mileage claims

Warwickshire County Council's 'Go Green' boss has been using his 4x4 vehicle to clock up almost 10,000 miles, costing taxpayers no less than £8,500. The council's 'environmental leader' hasn't exactly been leading by example as his expenses claims for mileage topped the list of all elected members, and yet he has brushed criticism aside by stating that the council can't 'go green overnight'.

June 2009 – Birmingham City Council boss takes home £200,000+

The Birmingham City Council Chief Executive enjoyed a very healthy 18.2 per cent pay increase between 2006/7 and 2007/8 making him a member of the "£200,000+ per year club". This increase might surprise taxpayers as the Audit Commission recently slashed the council's star rating from a three to a two.

July 2009 – Birmingham's bust lane

The bus lane that runs down Tyburn Road will finally be axed after costing taxpayers about £2.6 million. The signs are being dismantled and the road-markings painted over as a study reveals that the lane actually slowed traffic instead of easing congestion. The costs include £2.5 million to implement the scheme, a £17,000 public consultation and £88,000 to remove it.

CHAPTER 10

OUR PLUNDERING POLITICIANS

Thanks to some of the best journalism in decades, we are now all gruesomely familiar with how the majority of our supposedly honourable politicians have been avidly pocketing as much of our money as they hoped they could get away with. From the extravagant and often implausible expense claims made by senior politicians such as Gordon Brown, Alistair Darling, Jacqui Smith, Geoff Hoon, Hazel Blears, Jack Straw, Ed Balls, Yvette Cooper, Andy Burnham, Bob Ainsworth and Shaun Woodward to many hundreds of ordinary MPs grabbing tens of thousands for anything they could think of including flipping homes, mortgages which didn't exist, luxury furniture and all kinds of other attempts to squeeze every last penny from their allowances, our ministers' and MPs' plundering of our money has been brilliantly exposed.

It took nearly four years for the whole expenses saga to be revealed and even then the information was heavily redacted. Throughout these years, the TaxPayers' Alliance (TPA) continually worked to push the authorities to reveal how much MPs were claiming and co-author Matthew Elliott was regularly collared by MPs asking him to take the pressure off expenses. One senior Conservative MP emailed the campaign in 2006: 'Are you going to be a serious campaign, or a cross between student political tw*ts and Alf Garnett, occasionally having a bit of gratuitous fun in the *Daily Express*, but avoiding any real work? It seems that you've already made your choice . . . Anyway, you're c**ts.' As the expenses edged closer to being published, one said: 'The work you're doing on public sector waste is excellent, old boy, but you're barking up the wrong tree on expenses. There are a few rotten apples here, but they've been exposed – it's wrong to tar us all with the same brush.' Sometimes they were more brutal – another MP texted: 'You're a f**king idiot, Elliott. After your comments today, don't bother crawling back here when the TPA goes tits-up.' Needless to say, after the *Daily Telegraph* published stories based on the unredacted expenses, all these MPs went on the airwaves to say they had long advocated reform and transparency.

The expenses scandal has shown that the majority of our politicians have acted in a disgraceful manner. But some are more disgraceful than others. Following the tsunami of revelations, hopefully a few of the most foul-smelling MPs will withdraw to comfortable, financially secure retirement, which will be paid for by us taxpayers. However, less than a year after *Fleeced!* is published, there will be a general election. Then most of our sitting MPs will come around again grovelling for our votes so that they can dedicate another five years of their lives to the supposed public service of representing us in Parliament. As our elected representatives posture and preen themselves in order to win back our confidence, or at least our votes, there will be many who tell us that they personally have always been passionate supporters of openness and honesty and that they have battled vigorously for our right to know about their use of our money. So it might be instructive to look back to see whether their proclaimed reforming zeal is something which they have demonstrated over a longer period or whether it is a sudden conversion on the road to Damascus as they desperately attempt to keep their well-rewarded jobs.

One way of conducting an 'honesty health-check' is to remind ourselves of which MPs were most active in trying to prevent us finding out about their financial shenanigans and also which fought hardest to block any reforms to the current expenses system in order to preserve their privileged plundering of money that perhaps would have been better spent on schools, hospitals and equipment for our troops rather than MPs' luxurious lifestyles and growing property empires. Thus when they come along boasting about their reforming credentials, we can better identify the still insatiable wolves in their hastily purchased (probably with our money) sheep's clothing.

OPENING UP GOVERNMENT

Before being elected, Tony Blair promised that he would open up government through a Freedom of Information Act (FoI) that would completely change Britain's political culture:

> I don't believe that [an FoI Act's] impact would simply be in the pure matter of legislation . . . It would also signal a culture change that would make a dramatic difference to the way that Britain is governed. The very fact of its introduction will signal a new relationship between government and people: a relationship which sees the public as legitimate stakeholders in the running of the country and sees election to serve the public as being given on trust.

> I regard it not merely as simply a list of commitments that we give because at some point in time, someone got up and agitated for it . . . It is genuinely about changing the relationship in politics today.1

Explaining why we needed FoI, Blair went on to describe that it was necessary to counteract the public's disillusionment with politics and politicians:

> There is so much disaffection from politics, so much disillusion with it, and one of . . . the reasons is that we live in a modern and a far better educated and far more open and far more assertive democracy and country and it's good that people feel in that way. The irony is that the system

of government is about 50, 60, 70 years behind the actual feelings and sentiments of the broad majority of people. A Freedom of Information Act is not just important in itself. It is part of bringing our politics up to date, of letting politics catch up with the aspirations of people and delivering not just more open but more effective and efficient government for the future.

To his credit, Blair did give us the FoI Act and it has been extraordinarily effective in starting to expose the incredible scale of waste and corruption throughout the public sector. However, one group of public servants who were less than enamoured with the Act were the MPs who had passed it in the first place. Our honourable representatives seem to have been quite happy for other parts of the public sector to be pushed grudgingly into the new era of open government that Blair had announced, but felt they personally should be above the law that they had passed.

Macleans cleans whiter

The most serious attempt by MPs to avoid the FoI Act was a private member's bill in 2006–7 proposed by the Tory MP David Maclean to exempt the Houses of Commons and Lords from the Act. David Maclean was reported to have been the highest claiming MP in two out of the five years prior to his proposed bill.[2] He was also accused of having 'spent thousands of pounds' of taxpayers' money renovating his second home in the Lake District before selling it for £750,000 without paying capital gains tax on the sale 'because he said he considered it to be his main home'.[3]

One could argue that there is no link between Maclean's use of his expenses and his desire to exempt MPs' work from public scrutiny. In fact, Maclean's bill was so exquisitely presented as a measure designed purely to protect the confidentiality of his constituents that it is difficult to criticize those who supported it.

However, once you start joining up the dots between those who went the extra mile to push Maclean's bill through, those who also voted to preserve the existing expenses system and those who made most creative use of the expenses system, a few names do keep cropping up with sufficient regularity for voters to mull over whether these individuals are fit to govern us.

When first presenting his Freedom of Information (Amendment) Bill, Maclean stressed that this was intended as a protection for his constituents by guaranteeing that their correspondence with their MP and an MP's correspondence on their behalf could not be accessed by other people using a FoI request: 'I take the view that when we write on behalf of constituents or when a constituent comes to us we must be able to look them in the eye and say that in all circumstances what they tell us will not get out – it is like a relationship with a priest'.[4] The amendment bill therefore supposedly had absolutely nothing to do with trying to hide MPs' expenses, although this would have been one of the inevitable consequences. Furthermore, Maclean quoted a letter from the Speaker confirming that his bill would not inhibit the annual publication of MPs' expenses in a few broad categories for each MP, as had happened in previous years:

> Mr Speaker has confirmed that even if the Bill becomes an Act, and even if technically or legally we will not have to publish information, the view of the House of Commons Members Estimate Committee and Mr Speaker is that we should continue every October to publish the same information on travel, allowances, accommodation and secretarial costs that we have published in the past few years.

This admirable intention to protect constituents was strongly supported by Jim Dowd, Labour MP for Lewisham West: 'I congratulate the right hon. Gentleman on introducing an excellent private Member's Bill. For the avoidance of doubt . . . we are not seeking a blanket exclusion for everything that MPs do. We are seeking, for the benefit of our constituents, a necessary protection on their behalf.'[5] Fraser Kemp, the Labour MP representing Houghton and Washington East, also helped clarify the apparently laudable motives behind a measure that would incidentally prevent us finding out what our parliamentarians were doing with our money: 'What we want is really special protection for our constituents.' Moreover, Maclean evidently didn't see any problem with removing MPs from the FoI Act as he claimed all MPs were honest people: 'We are all honourable Members in the House.'

A small group of MPs opposed the bill as it seemed to put MPs above the law and made the publication of expenses voluntary. One said:

> After all our fine words in this place about openness, transparency and wanting everyone to see what is being done in the name of democracy, we are saying that when it comes to freedom of information we are giving ourselves an exemption. Such a proposal is ridiculous and it is extraordinary that the Bill has not been laughed out of court. It is nonsense.[6]

Another stated: 'It is wrong and it is against the interests of Parliament. We are in danger of bringing ourselves into disrepute.'[7] As MPs prepared to vote, they were warned: 'We ought to be ashamed of ourselves today, and anybody who votes for the Bill ought to be ashamed of themselves.'[8]

One key argument used by the bill's opponents was that the Data Protection Act already protected MPs' correspondence from FoI requests, so there was no need for this new broad-brush exemption for MPs from the FoI Act. To cut a long and involved story short, there were five votes on different aspects of Maclean's bill and there was a large majority supporting the bill on every single vote, with 117 voting for Maclean's bill on the most critical of these votes, with only 22 opposing it.

Prime Minister Gordon Brown claimed that the whole thing had nothing to do with him. His spokesman said: 'Gordon has also spoken about the sovereignty of Parliament. If MPs have voted this measure through, then that is a matter for them.'[9] However, although less than 140 MPs voted in each of the votes, no fewer than 29 government ministers voted (all in favour of the bill) with some such as Bob Ainsworth managing to find the time in their busy schedules to support the bill in all five votes. However, as the whole purpose of Maclean's bill was ostensibly to protect constituents' confidentiality and not shield MPs' expenses from public scrutiny, those voting for it could emerge as true champions of the rights of ordinary constituents, whose confidentiality was nonetheless already protected by the Data Protection Act.

But the efforts of the bill's supporters, however pure or impure their motives, were of no avail – the bill got bombed out in the Lords where it failed to find a single member willing to sponsor it.

You again?

The true colours of some of our MPs started to emerge about a year later in July 2008 when they voted on a proposal from the Commons Members Estimate Committee to reform their allowances system. By a vote of 172 to 144, the proposal was rejected so that MPs could continue to claim for furniture and household goods using the 'John Lewis list'; keep their £24,000 or so a year additional costs allowance rather than being reimbursed for overnight expenses; avoid any outside audit of their expenses; not require receipts for claims under £25; and maintain high allowances for outer London MPs. This time, although the government again professed neutrality, an impressive 33 ministers voted to block changes to the system they so often publicly claimed was in need of reform.

This brings us to an interesting group of people – the MPs who made the most effort to support Maclean's bill in 2007 and also voted in favour of protecting the existing expenses system in 2008 (see Figure 1). The '6 votes for privilege' column lists those MPs who made the greatest contribution by turning up for all five votes to give their support to Maclean's bill and then also voted for the successful 2008 move to block expenses reform and external auditing. The '5 votes for privilege' column includes those who only voted on four of the five Maclean votes but also voted to stop expenses reform and external auditing. A few of those on the list will thankfully be leaving politics, often in shame due to their milking of the expenses system, but most of them will be hoping to hold on to their profitable political positions. If readers see any of these other individuals canvassing for their votes at the next general election, they might be tempted to wonder whether any of them deserves to be returned to Parliament.[10] Perhaps only the 144 MPs who voted for the expenses reform package deserve re-election and we should all boycott the 474 MPs who did not support the reforms.

Figure I Openness: The Hall of Fame/Shame

6 votes for privilege	5 votes for privilege	
Adrian Bailey Lab	Graham Allen Lab	Tom Levitt Lab
Liz Blackman Lab	Janet Anderson Lab	Tony Lloyd Lab
Nick Brown Lab	Clive Betts Lab	Khalid Mahmood Lab
Harry Cohen Lab	Colin Burgon Lab	Gillian Merron Lab
Brian Donohoe Lab	John Butterfill Con	Elliot Morley Lab
Jim Dowd Lab	Alan Campbell Lab	Denis Murphy Lab
Thomas McAvoy Lab	David Clelland Lab	James Plaskitt Lab
Steve McCabe Lab	Wayne David Lab	Stephen Pound Lab
Shona McIsaac Lab	Angela Eagle Lab	Ken Purchase Lab
Tony McNulty Lab	Maria Eagle Lab	John Robertson Lab
George Mudie Lab	Mike Hall Lab	Jim Sheridan Lab
Anne Snelgrove Lab	John Heppell Lab	Angela C. Smith Lab
John Spellar Lab	Keith Hill Lab	Mark Tami Lab
Gareth Thomas Lab	Huw I-Davies Lab	Claire Ward Lab
Tom Watson Lab	Kevan Jones Lab	Ann Winterton Con
	Martyn Jones Lab	Nicholas Winterton Con
	Julie Kirkbride Con	Phil Woolas Lab
	Greg Knight Con	David Wright Lab
	Bob Laxton Lab	

Some of these people probably deserve a special mention for their ability to both turn up for so many important votes to preserve their own privileges while also putting in the time and effort to make expense claims which attracted the attention of several newspapers. It's difficult to choose the most worthy – there are so many fine contenders – but we only have room for a few, including Harry Cohen, Labour MP for Leyton & Wanstead. His constituency is just nine miles from Westminster, but he seems to have needed a succession of second homes which were each decorated using our money. When his doings were reported, Cohen gave an interview to one newspaper in which he didn't come out smelling of roses. He protested it had all been a stitch-up: 'I made a big mistake discussing parliamentary allowances with a tabloid journalist . . . The article was full of inaccuracies, including the headline which was false . . . My repeated emphasis was, and is, on the urgent need for major reform of the allowances system. This was clearly omitted.'[11] Yet it is not obvious that Cohen took any legal action against the newspaper which had allegedly misrepresented him so insolently. Moreover, if he was so keen on the issue of expenses reform, why would he vote against it? It's all very curious.

Chief whip Nick Brown reportedly 'claimed £18,800 without receipts in expenses for food over the course of four years'.[12] He also claimed a total of about £87,708 for his constituency home in 2004–8. This apparently included: '£23,608, just £15 below the maximum allowable amount' in 2007–8 when his mortgage interest repayments were just £6,600 by 'including the maximum £4,800 for food, £2,880 for "repairs and insurance", £2,880 for services' and various other bits and pieces. And we have Meg Munn, Labour MP for Sheffield Heeley, who claimed maximum second home allowances in three out of four years. Her husband, who worked at HM Revenue and Customs, was paid by several ministers to provide tax advice. Her office expenses reportedly 'include payments to her husband, who also works as her parliamentary assistant, for accounting advice'.[13]

I blame 'the system'

There is also another interesting line of investigation: to compare the list of the MPs who voted in July 2008 to block any changes to the expenses system with the list of those who, when caught making the most outrageously brazen expense claims, blamed the system rather than any personal moral failings for their difficulties. These people are too numerous to list here, but in passing let's just mention a few of our absolute favourites.

Number one must be Jacqui Smith, who we will discuss in the next chapter, who felt that 'the system' was in some way to responsible for her second-home irregularities: 'I think and all of us have said this, we knew if we thought about it that it wasn't a good system.'[14] Tory MP Julie Kirkbride also had a go at the system when her wildly imaginative use of expenses, including an apparently lucrative confusion between her and her MP husband Andrew MacKay about where they lived, was exposed: 'We had felt our expenses would not be queried and that, whilst the antiquated system is obviously in need of wholesale reform, we had claimed correctly.'[15] Her potentially ludicrous attempts to portray herself as an honest working mum and a victim are well worth a read for anyone interested in the ancient art of hagiography.[16] Given her apparent enthusiasm for reforming the system, it may seem surprising that both she and her husband voted against any reforms and any improved auditing. Like so many others, David Clelland also lashed out at 'the increasingly bureaucratic' nature of the Commons expenses system as part of the explanation for his interesting, taxpayer-funded domestic arrangements, which were approved by the obsequious Fees Office.[17]

PLUS ÇA CHANGE

As the barrage of press and public criticism of our parliamentarians intensified, the leaders of the two main parties jumped around, sometimes trying to dodge the mud that was flying around and sometimes jostling with each other to portray themselves as great reformers whom we could now trust to clean out Westminster's Augean stables. Given Brown's and Cameron's self-proclaimed enthusiasm for changing the heinous system, which had tempted so many of our innocent and honourable MPs away from the straight and narrow, it might be worth spending a moment testing our political leaders' qualifications as reformers.

Tender treatment for Tories

Even before the major expenses stories broke in 2009, Conservative leader David Cameron was hit by scandal following the revelations about MP Derek Conway giving quite large sums of our money to his two sons for work that may never have been done. Conway had the party whip removed from him, but was allowed by the Commons to stay in Parliament until the next election. That meant he had plenty of time to stock up with our cash and goodies bought on expenses prior to his eventual retirement. This apparently included getting us to pay for him employing his wife and generous office costs in his family home a few hundred miles from his constituency. The office costs reportedly included a digital camera, a fridge freezer, a TV, a £399 satellite navigation device (presumably in case he forgot where his office was as it was so far from his constituents), Wedgwood crockery, two folding Clifford James banqueting tables and £220 for repairs to a briefcase.[18] Conway also used 'most of his second home allowance to pay the mortgage interest on his flat in Pimlico, central London, despite representing a constituency which is on the outskirts of the capital'.[19] Once he finally departs, Conway will probably get generous resettlement allowances along with a massive taxpayer-funded pension. All in all, he will have done very nicely indeed from his years of 'public service'.

Cameron also had a couple of small problems at the European Parliament with MEPs Giles Chichester and Den Dover. Chichester admitted making a mistake by paying about £445,000 of our money to a company of which he was a paid director, 'in connection with secretarial and assistant services for the European Parliament constituency and committee work'.[20] Cameron made much of the fact that Chichester stepped down as Conservative leader in the European Parliament, but Chichester kept his well-rewarded MEP job. Then to add insult to injury for us taxpayers, in the June 2009 EU elections Chichester was chosen by the Tory leadership as their top candidate for his region, guaranteeing him another five wonderfully lucrative years representing Britain's interests in Brussels. Shortly after Chichester hit the headlines, there was a kerfuffle regarding about £750,000 paid by Den Dover, Tory chief whip in Europe, to a company owned by his wife and daughter. Dover was replaced as chief whip, but of course kept his MEP job. He was later asked by the European Parliament to repay around €600,000. He refused and there's currently a bit of argy-bargy going on. As he was over 70 by the time of the 2009 EU elections, he retired without seeking re-election. It would not be totally surprising if not one cent is ever repaid and he's allowed to walk away with our money to enjoy his well-remunerated retirement.

We'll fight them on the beaches

In January 2009 Gordon Brown and Harriet Harman made one last bold attempt to block publication of MPs' expenses even though the information commissioner had ruled that MPs' receipts should be published and the House of Commons had already spent hundreds of thousands of pounds of our money preparing them for release. Brown and Harman tried to rush through an amendment to the FoI Act excluding MPs' and Peers' expenses from the scope of the Act. Moving with remarkable speed, the proposal was announced by Harman, the Leader of the House, on 15 January 2009 and scheduled to be voted on in both the Commons and the Lords on 22 January and then become law the next day. Brown must have mislaid his moral compass at the time as he reportedly imposed a three-line whip to force Labour MPs to back the move and threatened sanctions on any rebels. The purpose of preventing us seeing MPs' receipts was apparently to improve transparency, as Gordon Brown's spokesman implausibly explained: 'The aim was to finish up with a system that was more transparent.'[21] Harman also gave her understanding of how greater transparency could be introduced by blocking publication of MPs' receipts: 'What we've said is receipts must be produced and they must be audited but we didn't think it was right that there should be 1.2 million receipts, every single receipt for every ream of paper that is bought should be necessary, and then published.'[22]

However, in circumstances which are not entirely clear, Brown and Harman did an acrobatic U-turn and abandoned the proposal within a couple of days. Brown claimed that the Tories had originally supported the measure: 'We thought we had agreement on the Freedom of Information Act . . . Recently that support that we believed we had from the main opposition party was withdrawn.'[23] Harman backed her master's version of events: 'At the last minute the Tories have pulled the plug and I will have to talk to them about why.' Cameron seemed to have a different version of events: 'We welcome this embarrassing U-turn by the government. To exempt MPs from the FoI Act would be completely wrong. They should be treated the same as everybody else.' But there are indications that the Conservative leadership may have had a last-minute change of heart and that they might previously not have been as allergic to the proposed exemption as several of them later made out.

My reforms are bigger than yours

Once the *Telegraph* started printing the real, unredacted details of MPs' expenses receipts both party leaders seemed to be caught on the hop. In the first two days, Brown failed to take any action against the apparently excessive claims of many of his top brass – Hazel Blears, Shaun Woodward, Caroline Flint, Margaret Beckett, David Miliband, Alistair Darling, Andy Burnham and Keith Vaz amongst others. This allowed Cameron to steal a march on the dithering Brown by making a rather vague threat that MPs who broke the rules 'could be sacked'. Then the next day Cameron further outwitted the plodding prime minister by ordering his shadow cabinet to refund any excessive expenses. Finally, almost two weeks after the flood of revelations began, Brown promised a radical reform of the expenses system, which he had previously resisted, and said that no Labour MP who had broken the rules would be allowed to stand again as a Labour MP. But they would, of course, be permitted to stay on, potentially milking the system, until the next election, which would also make them eligible for large resettlement allowances. Harman popped up a couple of days later with plans for a new expenses system that would put MPs 'above reproach'.

Then, as the scandals kept coming, both leaders mysteriously began promising all sorts of things which had little or nothing to do with the basic problem, that most of our MPs, aided and abetted by the Fees Office, had simply acted like thieves. We were offered supposedly 'independent' committees to audit MPs' expenses: that was what we already paid the Fees Office to do. This was followed by highfalutin' commitments to constitutional changes and all kinds of other smokescreens and diversionary tactics to give the impression that Brown and Cameron were tackling the problem. But our political leaders' true feelings about bowing to public demands for the punishment of offenders and cleaning up the filth, can be tested by looking at the reputations of those who still form the current government and those who would like to make up the next one.

Business as usual

At the top of the government pile is Gordon Brown who flipped his designated second home from a London flat to his Scottish constituency home shortly after moving into Downing Street. Moreover, in spite of the multitude of assistants and secretaries serving him and in spite of his own financial genius, he was found to have mistakenly submitted some bills twice and equally mistakenly to have claimed for utilities and service charges on the 'wrong properties'. Next we have Peter Mandelson. With his Brussels pension and ministerial salary, he has no need to milk his expenses. However, commenting on his younger days as a constituency MP a newspaper wrote that Mandelson had: 'claimed thousands of pounds for work on his constituency home in Hartlepool shortly after announcing his resignation as an MP, it was reported. He renovated the terrace house in 2004 and sold it for a £136,000 profit. Lord Mandelson's spokesman insisted the expenditure was to repair the property, "not improve it"' and Lord Mandelson dismissed the allegations as 'smears' without 'a scintilla of evidence' and explained that the work on the house was necessary to stop trees damaging a dividing wall and his neighbours' property.[24] Alistair Darling, our chancellor, seems to have been much more successful in running his own economic affairs than those of the country. He gained a reputation as a serial 'flipper', having changed the designation of his second home no less than four times.

Jack Straw, our justice minister, retained his job after actions that would have brought any normal person before his courts. It's unlikely most benefit cheats could have got away with Straw's excuse that 'accountancy does not appear to be my strongest suit' when he was caught obtaining a 50 per cent 'zero occupancy' discount for his second home in his Blackburn constituency, yet claiming for reimbursement of full council tax from us. Ed Balls and Yvette Cooper designated as their second home the London house where they lived with their children, meaning they could claim second-home allowances even though the rules make clear that: 'Members can nominate either their constituency home or one in London as their second home but your main home will normally be the one where you spend more nights than any other.' Then once you chuck in David Miliband, Liam Byrne, Bob Ainsworth and many others' wildly generous ways of helping themselves to our money, Gordon Brown's blustering and boasting about how he was dealing with excessive expenses claims to put his MPs beyond reproach start to look more than slightly ridiculous.

Over on the Tory benches, things didn't look squeaky clean either. David Cameron himself has kept his nose relatively clean and can only really be accused of admirable magnanimity to himself rather than deliberately abusing the system. Shortly after being elected, 'He took out the £350,000 mortgage – close to the maximum amount that can be claimed for – to buy a large house in Oxfordshire.'[25] Shadow chancellor George Osborne, on the other hand, seems to have been sailing a little closer to the wind, and not just on his Greek holidays. Osborne bought a Cheshire farmhouse close to his constituency just under a year before winning the seat in June 2001. Rather than taking out a mortgage on the new property, 'he funded the purchase by increasing his borrowing on the London home where he and his wife had lived since 1998.' Then came the stroke of genius: 'After his election he designated the London house his "second home" with the Commons authorities.'[26] This allowed him to claim the mortgage interest payments on his expenses even though the mortgage in question looked awfully like it had been taken out on his main home. Then two years later, he took out a mortgage on the Cheshire house and made it his second home so he could claim those interest payments on expenses. His spokesman explained that all these mortgages and changes were: 'Entirely reasonable as all the costs are associated with his need to have a second home in Cheshire, and his arrangements have always sought to minimise the interest costs to the taxpayer.'

Michael Gove reportedly spent thousands of pounds furnishing his London home before flipping his second home designation to a new property in his Surrey constituency and submitting a £13,259 bill for the move including stamp duty and other fees. He agreed to pay back £7,000 claimed for furniture.

On and on and on the list goes; pick a leading Tory MP and you'll probably see some expenses manure sticking to him or her. Perhaps the most gruesome of all the Tories implicated in possible over-expensing was the well-dressed Alan Duncan. On 'Have I Got News For You', he famously said, rather smugly, about the expenses system: 'Fabulous system, isn't it?' When the always perfectly coiffed Mr Duncan found himself mired in accusations of greed, he popped up on television once again, this time looking somewhat more contrite and declaring: 'The House of Commons is in such a mess. These allowances have got to stop.' The difference between the elegant Alan Duncan's two appearances is highly recommended viewing.[27]

We promise...to take more of your money

Of course, following the expenses scandals, the two main parties have allowed a few of the most ridiculous transgressors the well-rewarded soft landing of a gentle withdrawal come the next election. Real punishment has been in worryingly short supply. And all those who do withdraw will be laughing their socks off as they spend the rest of their lives in taxpayer-funded luxury while the rest of us can look forward to decades of increased taxes in order to help pay for our cheating MPs' lifelong financial security.

Gordon Brown has made many great promises in his time, most recently in a wordy pledge to clean up politics. This latest commitment is worth repeating in full for its unintentional humour, as it is clearly so many billions and trillions of miles away from what Brown is actually trying to do:

> The first thing we've got to do is to clean up politics once and for all. We've got to make sure that people see that their Members of Parliament and those who seek to represent them are acting in the public interest and not in their self interest.
>
> We've got to make sure that people see that their politicians are in it not for what they can get, but for what they can give. That's why today we promise that we will uphold the highest standards of integrity, we promise that there will be transparency in everything we do, we promise that we will report to our constituents and do so as regularly as possible. Report not only to our own party but to all sections of the community in our constituencies so they can raise their concerns with us and we can be true and honoured servants of the people of this country.
>
> I believe that our pledge to clean up politics, complemented by the new Parliamentary Standards authority that Harriet Harman is introducing, complemented by the new code of conduct for MPs and complemented by the review that is now taking place of four years of previous expenses, so we deal with any abuse, we deal with any repayment, we deal with anything that has been wrong and discipline people as necessary, is the first start to making sure that the politics of our country are based on these principles: that we will always act responsibly and in a fair way.[28]

However, if anyone is expecting real reform from either of the main party leaders, they'll be waiting an awfully long time. Anyway, just to give a final, contemptuous two fingers gesture to us taxpayers, in July 2009 as MPs departed for their long summer break they awarded themselves a new £25-a-night subsistence allowance payable without a receipt when staying away from their main home. This could net some of them thousands of pounds a year tax-free over and above all their mortgage, rent, food, utility bills and council tax allowances.

Moreover, with the MPs' new wheeze of appointing supposedly independent auditors to review their expense claims, it won't be long before they're telling us that with such a 'tough', 'robust' new system, it would be wasting taxpayers' money to carry on publishing their receipts. Much better, they will suggest, to let the 'independent' professionals get on with the job. But any firm of accountants given the auditing task will know that asking too many difficult questions of MPs could lead to the loss of their lucrative auditing contract. So we can expect that a Stygian darkness will soon descend again on the whole area of MPs' expenses and we will once again be prevented from finding out what is happening when our rulers shove their faces well and truly back into the trough of our money.

Time for a cull?

As one looks through the pages and pages of evidence against MPs who have been filling their pockets with our money, one thing that is striking is that most of them seem to be insignificant nonentities whom most people have never heard of, and who may not have contributed anything of any great value to anyone. Yet, as another obedient commission produces another report and proposals on MPs' expenses, we can be absolutely certain that nobody will ask the real questions that need to be asked, such as: 'Why do we need 646 MPs anyway?' and 'Now that the EU produces over 80 per cent of our laws, why can't we reduce the number of MPs to 200, or at most 300?'

CHAPTER 11

SNOUTS IN THE TROUGH

LEST WE FORGET

As 2008 turned into 2009, our politicians started riding a wave of public disgust over the way bankers had behaved. The talk was of new 'controls', 'crackdowns', 'returning to old-fashioned values' and 'transparency'. This culminated in a hearing of the Treasury Select Committee in February 2009, portrayed in the press as a show trial, in which the former chief executives and chairmen of RBS and HBOS were harangued for their part in the financial chaos and Fred Goodwin's pension arrangements were vilified. In an interview with Andrew Marr on the BBC, Harriet Harman explained that although Goodwin's pension arrangements might be enforceable in a court of law, they were 'not enforceable in the court of public opinion, and that is where the government steps in'. If the court of public opinion was fed up with bankers, it was about to be enraged by the behaviour of politicians.

May and June 2009 were devastating months for MPs as the *Daily Telegraph* unleashed its torrent of stories detailing the many inventive ways our plundering politicians stuffed their pockets with our money. But by July, with the horrific and unnecessary death toll in Afghanistan forcing its way on to the front pages and unemployment shooting up towards two and a half million, the media started to move on from the expenses scandal to other stories. MPs leaving for their 12-week summer break on 22 July had good reason to believe that by the time they returned in the middle of October, relaxed and well rested from their extended holidays, much of the expenses storm would have blown over and a few cosmetic changes to the expenses system would allow their scamming, and sometimes blatant thieving, of taxpayers' money to continue much as before.

For this reason, it is worth revisiting some of the worst abuses so that, come the next election, we remember the people who were most rapacious in misusing their position to fleece those of us unfortunate enough not to have gone into politics as a career. There were about ten main dodgy techniques liberally used by MPs to enrich themselves at our expense (see Figure 1). As the table only shows what a few of our MPs were up to in the five years from 2002–3 to 2007–8, the real figures for the number of MPs using each technique are certainly much higher than those listed here.

Figure I Many MPs have been enthusiastic expensers

Technique	No. of MPs
1. Creative 'second-homeing'	81
2. Mortgage games	51
3. Flipping	57
4. Outer-London MPs with second homes	24
5. Capital Gains Tax avoidance	24
6. Council Tax overclaims	12
7. Fit, furnish and flog	66
8. Benefiting their families	139
9. Questionable gardening	40
10. Frivolous/Unnecessary/Ridiculous claims	410

THE TOP TEN

I. Second home is where the heart is

Perhaps the most brazen scam used by MPs was the way they imaginatively chose which was their main home and which was their second home. This choice was important as they could claim up to £24,000 a year for their second home, but very little for their main home apart from a few thousand pounds if they conducted parliamentary business there. When caught playing the second-home game, MPs usually said either that they had acted within the rules or that the rules were unclear. But a 2008 ruling by the Parliamentary Commissioner for Standards, John Lyon, seemed to specify in very straightforward and easily comprehensible terms what was a main and what was a second home: 'If a Member has his or her family living permanently in their constituency home and has modest accommodation in London big enough only for themselves, and which they use only when Parliament is in session, then it would clearly seen to be a matter of fact that the Member's main home is in the constituency'.[1]

Jacqui, you take my breath away

The clear winner of the unlikely second-home prize has to be, of course, the Second-Home Secretary Jacqui Smith. By declaring a room in her sister's house as her main home between 2001–2 and 2007–8 she was able to bank about £140,000 in additional cost allowances for the constituency home where her porn-watching, taxpayer-paid (£40,000 a year) husband lived with her two children. If, as seems likely, she had been claiming her constituency house was her second home since she became an MP in 1997, she has probably got away with closer to a tax-free £200,000. By dreaming up this wheeze, Jacqui Smith was able to furnish her much bigger 'second home' with an impressively wide range of fixtures and fittings at our expense. These included a stone sink and console (£550), an Ariston washing machine (£249), a Hotpoint electric cooker (£414), a Hotpoint tumble dryer (£209 including fitting), a Zanussi washing machine (£319.95 including fitting), a fireplace (£1,000), doors, garden materials and many other goodies which probably couldn't have fitted into the spare room which was her 'main home'.

Smith's curious interpretation of the second-home opportunity became even more absurd when she was made home secretary from 2007 to 2009 and declined to use a grace-and-favour residence provided to her rent-free. One of the rules is that MPs must get 'value for money' from their second-home claim. Yet by living at her sister's for a few nights a week while serving as home secretary, rather than taking her grace-and-favour accommodation, Jacqui landed us taxpayers with the extra, and completely avoidable, £200,000 a year expense of providing police protection for her – possibly more than £400,000 in two years just so she could pocket about £40,000.

The reasons, excuses and obfuscations given by Smith and her various lackeys truly deserve some kind of award. She told us: 'What I claim is what I think are fair and reasonable expenses for the fact that I have to live in two places' and 'I think that I have abided both by the letter of the law and by the spirit of the regulations.' Her spokesperson defended her arrangement: 'She has lived with her sister in London since she was a backbench MP and is perfectly happy with it. Most people would think that is a nice thing.'[2]

Yet Jacqui Smith's claims that her sister's London house was her main home were contradicted by her neighbours. One commented: 'When I read that she spends most of the nights here, I thought "That is a fabrication".'[3] The neighbour went on to explain: 'You can tell when she is here because the police guards arrive first. They turn up mid-morning on Monday and leave mid-morning on Thursday.' Moreover, Jacqui's own spokesperson seemed to contradict her boss's story that her sister's house was her home when she told the press: 'She tends to go home Thursday evenings and returns on Sunday or Monday.'[4] One of the rules states that MPs should: 'Avoid any arrangement which may give rise to an accusation that you are, or someone close to you is, obtaining an immediate benefit or subsidy from public funds.'[5] It's difficult to square that with Jacqui Smith's living arrangements.

Over the last seven years, Jacqui Smith has probably cost taxpayers over £2 million in salary, expenses and other bits and pieces. Jacqui Smith had a small majority of only 2,716 at the last election. With subsequent boundary changes this may have been reduced. If she has the nerve to stand at the next election, hopefully Redditch's voters will have the good sense to send her packing. It would perhaps also be fitting if she was given the choice between repaying a few hundred thousand pounds or facing a police investigation for fraud. Moreover, if it is found that officials at Westminster, such as Andrew Walker in the Fees Office, helped her with her arrangements, perhaps they should be investigated for conspiracy to defraud the taxpayer. But that's daydreaming – the most likely outcome is that Gordon Brown will try to bounce her into the Lords so she can carry on sponging off taxpayers for the rest of her days as a reward for her years of 'public service'.

The Jacqui Smith fan club
A few other MPs also deserve a mention for the diligent way they seem to have followed Jacqui Smith's example in creatively interpreting which was their second home. First up must be children's secretary Ed Balls and his wife, chief secretary to the Treasury Yvette Cooper. They were reported to have switched their 'second home' designation from their house in West Yorkshire to their £655,000 London home even though their children go to school from this house. This arrangement probably helped them pay their £438,000 mortgage.[6] However, rather than criticizing them for their liberal interpretation of the words 'second home', perhaps we should be grateful to them for their restraint – after all, in 2007–8 they only claimed a modest £24,000 between them when they could have claimed about £46,000. But as they pick up around £280,000 in salaries alone from taxpayers every year, they won't be going hungry.

Former minister Tony McNulty should also get special commendation. It was reported that although he and his wife, chief inspector of schools Christine Gilbert, lived 'in a house that she owns just three miles from Westminster, the minister has been claiming up to £14,000 a year in parliamentary expenses to help pay for a second house in Harrow where his parents live, eleven miles from the Commons'.[7] The house for which he obtained at least £60,000 tax-free was in his Harrow constituency and McNulty said he occasionally used it for constituency work and that this was 'within the rules'. Then he announced he had stopped claiming and that MPs who lived within 60 miles of Parliament should be banned from getting the £24,000 second-home allowance.

2. The marvels of mortgages

Non-existent mortgages

The closest the expenses scandal came to outright criminality was in the revelation that a number of MPs had claimed for mortgage payments that they hadn't actually made. Elliot Morley, a junior minister under Tony Blair, claimed more than £16,000 for the mortgage interest on his constituency home despite having already paid off the mortgage in full and not making any further payments to the mortgage company from his own bank account. Land Registry records show the mortgage on his Scunthorpe home had been paid off by 1 March 2006. This did not stop Morley from claiming £800 in mortgage interest each month throughout 2006 and into 2007. When the parliamentary authorities asked members for proof of their mortgage expenses in 2007, Morley did not provide any.

At the end of 2007, Elliot Morley designated his London address as his second home. There was nothing wrong with this, except that it is thought he had previously rented the property to his friend and fellow MP Ian Cawsey, who designated it as his second home. This meant that for some months there may have been two MPs claiming full expenses on the same house, with Morley receiving expenses and rent.

David Chaytor, the MP for Bury North, also admitted to

claiming £13,000 mortgage interest expenses for his London flat between September 2005 and August 2006 despite records at the Land Registry showing the mortgage on the property had been paid off in January 2004. Chaytor claimed to have made an 'unforgivable error' and has announced his decision to stand down at the next election.

Members of the public are furious that MPs caught like this still receive a full salary and expenses until the next election. None of the disgraced MPs who will be standing down as a result of the expenses scandal will have to forfeit the Resettlement Allowance of between 50 per cent and 100 per cent of their £64,766 salary, nor for that matter will they have to go without the £42,068 Winding Up Allowance when they cease to be a Member of Parliament. There has been some interest in pressing charges against MPs who have wrongly claimed payments for 'phantom mortgages', with the 2006 Fraud Act and the 1986 Theft Act being cited as laws likely to be used.

Some of the incorrectly claimed mortgage-related expenses which have been repaid:

Elliot Morley (L)	£36,800
Rosie Winterton (L)	£8,247
David Chaytor (L)	£4,812
Tony McNulty (L)	£4,277 (inc. council tax element)
David Miliband (L)	£434

Claiming for mortgage interest and capital

Compared with the byzantine ways some MPs have found of shifting their primary residence, this wheeze is relatively straightforward. MPs are only allowed to claim for interest on the mortgage for their second home. They are not allowed to claim for capital repayments and have been specifically prohibited from submitting claims for things like endowment mortgages which should accumulate capital over the lifetime of the policy. However, this hasn't stopped our enterprising representatives from trying to reclaim their capital repayments. Making this scandal even worse is the fact that so many of them have succeeded.

Mark Hendrick, the Labour MP for Preston, repaid £6,805.52 to the Fees Office in 2008 after the House authorities noticed he had submitted claims for the capital repayment element of his second-home mortgage, as well as for the interest. The confusion arose when the MP paid off the mortgage on his London home, then moved his second-home designation (and the mortgage) to his constituency base. The claim first came to the attention of the Fees Office when it noticed the amount claimed varied from month to month. This was because the MP 'estimated' his monthly expenses and submitted claims accordingly.

Clare Short, the former international development secretary who now sits as an Independent Member for Birmingham Ladywood, also repaid money. She claimed for the capital element of her mortgage for over two years. When the Fees Office asked her to repay more than £8,000, she said that she 'was not clear about the rules on capital and interest', in spite of the rules being unusually straightforward. Moreover, she felt that officials should 'accept some responsibility for the situation' because they allowed the claims and didn't correct her earlier. These are exactly the type of explanations that ordinary taxpayers find are highly unlikely to go down well with HMRC when they investigate a small business, or with the police when ticketing somebody for driving at 35mph in a 30mph zone.

Trust fund fun

Just because an MP has paid off the mortgage on their second home, it doesn't mean they have to go without their much-loved expense claims. For example, the Tory MPs Nicholas and Ann Winterton designated a London flat as their second home. No problem there, you might think. Surely it is cheaper to have two MPs at the same address, with only one mortgage to pay. Sadly not. Since 2002, the flat used by the Wintertons had been controlled by a Winterton family trust, believed to benefit Nicholas and Ann's children. Although it is thought that the flat was previously owned outright by the couple, they could now claim £900 a month, each, whilst ensuring any inheritance tax payable on their estate by their children would be reduced because the flat was administered by a trust.

3. Flipper

In 2008 the *Oxford English Dictionary* released a list of new words that had entered the English language that year. These included 'sub-prime', 'wantaway' and 'jasm'. The 2009 list will most probably include 'flipping'. This occurs when an MP changes the designation of which of their houses is their main home, for which they can't claim the cost of new televisions, decorating, wardrobes, soundproofing the bedroom, etc., and their second home, for which they can claim for all of the above plus a whole lot more – up to £24,222.[8]

The best-known flipper is probably Gordon Brown himself. As chancellor, Brown used his Westminster flat as his second home despite having access to a flat in Downing Street. He claimed for items like a £265 vacuum cleaner and a £9,000 kitchen from IKEA. The kitchen claim seems to have been spread across two separate financial years to maximize the total he could claw back as it exceeded the maximum allowed for a kitchen in one year. Shortly after moving into Downing Street, Gordon Brown changed his designated second home from his Westminster flat to his house overlooking the Firth of Forth. Now that he has moved his second home to Scotland, he can claim for the same items again if he so wishes, just for a different home.

Alistair Darling, on the other hand, has been a far more energetic flipper. He changed his designated second home four times in four years. In 2004–5, Darling claimed his main home was in a small flat in Lambeth, previously owned by Gordon Brown who sold it to Lewis Moonie (the current Lord Moonie, who sits in the House of Lords and was a minister in Tony Blair's government) in 1992. Moonie rented a room to Darling who claimed his Edinburgh house was his second home – for which he could claim expenses. In September 2005, he bought a flat near the Oval cricket ground for £226,000, which, as his newly designated second home, meant the public purse covered his £2,260 stamp duty and £1,238 in legal fees, amongst other items. In 2007, the newly promoted chancellor claimed Downing Street was his second home and submitted expense claims for living in the property whilst renting out his Oval flat. This arrangement, however, meant he could only claim for items like utility bills, and not for items that were already present in the flat. This might have been one of the reasons why he changed his second home designation yet again to his house in Edinburgh.

Perhaps the pressure of the onset of the credit crunch is the most charitable explanation as to why Darling mistakenly claimed for two homes at the same time in late 2007. Shortly before moving to Downing Street, Alistair Darling submitted a £1,004 bill for the service charge for his flat near the Oval, which was within the rules. However, the bill covered the period to the end of December 2007, by which time he had already moved his designated second home to Downing Street and started claiming for expenses incurred there. Parliamentary rules forbid claiming expenses for two different properties at the same time. In June 2009, after this was revealed in the press, the chancellor agreed to repay any wrongly claimed expenses.

It would be impossible to write any piece on parliamentary expenses without mentioning Geoff Hoon. As a former MEP, maybe the Labour MP for Ashfield had a head start on some of his colleagues in the energetic expenses stakes. In the last few years the former defence secretary has built a property empire which far exceeds what most people can dream of acquiring during a lifetime's work.

Between 2004 and 2006, Hoon claimed thousands of pounds for renovations and new furnishings at his constituency home. In 2004–5, he claimed the maximum permissible from the taxpayer for the property: £20,902. The house was bought for around £135,000 in the 1980s, and is now believed to be worth in excess of £600,000. As defence secretary, he was allocated a flat in Admiralty House, the imposing building located between the Cabinet Office and Admiralty Arch. After leaving this flat in 2006, Hoon is believed to have sold the flat he previously owned (and rented out, whilst living rent-free in his official residence) and acquired another, rather grand home in a fashionable Georgian square near Parliament. The monthly mortgage interest bill is believed to be around £900, which is what he claimed on expenses. Other claims exposed by the *Daily Telegraph* investigation include more than £500 for new flooring and a £449 television – the second TV he claimed for in the space of two years. In 2007–8, Geoff Hoon again spent the maximum allowed under the expenses scheme, this time £23,083.

Including the cottage Mrs Hoon is reported to have bought on the Suffolk coast, the Hoons now have a property empire valued in the region of £1.7 million – doubtless a great comfort to all of the service families who lived in clapped-out military housing whilst Geoff Hoon was their secretary of state.[9]

Some of the serial flippers:

Geoff Hoon (L) flipped four times in four years.

Hazel Blears (L) claimed for three properties and nights spent in a series of hotels in just one year.

Alistair Darling (L) made four separate second-home designations in about four years.

John Bercow (Speaker) flipped twice in the space of a year when he sold two houses, avoiding capital gains tax on both properties.

Kitty Ussher (L) flipped homes for a month, coinciding with sale of a property.

4. Maybe it's because I'm a Londoner

It is argued that MPs need a second home so they can do their jobs better by being available near Parliament at short notice, allowing them to stay for late debates and the like. As the expense regime has become ever more generous over the years, these underlying assumptions have gradually become less compelling. Since the late 1990s, the Commons has progressively sat for fewer and fewer late-night sessions. This is regarded as a triumph of modernization by making Parliament more 'family friendly'. Most Wednesdays, the House has risen by around 7 p.m.; on Mondays and Tuesdays it rarely sits much past 10 p.m.; Thursdays are generally fairly relaxed affairs with many members already having left London for their constituencies by lunchtime; Fridays tend to be given over only to private members' bills, for which very few MPs actually attend. There is also an almost indecent number of holidays. In 2008–9 slightly in excess of 20 weeks 'holiday' were available to most MPs when the Commons did not sit.[10] Parliament was believed to have been in session for fewer days than at any time since 1945. In spite of an easier working life, MPs with seats within easy commuting distance of London and who represent constituents who travel further for work every day for more days than they do, get to claim for a second home in central London on which they can accumulate capital and can sell once they cease being an MP.

People like Tony McNulty, with two homes just a few miles apart in Harrow and Hammersmith, have some serious questions to answer in Harriet Harman's 'court of public opinion'. Others include Harry Cohen, the MP for Leyton & Wanstead who has claimed £104,701 in housing allowances since 2002. Derek Conway, the former Tory and current partyless MP for Old Bexley & Sidcup, claimed a total of £104,651 in the same period. Mike Gapes, the Labour chairman of the Foreign Affairs Select Committee and MP for Ilford South, claimed £104,650. Last, but by no means least, Jon Cruddas, the MP for Dagenham and all-round hero of the workers, claimed £103,117. It has been unkindly noted that he acquired his £500,000 Notting Hill home around the time his child was due to start school. Fortuitously, the home is in the catchment area for the highly sought-after Cardinal Vaughan Memorial School, which is generally considered far superior to any of the schools in his Dagenham constituency.[11]

In total, over the five years of claims which have been revealed, 27 outer-London MPs claimed £1.7 million in second-home allowances, an average of £63,000 each (see Figure 2). However, another 22 MPs living similar distances from Westminster made no second-home claims at all.

Figure 2 Outer-London MPs: Top ten claimants

MP	Constituency	Claims*	Distance**
1. Harry Cohen	Leyton & Wanstead	£104,701	11.4m
2. Andrew Rosindell	Romford	£104,699	18.5m
3. Derek Conway	Old Bexley & Sidcup	£104,651	12.3m
4. Mike Gapes	Ilford South	£104,650	13.2m
5. John Cruddas	Dagenham	£103,117	13.5m
6. Richard Ottaway	Croydon Sth	£101,808	13.1m
7. Andrew Love	Edmonton	£100,303	9.6m
8. Joan Ryan	Enfield North	£95,932	13.6m
9. Jacqui Lait	Beckenham	£93,468	8.8m
10. John Austin	Erith & Thamesmead	£87,328	12.6m
*2001/2 to 2006/7		**by road from constituency office to Westminster	

5. Avoiding capital gains tax

Main homes are one of the few asset classes in Britain to be exempt from capital gains tax (CGT) – a levy currently set at 18 per cent on the sales of assets which generate a gain on the original capital invested. In 2008–9, it is expected to raise less than £5 billion (or less than 1 per cent of government expenditure), so isn't a very effective revenue raiser.

Although quite a small tax compared with many others Parliament is responsible for, MPs seem rather disinclined to pay it themselves when they make profits from selling their many homes. Greg Barker, the millionaire Conservative MP for Bexhill & Battle, made a profit believed to be in the region of £320,000 in slightly over two years by buying and then selling a flat in Chelsea, funded partly with the help of parliamentary expenses. In order to qualify for these expenses, he designated the flat as his second home, but when he came to sell it he designated it as his main home, thereby saving himself many thousands of pounds in CGT.

Other similar transactions were completed by Hazel Blears who took to the nation's TV screens brandishing a cheque for £13,000 which she made payable to HMRC as a 'voluntary contribution' in lieu of CGT she might have been liable for on the sale of two flats in East London;[12] Kitty Ussher left her post as a junior minister in the Treasury after it was revealed that she changed the designation of her main home for a single month when she sold her constituency home for a £40,000 profit; Eleanor Laing, the Tory MP for Epping Forest, made a reported £1 million profit on the sale of the flat in London she had purchased with the help of parliamentary allowances and after avoiding CGT on the transaction;[13] and finally Geoff Hoon didn't incur any CGT liability on the London flat he is believed to have sold for a profit of around £300,000 in 2006 because he designated London as his primary residence for tax purposes. Yet, as discussed, he then moved upmarket and bought a smart London house, located in a Georgian square. By designating this new London home as his second home to the Commons Fees Office, he could claim expenses on his latest acquisition.

Another way of getting a little tax-free windfall at the taxpayers' expense was when at least 13 MPs who rented flats in the Dolphin Square estate in Westminster all received big cash payments (one was reported to have been offered £42,000) from their landlord in return for giving up their rights to low rents. The result was that once they took the money to allow their rents to increase, they just charged us more on their expenses.

6. Council tax, too

Council tax comes just ahead of inheritance tax for the title of Britain's most hated tax. Maybe one of the reasons why MPs have allowed council tax to double in the past decade is because the way many of them encounter the tax bears no relation to the way most families have to deal with it. Any MP who claims for a second home is eligible to offset all of the council tax against expenses. If their family lives at the address they designate as their second home, and only the MP appears on the paperwork for their other address, then they will be eligible for the 25 per cent discount given to single people who pay council tax and live alone. Even with this cushy arrangement, some MPs still mess up. Shahid Malik, for example, was actually summonsed for failure to pay council tax he could have claimed on expenses. Astonishingly, he was reimbursed for the £65 summons, although he has now repaid this.

More commonly, MPs simply claimed more from expenses than they actually paid for council tax, turning it into a tidy little earner for themselves. Even before the scandal broke over the summer, more than 18 MPs are believed to have privately repaid money they over-claimed. David Willetts and Jeremy Hunt, the Tory frontbenchers, both admitted to claiming more than £500 too much for their council tax bills. The government whip, Mark Tami, is believed to have over-claimed around £1,500 for his Band C property in south London, and the former home secretary, David Blunkett, is also thought to have over-claimed on council tax bills submitted for the cottage he rents on the Duke of Devonshire's estate at Chatsworth.

Council tax claimed 'in error' and repaid:

David Kidney (L)	£2,505	Council tax error
Michael Meacher (L)	£2,019	Council tax double claim
David Amess (C)	£106	Council tax overpayment
Julie Mason (L)	£90	Council tax late payment charge
Lembit Opik (LD)	£40	Council tax summons

7. Fit, furnish and flog

This gem does what it says on the tin: an MP buys a home, uses their expenses to renovate the property and then sells it on. This is in clear breach of the rules which state that MPs are allowed to claim back the cost of repairs that 'make good dilapidations' but they cannot claim for work that 'enhances the property'. This scam is often used in conjunction with CGT avoidance (see above).

Andrew Lansley was alleged to have engaged in this when he spent £2,000 having his Cambridgeshire cottage repainted and £500 resurfacing the driveway shortly before selling the property for £433,000. His colleague on the Conservative frontbench, Chris Grayling, came up with a slight variation. He owns four homes within the M25: his family home in Surrey, his expenses-subsidized flat near Westminster and a couple of buy-to-let flats. He spent some rather lavish sums on his central London flat including £4,250 for redecoration in the summer of 2005, followed shortly after with £1,561 on the bathroom and £1,341 on the kitchen. He also negotiated a special dispensation from the normal rule against claiming for more than one residence (so, it was quite within the rules for him to bill the taxpayer for two of his four London area homes).

Possibly the most interesting example of this is the aforementioned David Maclean (see Chapter 10 *Our Plundering Politicians*), the former Conservative Chief Whip who was a leading figure in the campaign to keep MPs' expenses secret.

He submitted bills for more than £40,000 towards the cost of renovating his Cumbrian house before selling it for a reported £750,000. Although he claimed the expenses by nominating this as his second home, he also avoided CGT by telling HMRC that he considered it his main home.

Ian Gibson, the former Labour MP, was banned from standing as a Labour candidate after it was found his daughter had lived rent-free in a London flat for which he had claimed more than £80,000 over four years. He sold it to his daughter and her boyfriend in 2008 for £162,000 – approximately half its market value.

Furniture and refurbishment claimed 'in error' and repaid:

Keith Vaz (L)	£18,949	Furniture
Richard Younger-Ross (LD)	£8,338	Furniture
Chris Grayling (C)	£5,061	Furniture and double claim
Andrew Lansley (C)	£2,641	Renovation
Ed Vaizey (C)	£2,449	Furniture
Menzies Campbell (LD)	£1,772	Interior designer
Huw Irranca-Davies (L)	£857	Garden furniture

8. Keeping it in the family

You might think the days of political dynasties in Britain died out sometime around the Glorious Revolution in 1688. But no, they are alive and kicking. Just as America has the Bushes, Clintons and Kennedys, we have the Wintertons, the Keens and the Mackays. As briefly mentioned previously, married MPs Andrew Mackay and Julie Kirkbride each designated a separate second home (meaning that between them they had no main home but two second homes). Furthermore, Julie Kirkbride employed her sister as a secretary, out of her office expenses budget, despite the sister living 125 miles away, and also allowed her brother to stay in her constituency home which was against Commons rules because the house in question was funded out of expenses.

Alan Beith, Liberal Democrat MP and candidate in the race to replace Michael Martin as speaker of the House of Commons following the expenses shambles, claimed £117,000 second-home expenses while his wife, Baroness Maddock, claimed £60,000 in House of Lords expenses for staying at the same address.

Stephen Byers claimed more than £125,000 on a flat owned by his long-time partner, Jan Cookson. There doesn't seem to have been a mortgage on the London property and Byers claims to have paid no rent. The total figure for his expenses appears to have been made up of claims like £4,867 for general repairs, £381 for a Bosch washing machine and £240.50 for replacement bathroom tiles.

Alan and Ann Keen, 'Mr and Mrs Expenses' as they are known in Westminster, have claimed nearly £40,000 each year for a central London flat. They appear to have been claiming interest on a total debt of £520,000, even though records show their flat only cost £500,000. One mortgage was secured against the London flat for £350,000, with a second secured against their other home for a total of £170,000 – an arrangement not normally allowed. The Keens also own another home in Brentwood about ten miles away, which is less distance than many of their constituents commute to work every day.

Family offenders:

Anne Cryer and son John (L): in 2004 each designated a flat owned by third family member as a second home and claimed accordingly.

Anne Main (C): let her daughter use flat funded on parliamentary expenses.

Peter and Iris Robinson (DUP): each submitted the same £1,223 bill in 2007.

Malcolm Bruce (LD): used office allowance to fund activity at his constituency home (having used his housing allowance on his London property) because he employed his wife who worked from there.

9. Gardeners' question time

Some of the rare moments of light relief in the expenses scandal came from claims submitted for gardening. Simon Heffer, the associate editor of the *Daily Telegraph*, was so incensed with the claims made by his local MP, Alan Haselhurst, who also served as deputy speaker, that he threatened to stand against him at the next election. Haselhurst claimed more than £12,000 for gardening at his Essex country house between 2004 and 2008, out of a total claim of £142,119 in Additional Costs Allowance claimed since 2001, despite it being reported that there was no mortgage on the property.

In a three-year period, Alan Duncan tried to claim £7,000 in gardening expenses, successfully obtaining more than £4,000. When the scandal broke, he agreed to repay certain sums, including his claim for expenses incurred in relation to his ride-on lawnmower. This wasn't enough for some activists who invaded his garden and cut a new flower bed – in the shape of a pound sign – in his lawn.[14]

David Heathcoat-Amory, the Tory MP, submitted 19 claims for several hundred bags of manure at a cost of around £388. He has since repaid the money. Margaret Beckett, known around Westminster as a keen gardener, claimed £600 in 2006 for 'the supply of plants for hanging baskets, tubs, pots, planters, pouches and garden', and separately for £711 in respect of 'labour and materials for planting of summer house, shed and pergola'. This was too much even for the Fees Office who reminded her that expenses could only be claimed if they were 'wholly, exclusively and necessarily incurred' staying away from the designated main home for the purposes of parliamentary business. When the story broke, Mrs Beckett explained the gardening bills had been submitted by mistake.

Even David Miliband's gardener seemed to query the MP's gardening bills. In April 2008 the gardener submitted a bill to the foreign secretary for £132.96 and asked if so much work was really necessary, given the relatively short periods of time the minister spent at his house and the labour-intensive nature of much of the work. In those few short words the gardener spoke more sense than the whole of the political class put together. Real people in the real world want to see value for money.

Gardening & grounds, claimed 'in error' and repaid:

Alan Haselhurst (C)	£15,574	Gardening
Jonathan Djanogly (C)	£25,000	Gardening and gates
Alan Duncan (C)	£4,704	Gardening
Stewart Jackson (C)	£1,180	Swimming pool
James Arbuthnot (C)	£767	Swimming pool
Oliver Letwin (C)	£2,000	Pipe under tennis court

10. Horror show

Although our 646 MPs pocketed tens of millions in dubious claims, sometimes the public seemed angrier over some of the little or frivolous items. There were the iconic claims such as Douglas Hogg's moat dredging (£2,115), Peter Viggers' duck island (£1,645), Margaret Moran's treatment of dry rot at a house in neither her constituency nor central London (£22,500) and the claims for pornography submitted by Jacqui Smith (£10 – though watched by her husband). Then we had the ice cube tray for £1.50, the box of matches for 59p and the £4.47 for dog food – even though the dog wasn't an MP.[15]

Never again will politicians be able to portray all public spending to be 'good' as an end in itself. Moreover, people are furious that MPs are insulating themselves from the policies they force on everybody else by using everybody else's money. If Barbara Follett really feels so unsafe in London after 12 years of a government she supports, then why doesn't she lobby for some change in policing policy, rather than claiming £25,000 for security guards on expenses? As the wife of a multimillionaire novelist she could presumably afford her own security guards, or move to another part of London or, indeed, to one of her many other homes.

Irritating payments:

Mark Francois (C)	£4.36	Two five-packs of Peperami
Melanie Moon (L)	£1	IKEA gift wrap
Adrian Bailey (L)	£9	Toothbrush, shampoo and conditioner
Austin Mitchell (L)	£0.68	Branston Pickle
Chris Huhne (LD)	£119	Trouser press
Hazel Blears (L)	£2.50	Kit Kat
Charles Kennedy (LD)	£35.75	Gifts from Commons shop
Ed Balls (L)	£7.99	Book called *Reasons to be Cheerful*
Michael Ancram (C)	£98.50	Swimming pool maintenance
Jeremy Brown (LD)	£16.50	Commemoration wreath

IF YOU WANT IT, HERE IT IS, COME AND GET IT

The House of Commons Fees Office is supposed to act as the arbiter of the acceptability of claims, and also to defend the interests of the taxpayer. Occasionally, it does reject claims or pay out less than the total submitted. However, in too many cases it seems to take the attitude that it was okay for MPs to claim as much as they could, rather than as little as necessary. In some cases the Fees Office seemed more interested in aiding and abetting MPs rather than looking after taxpayers' money.

One example was the way Douglas Hogg was allowed to structure his claims. In 2004 the MP for Sleaford, who is also Viscount Hailsham and the second generation cabinet minister in his family, was allowed to negotiate a special deal for administering his expense claims. This entailed him being paid a twelfth of the maximum annual allowance each month. The former agriculture minister, who is married to a member of the House of Lords, claimed this was necessary as the costs of running the home 'greatly' exceeded the allowance and the arrangement 'will certainly make my life a lot easier'. Perhaps it is easier to forgive Hogg for trying this on than it is to forgive the Fees Office for letting him.

Another example is the Fees Office permitting Ben Chapman, Labour MP for Wirral South, to over-claim around £15,000 for part of his mortgage that had already been cleared between December 2002 and October 2003. Unlike Elliot Morley, who excused himself by saying his overpayments were accidental, Ben Chapman seemed to have claimed that his additional payments were with the prior approval of the Fees Office. At the end of 2002 or at the very start of 2003, Chapman paid £295,000 capital off his mortgage. This cut the amount he could claim under the Additional Costs Allowance. However, because he complained about 'forgoing interest and investment opportunities elsewhere', the Fees Office agreed that his expense claims could continue to be made at the previous, higher level.[16]

One possible reason for the ineffectiveness of the Fees Office could be the institutional schizophrenia which affected most House of Commons bodies under Speaker Michael Martin. The head of the Fees Office, Andrew Walker, who earns around £125,000, is reported to have warned Michael Martin several years ago about the scope of expense claims, but felt pressured into dropping his concerns.[17] His immediate boss, Malcolm Jack (who was revealed to have four homes of his own), was believed to enjoy a close friendship with Michael Martin and neither man was thought to have any accounting qualifications or experience in dealing with financial claims of this complexity. One would hope matters will improve under the new speaker, who should take care not to cultivate the 'climate of fear' that was readily associated with his predecessor in matters relating to MPs' 'entitlements'. However, Speaker John Bercow's own flipping and

CGT avoidance, which led to him 'voluntarily' repaying £6,508 plus VAT, and the fact that he employed a family member, hardly inspire any confidence that there will be any clampdown on the creative use of the Commons expenses system.

PARLIAMENTARY COMMISSIONER FOR LOW STANDARDS

Another link in the chain that failed was the office of the Parliamentary Commissioner for Standards, a post responsible for regulating the conduct of MPs, currently held by John Lyon. Before the scandal broke over the summer of 2009, John Lyon had gained quite a reputation for taking a very hands-off approach to MPs' arrangements and he sparked controversy just as the full scale of the scandal was emerging by refusing to look into the various complaints he had received relating to Jacqui Smith's designation of her sister's spare room as her main residence.[18]

During John Lyon's first three months in post around the beginning of 2008, 113 complaints were lodged. Only one was resolved by March 2009. Of the rest a huge 93 were quickly dismissed, 3 more thrown out after a brief investigation, and 16 carried forward and possibly still under investigation.

His apparently dismal performance hardly compares with the much more robust approach of one of his predecessors as Parliamentary Commissioner, Elizabeth Filkin. She had a rather more ferocious reputation and led a number of high-profile investigations into the conduct of MPs, including Keith Vaz, John Major and William Hague. Her persistence was rumoured to have displeased her political masters and she was widely believed to have been forced out of her job after a whispering campaign against her.[19]

THE 'OTHER PLACE'

The big scandal to hit the House of Lords in 2009 predated the Commons expenses scandal by a few months. This was the revelation in the *Sunday Times* that some members of the House were allegedly willing to help change legislation in return for lobbying fees.[20] But peers, who claim almost £20 million a year in expenses, are also beginning to be implicated in the expenses furore.

Peers who register their main home outside of London could claim so-called 'subsistence' payments of £165.50 a night in 2007–8 and another daily payment of £82.50 to cover the cost of food for every day a member is in London and attends a session, irrespective of whether they contribute. These rates increased substantially in 2008–9. Peers can also be paid office, attendance and travel costs – almost all of these without having to show a single receipt. However, looking at some of the amounts claimed and the limited activity of some peers making the largest claims, one could get the impression that some were using their allowances as a steady income stream (see Figure 3).[21]

Figure 3 Not all peers seem to provide the same value

Peer	2007/8 claim	Questions tabled	Debates spoken in	Votes
1. Lord Laird	£65,910	672	6	36
2. Baroness Smith	£60,026	0	0	22
3. Lord Taylor	£59,413	0	8	61
4. Lord King	£58,317	0	0	66
5. Baroness Bonham-Carter	£58,119	0	6	58
6. Lord Kingsland	£57,726	0	47	49
7. Lord Addington	£57,392	4	53	85
8. Lord Razzall	£56,114	0	26	52
9. Baroness Gardner	£56,004	1	71	48
10. Lord Hunt	£55,999	0	29	46

Around £50,000 to £60,000 tax-free a year is quite a reasonable sum of money when added to all the other cash peers can earn from being prominent figures in public life. Several peers do exceptionally well from taxpayers' generosity as they are either married to or living with other peers and so can bank closer to £100,000 a year tax-free between them.

Although he is far from being among the highest claimants, perhaps special mention should be made of Lord Oxburgh who claimed £41,410 while tabling no questions, speaking in just nine debates and voting only twice in a year – about £4,600 a speech or £20,000 a vote. There is also Lord Birt, Tony Blair's former 'blue skies thinker', who took £30,709 while tabling no questions, speaking in three debates and voting a modest five times. And we are lucky to have the services of the possibly appropriately named Lord Eatwell who picked up £44,861 in 2007–8 while tabling no questions, speaking in ten debates and only voting 18 times, making us pay almost £4,500 for each of his speeches or £2,500 for each of his votes.

Although there has been less attention paid to peers' expenses, there are strong indications that many of the abuses used by MPs may also be widespread in the Lords. Several peers have registered their French homes as their main residence, allowing them to claim generous expenses for visiting London. In words that were slightly reminiscent of the Jacqui Smith second-home affair, a neighbour of one such peer was quoted as saying: 'I am certain they do not live here all the time. They are only here one or two weekends a month. It is a second home.'[22]

Baroness Uddin reportedly failed to provide sufficient evidence in support of her £83,000 claim relating to owning a home outside London between 2001 and 2005. Since 2005, it is not clear if she has actually maintained a home (as opposed to just owning property) outside London. After she was confronted by the *Sunday Times*, she was allegedly spotted moving furniture into a two-bedroom flat in Maidstone in an attempt to give it a 'lived-in look'. It is now believed that the Baroness, along with Elliot Morley and Ben Chapman, has been asked to help the Metropolitan Police with their enquiries.

Other interesting main-home designations include Baroness Thornton who was reported to have 'claimed up to £22,000 a year in expenses by saying that her mother's home in Yorkshire was her main home'.[23] Lord Ryder, a former acting chairman of the BBC, 'claimed more than £100,000 by saying that a converted stable on his parents' country estate was his main home'. Lord Clarke of Hampstead admitted that he had 'fiddled' his expenses by claiming close to £18,000 a year while often staying with family or friends.[24]

The Sunlight Centre for Open Politics, a new group dedicated to scrutinizing political institutions, has reported the former Liberal Democrat chief executive, Lord Rennard, to the House of Lords Committee for Privileges for allegedly abusing his second-home allowance by claiming his main home is in Eastbourne when they believe it is really in London, just two miles from Westminster. One of his neighbours at his Eastbourne flat said: 'We only see him a few times a year. We call him the "Holiday Home Man".'[25] Lord Rennard, who was said to earn about £90,000 as the chief executive of the Liberal Democrats, claimed £41,678 over six years up to 2007–8. A former adviser to the Lib Dems was quoted as saying: 'His colleagues know he lives in Vauxhall – and has to, to do his job.'[26]

Judging from these first glimpses into their Lordships' behaviour, we can expect plenty more of these types of allegations and inquiries from the press in the future. No doubt all wrongdoing will be indignantly denied by the ennobled perpetrators and none of their many suspect expense claims will ever be investigated by the compliant authorities.

CHAPTER 12

THE BANK ROBBERS

WHAT GORDON FORGOT TO TELL YOU

Ask and it shall be given

In 2007, Britain's bankers started calling on Gordon Brown and Alistair Darling to say that after years of big betting blow-outs and spending vast amounts of cash on themselves, they had got into a bit of difficulty. In addition to asking for immediate handouts of tens of billions, they wanted the government to offer guarantees potentially worth more than Britain earned in a year. The bankers had our government over a barrel. To refuse to bail them out could bring economic collapse. Brown claimed that he was acting to protect ordinary people: 'The recapitalization programme was not to subsidize bankers; it was to ensure that no depositor or saver lost money.'[1] But Alistair Darling was a bit more forthright in seemingly admitting that the government was powerless in the hands of the banks: 'If we had not intervened . . . the banking system would have gone down, taking millions of families, millions of businesses with it.'[2] Treasury minister Stephen 'Lurch' Timms confirmed our government's determination to do whatever the bankers wanted: 'We have made very clear throughout this whole period that we will do what is needed to maintain the stability of the UK financial system.'[3] But the unpleasant problem with the guarantees our government gave on our behalf is that they could be far in excess of our national income.

The assets and thus liabilities of Iceland's banks were about ten times their total national earnings (GDP). So when the banks went bankrupt, the whole country rapidly followed. Britain is not quite in the same league, as the liabilities of our banks are only around four-and-a-half times our GDP. However, Britain's numbers are still quite frightening. In 2007, with a massive balance sheet of £1.9 trillion the Royal Bank of Scotland (RBS) had total potential liabilities that comfortably exceeded what Britain earned in a year, our £1.4 trillion GDP. Barclays' balance sheet at £1.2 trillion was almost equal to one year's GDP and the combined Lloyds TSB plus HBOS figures weren't far behind (see Figure 1).

Figure 1 We had banks that were bigger than or as big as Britain

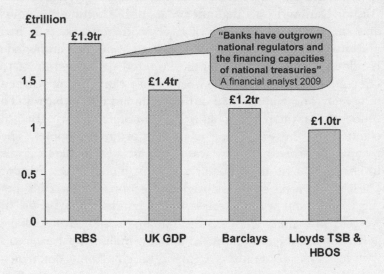

In comparison, the largest US banks like Bank of America, J.P. Morgan Chase and Citigroup only had potential liabilities in the region of $1 trillion each, less than one tenth of the US's $14 trillion GDP.

To give an idea of how vulnerable we were, on just a few deals the RBS lost more money than the UK's annual defence budget.

Furthermore, when Barclays' share price plunged towards the end of 2008 and beginning of 2009, the bank lost more value in a few months than the government spends on policing and criminal justice in a year. Barclays' share price has since recovered and it has not needed to seek support from taxpayers. However, with the banks which have been thrusting their begging bowls in the government's face, we taxpayers will end up buying toxic loans, generously made to Russian oligarchs and other wild and wonderful beneficiaries, which will probably cost us more than a year's budget for the NHS, education and defence. This hopefully starts to give some feeling for the size of the disaster for which we are all going to have to pay for years and probably decades to come.

Many commentators have said that the British financial sector became too large as a proportion of our GDP. However, Britain's financial sector only accounted for about 9.4 per cent of GDP at the height of the boom, while Switzerland's was over 12 per cent. There are probably many of us who wish we were living in wealthy Switzerland right now – a strong currency, clean air, mountains, skiing, lakes, low taxes, law and order – rather than in shabby, decaying, dangerous, virtually bankrupt Britain.

Under my thumb

Following the government's humiliating capitulation to the banks, Brown and his acolytes all started talking tough about how they were going to clamp down on the 'greedy' bankers. Brown told us: 'But as a condition for putting taxpayers' money into banks, we must also take action to end the old short-term bonus culture – the one-way bet culture – that encouraged banks to make reckless decisions.' Possibly not realizing how ridiculous he sounded, Brown put on his best moral-compass tone: 'I am certain that the values that we celebrate in society – hard work, entrepreneurialism and responsibility, not irresponsible short-termism – must underpin the future of our financial sector and its rewards.' Perhaps most famously, Brown declared: 'First, there must be no reward for failure.'

The City's response to our prime minister's call for a new Age of Responsibility was not slow in coming. First, despite the bank's failure, the RBS colleagues of Sir Fred Goodwin, colloquially referred to as 'the world's worst banker', let him waltz off into the sunset at the tender age of 50 with tens of millions of pounds of taxpayers' money in severance payments and pension benefits when he should have been sacked and probably dragged to court for breach of fiduciary duty, false accounting, negligence, making misleading statements to shareholders and numerous other transgressions. Other banking bosses were similarly given the nod and wink by their mates in the government and the regulatory agencies to snaffle millions of pounds of our money in return for leaving quietly and not rocking the boat. Then Northern Rock gave its staff bonuses of 10 per cent of their salaries in spite of the bank's collapse and later announcement in August 2009 of losses of £724 million. Vince Cable was one of the few to speak out: 'This is an extraordinary action from a state-owned bank which still owes billions to taxpayers. When millions of people are facing pay cuts or even unemployment, this is indefensible.' Gordon Brown, who had promised to control bankers' excesses, could only lamely comment: 'Operational decisions such as this are a matter for Northern Rock.' Perhaps he had forgotten that thanks to his blundering we now owned the bank.

The RBS went even further, promising its staff £1 billion in bonuses just months after it was rescued with £20 billion of our money and while it had a huge deficit in its pension fund.[4] Strangely, its chief executive had previously commented: 'I empathise 100 per cent with the public mood and it would give me no joy whatsoever to pay any bonuses to anyone, and if that was the responsible thing to do I would recommend that in a heartbeat.'[5] At the top of the RBS, executives who had earned millions a year in salaries and bonuses while destroying the bank still kept their jobs and salaries of over £700,000 a year and the

13 non-executive directors would be getting £70,000 a year each for just a few days work. As for Stephen Hester, the new chief executive of the RBS, in June 2009 he was offered a pay deal worth up to £9.6 million including a £1.2 million salary, about £2 million of annual non-cash bonus payments and almost £6.4 million of long-term share options.[6] This news came out just a few months after he had informed us: 'Banking pay in some parts of the industry is far too high and needs to come down, and we intend to lead that process.'[7] He has agreed to delay taking part of his shares incentive, but only following pressure from investors and the unions.

If newspaper reports are to be believed, Eric Daniels, the chief executive of Lloyds TSB, another bank expensively rescued by the taxpayer, could potentially earn up to £7 million in pay and bonus for 2009.[8] At Bradford & Bingley, wholly owned by the taxpayer, the chairman Richard Pym was reported to be on a £750,000 salary and to be in line for a bonus of £187,000.[9]

And now it looks like many banks, having dumped their losses on to us taxpayers, will soon be reporting big profits – and big profits, of course, mean big bonuses. One commentator may not have been completely misguided when he wrote: 'All over the world bankers have managed to con governments into giving them billions of dollars, without either side knowing what the true financial situation actually was.'[10] It looks like Christmas 2009 is going to be another bonus bumper year for the bankers, including many at banks bailed out by British and American taxpayers.

Be afraid. Be very afraid

Following their supine surrender to the financial interests of the bankers, the government and the regulators started to beat their chests and bellow loudly as they announced lots of 'tough' and 'robust' new regulatory controls which they planned to introduce. The chief executive of the Financial Services Authority (FSA) told the taxpayers who pay his considerable salary: 'There is a view that people are not frightened of the FSA. I can assure you that is a view I am determined to correct.'[11] However, while reporting the speech one financial blogger commented in an open letter to the FSA's head: 'Is it just me, or did anyone else find your speech yesterday as head of the City watchdog, the Financial Services Authority, hilarious and galling in equal measure?' The letter went on: 'Well, Mr Sants, people are frightened of the FSA, but for all the wrong reasons. Lax executive directors and the so-called heads of risk at banks are not frightened of the FSA, but ordinary people certainly are. Frightened of what it is not doing. People should be very frightened of the FSA.'[12]

After all, this is exactly the same FSA which in April 2008 prevented institutional shareholders voting against Sir Fred Goodwin on the clearly mistaken grounds that a mass rebellion against the RBS board could further destabilize the bank. This is the same FSA that in February 2009 claimed it had fully investigated claims made by the former HBOS head of Group Regulatory Risk in 2004 that the bank was making excessively risky lending and said it was satisfied that HBOS had taken action to deal with any concerns. In fact, the FSA maintained it had been on to HBOS's case long before the 2004 warnings: 'In conclusion, the FSA confirms that the allegations made by Mr. Moore were taken seriously, and were properly and professionally investigated. It should also be noted that the FSA's concerns about HBOS's risk management framework considerably pre-dated the allegations by Mr. Moore.'[13] This piece of typically bureaucratic self-absolution is all very well, but it doesn't fully explain how HBOS could disappear in 2008 in an almost nuclear-sized explosion with hundreds of billions in toxic debts if the FSA was, as it claimed, already hard at work on the case. Moreover, this is the same FSA for which we will pay over £350 million a year (increasing by the day), which has allowed mis-selling scandal after mis-selling scandal. There are reasonable grounds for agreeing with the blogger that British taxpayers and savers really should be very frightened, even terrified, of the FSA both for the damage it has allowed to happen in the past and for all the horrors it may choose to overlook in the future.

As for our government's commitment to regulation – well this can appear to be slightly ambivalent. The government is in a bit of a Catch-22 situation of its own making. If it imposes too much regulation on the financial sector, profitability will fall and it will never be able to sell off all the banks it has nationalized. However, too little regulation and there will be the risk of another damaging financial bubble and bust. So while our leaders were playing to the gallery by blustering on about their new determination to regulate financial services, at the same time they were frantically fighting European Union proposals to regulate financial services as they tried to protect their friends, or maybe masters, in the City from what they called 'over-regulation'.

On borrowed time

Then there was the small matter of the vanishing hundreds of billions. As 2007 turned ominously into 2008, the government kept on pouring money into various banks in order to supposedly 'recapitalize' them to restore confidence in the banking sector so that lending to homeowners and businesses could resume. Lots of money went into the banks, but very little seemed to come out again. As usual, Vince Cable was one of the few people to call what seemed to be a rip-off a rip-off: 'It is clear that the conditions set by the government over the original capitalisation were a sham. No effective monitoring and controls were put in place to ensure that the money went where it was intended'.[14] Actually, the disappearance of our money was to be expected. At the same time as the government was telling us that rescuing the banks with our hundreds of billions would lead to more lending, it was also telling the banks to build up their asset bases to protect themselves against a worsening economic situation that was being largely caused by the banks cutting off lending. It's a bit confusing really, prompting one writer to notice that: 'Banks were bailed out but somehow none

of the billions of pounds actually reached your local bank manager
to help small businesses pay the wages at the end of the month.'[15]

All in all, it looks like anything from £200 billion to £500
billion will be promised to the banks as insurance against potential
losses in return for them increasing lending by something like
£40 billion. An observer might think it would have been cheaper
for taxpayers if the government had allowed a few big banks to
go to the wall, leaving their big bosses without their massive payoffs. The government could then have brought in emergency
legislation giving some more efficient businesses such as Tesco,
Asda, Marks & Spencer and Sainsbury's £100 billion or so to
set up temporary new financial institutions to lend to companies
and individuals to keep the economy going for a year or so while
the previous banking system was thoroughly purged. Meanwhile,
with the lending drought caused by the banks hoarding our
cash, thousands of perfectly viable businesses are going to the
wall when their cashflow dries up because they cannot get their
hands on any of the money that the taxpayer-subsidized banks
are supposed to be lending to keep the economy from collapsing.

WHO WANTS TO BE A MULTIMILLIONAIRE?

Rich Uncle Sam and Dick and Stan and John

Most of us will be losers from the great banking bust. Many of us
have probably not fully realized the huge amounts of money we
are going to have to earn and which will then be taken out of our
pockets by the government and financial institutions in order to
pay for the bankers' rapaciousness and short-termism. But there
have been a fair few winners from the recent economic turmoil.
Some of us, for example politicians, top civil servants and leading
bankers, have probably never had it so good. The biggest winners
of the years of boom and bust have been US bank chiefs who
have been able to walk away from the economic wreckage with

their bank accounts stuffed with almost unimaginable amounts of cash, leaving us to pick up the bill.

There was Richard 'Dick' Fuld from the now sadly defunct Lehman Brothers who was reported to have managed to collect up to $200 million over his years at the bank before its collapse. Lehman Brothers was the largest bankruptcy in American corporate history. In his last year running the firm deep into the ground, Fuld was paid about $22 million, though he didn't receive any severance or bonus when he left the ruins in 2008. After his departure, Fuld appeared in the media when the press found out that he had transferred the $13 million Florida mansion he had jointly owned with his wife into her name alone in return for just $100. We realize that the US housing market has gone a bit slow over the last couple of years, but it seems incredible that a mere $100 was the best price he could get for such a palace. Coincidentally, Fuld was about to face a barrage of lawsuits from furious shareholders. Florida has particularly favourable home protection laws that would mean moving the property into his wife's name would ensure Fuld and his wife could keep their home in the event of bankruptcy.

Over at Merrill Lynch, former chief executive Stan O'Neal is believed to have banked about $161 million before he was pushed out after record losses. Like Fuld, O'Neal didn't receive any bonus for his final year or any severance pay. O'Neal was succeeded by John Thain in November 2007. Thain came from Goldman Sachs where he was reported to have made about $300 million from Goldman's stock-market flotation. He then moved to run the New York Stock Exchange before taking over at Merrill where he was welcomed with a $15 million signing-on bonus. Just as Merrill Lynch was about to collapse having lost billions of dollars, Thain sold it to the Bank of America (BoA) for $44 billion. US government officials don't seem to have been amused when they found out that shortly before finalizing the BoA deal, Thain pushed through bonus payments of about $4 billion for Merrill executives while the company was receiving $10 billion of taxpayers' money. The New York attorney general wrote in a letter to Merrill's board of directors: 'Clearly, the performance of Merrill's top executives throughout Merrill's abysmal year in no way justifies significant bonuses for its top executives, including the CEO.'[16] BoA bosses were not too happy either as, following the takeover, it needed to lobby the US government for billions more to make up for the losses made by Merrill Lynch.

Thain's spending of over $1 million decorating his office, including an $87,000 rug, a $35,000 'commode on legs' and a $1,405 trash can while Merrill Lynch was haemorrhaging money and firing thousands of employees probably didn't endear him to his new bosses, government officials or the public at large. Then of course there was the $230,000 of company money reportedly paid to Thain's chauffeur.[17] When Thain asked for a $10 million bonus, the attorney general called the request 'nothing less than shocking'. Thain later withdrew his bonus request before leaving Merrill's employment.

There were many others who rode away with anything from $40 million to $60 million each. Citigroup's Charles 'Chuck' Prince was rewarded for huge sub-prime losses and a plunging share price by being given a final year bonus of $12.5 million and a package of salary, stock and benefits worth $68 million. However, this bonus was down slightly from the previous year's $13.8 million. Then, much lower down the food chain, were the heads of the collapsed and rescued Fannie Mae and Freddie Mac. Their CEOs walked away with packages worth $9 million and $13 million respectively.

You would have thought that of all people, Wall Street bankers would have been most aware that there was incredible financial turbulence and that profits and share prices had collapsed. Apparently not. The top five US banks paid out $38 billion in bonuses in the Armageddon year of 2007–8, up from $36 billion in 2006–7 when they made record profits. This extraordinary dislocation of results and rewards was explained away by one Wall-Streeter: 'Joe six-pack is never going to get this, but if we don't pay the bonuses we lose the talent.'

Making millions bankrupting Britain's banks

The Brobdingnagian mountains of money which were given to failed US bankers past and present make the sums pocketed by Britain's worst bankers look quite small.

Britain's largest bank failure was the RBS, named Global Bank of the Year by the *Banker* magazine a year or so before the bank's implosion, and the number one failed banker was former Deloittes accountant Sir Fred Goodwin, *Forbes Magazine* Businessman of the Year in 2002. After the RBS collapse and his resignation, it was revealed that he would retire with a £700,000 or so a year pension worth about £30 million, which he may or may not take. Probably we'll never be told how much he eventually really gets as, once the fuss has died down and the media have got bored of the story, knowing looks will be exchanged between politicians, bureaucrats and bankers and enormous quantities of our money will continue to flow lucky Sir Fred's way. At the time of the bank's failure, its pension schemes had a deficit of about £1.9 billion, including the pension promises that have been so generously made on our behalf to Sir Fred. This deficit will probably also be dumped on UK taxpayers even while the bank is paying special bonuses to its staff.

In early 2008, Sir Fred was able to announce record results for 2007: 'For the Royal Bank of Scotland Group, 2007 was defined by another strong operating performance and by the acquisition of ABN Amro.'[18] Sir Fred helpfully explained to the world at large why his bank was so successful: 'Delivering such a robust financial performance in this environment is the consequence of action in two areas: over a number of years we have diversified the Group's income streams and last year also saw us benefit from our focus on credit quality and risk management.'[19] As tens of billions of pounds of our money pour into the black hole that was and unfortunately still is the RBS, some of us might be tempted to wonder whether the bank's claim of 'focus on credit quality and risk management' might not constitute a crime for gross misuse and abuse of the English language. It might even be construed as misleading shareholders. Just before the bank's ignominious collapse, Sir Fred's chairman, the £750,000-a-year former pharmaceuticals boss Sir Tom McKillop, also seemed proud of the bank's diversification strategy and admirable credit control: 'We have witnessed the benefits of the Group's long-standing focus on credit quality and the diversification of our income streams which have allowed us to deliver record profits.'[20]

After Sir Fred and Sir Tom had departed, RBS's new bosses seemed a little more careful with their next report to shareholders, as if aware that previous versions had possibly stretched the English language beyond breaking point. Plus, they probably didn't want to get sued:

> Certain statements made in this document constitute forward-looking statements within the meaning of the United States Private Securities Litigation Reform Act of 1995. Forward-looking statements can be identified by the use of words such as 'may', 'will', 'expect', 'intend', 'estimate', 'anticipate', 'believe', 'plan', 'seek', 'continue' or similar expressions. Such statements are based on current expectations and, by their nature, are subject to a number of risks and uncertainties.[21]

If you ever want to slip a few words into a contract in order to absolve yourself from any responsibility in perpetuity, the above extract might serve as a pretty good template.

Over at HBOS, there were losses of £10.8 billion and still counting. We would have liked to have brought you a couple of choice extracts from the 2007 HBOS annual report, just before the bank imploded, but the report is proving difficult to locate. Perhaps it's being redacted. Instead, we'll have to settle for a press release from Andy Hornby, chief executive of HBOS plc:

> In 2007, the disciplined execution of our strategy has resulted in good earnings growth for our shareholders despite difficult market conditions. With our multi-brand distribution strength, strong balance sheet and low cost operating platforms, we are well placed to take opportunities presented by these difficult markets and deliver good growth in shareholder value over the next few years.[22]

Unfortunately, HBOS didn't 'deliver good growth in shareholder value over the next few years' because it didn't last a 'few years' – it actually delivered a total wipeout of shareholder value within just a few months. In addition, it also took Lloyds TSB down with it when the gruesome scale of its losses was revealed. Prior to the disintegration of the bank for which he was responsible, Hornby had reassured us: 'The Total Capital Ratio stood at 11.1 per cent in 2007, which is significantly more than the regulatory minimum Total Capital Ratio of 8.0 per cent.' For its wonderful annual reports HBOS received the 2007 Institute of Practitioners in Advertising award for the Best Narrative Reporting for a Top FTSE 100 company. Perhaps a fiction-writing prize would have been more appropriate.

HBOS gave us three individuals who were able to saunter nonchalantly away with megabucks in their bank accounts from the smoking, dust-covered ground zero which once was a healthy, well-respected bank.

There was Peter Cummings, former head of HBOS's corporate lending division and once the highest paid executive at the bank. His share of the damage was about £7 billion in bad loans, largely due to losses on property loans. At the height of his lending splurge, in an *Observer* article titled 'Cummings keeps his nerve in the face of property downturn', he was quoted as being almost dismissive about those who were worried that property prices had risen to unsustainable levels: 'Some people look as though they are losing their nerve, beginning to panic, even in today's testing real estate environment. Not us.'[23] Meanwhile a spokesman for HBOS also seemed bullish: 'We make no apologies that we are an asset-backed lender. We lend to companies whose business model we know and understand.' The rest, as they say, is history. Just Cummings' actions will probably cost every man, woman and child in this country over £110 each. Cummings was reported to have left in January 2009 with a £660,000 payoff and pension entitlements of £6 million.[24]

HBOS also gave us Sir James Crosby. Sir James was chief executive of HBOS and is generally credited for overseeing its slightly risky reliance on wholesale credit markets for finance rather than something safe and old-fashioned like customers' deposits. Either by good judgement or luck, he left HBOS aged 50 at the height of the bubble earning £858,000 in his final year and collecting bonuses of £2,147,000 between 2002 and 2006. A spokeswoman for the bank confirmed that his pension would be £572,000 a year.[25] Sir James later came under a bit of a cloud when a former risk manager at HBOS claimed he was fired for questioning the bank's strategy. Sir James said there was 'no substance' to the allegations.

Finally, the man left holding the exploding parcel at HBOS was the aforementioned Andy Hornby, the youngest head of a UK bank, then, following the mysterious disappearance of the bank he was running, he became the youngest ex-head of a British bank. In his final year at the recently deceased bank, Hornby had a £1.9 million remuneration package and is probably getting a pension of about £184,000 a year. Unfortunately, he didn't last long enough to get a knighthood like so many of his disgraced peers.

As we've touched on the HBOS catastrophe, we ought to mention Lloyds TSB, the bank that took over HBOS. Lloyds TSB's is an interesting story as it shows us what happened when Prime Minister Gordon Brown briefly applied his economic skills fairly directly to the banking sector. Until the HBOS debacle, Lloyds TSB's share price had languished behind other banks and it had been much criticized by City insiders and financial journalists for being too boring and unambitious because it hadn't followed the aggressive growth strategies of its competitors. But this made the bank attractive to shareholders, as a spokesman for the UK Shareholders' Association explained: 'People bought Lloyds shares because it was seen as a safe, plodding company and no one thought they would do anything risky.'[26] However, in spite of more modest expansion than other banks, Lloyds TSB's executives seemed to be making a comfortable living (see Figure 2). At a House of Commons select committee meeting, Lloyds chief Eric Daniels memorably said that he received a 'relatively modest salary' – at the time his basic salary was about £1 million a year – around £20,000 a week.

Figure 2 Life can be good, even at a 'boring' bank like Lloyds TSB

Person	2007 Remuneration
J.E. Daniels	£2,884,000
M.E. Fairey	£1,440,000
T.A. Dial	£1,995,000
A.G. Kane	£1,377,000
G.T. Tate	£1,386,000
H.A. Weir	£1,586,000

Lloyds TSB's annual reports were closer to fact than the fiction churned out by other banks' marketing departments, especially the 250 pages of fantasy produced by the RBS. As the bank moved into 2008, its chairman Sir Victor Blank seemed to be looking forward to another cautious but successful year: 'The progress made over the last four years means that we have a strong capital position from which we can continue to grow the business.'[27]

Throughout 2008, as other banks went crashing into the dust, Lloyds TSB soldiered on. Then in autumn 2008 the chance of a lifetime seemed to present itself. HBOS was about to collapse, the government couldn't afford another banking failure and Gordon Brown allegedly waived competition rules to encourage Lloyds TSB to save the government money and further embarrassment by taking over the failing HBOS. Lloyds chairman Sir Victor Blank explained the logic behind the move: 'This will be a unique opportunity to accelerate and extend our strategy and create the UK's leading financial services group.'[28] Some commentators worried that the decision was made too hastily without sufficient time being spent checking out how financially sound or otherwise HBOS really was. But Eric Daniels refuted the suggestion of a rushed job: 'There shouldn't be any impression this is a shotgun marriage or a forced marriage, this is something that's been looked at for a good long while.'[29] Gordon Brown joined in the optimism: 'I believe that we have taken not only the right action, but that by taking that action we have brought more stability to the financial system.' In addition Lurch (Treasury minister Stephen Timms) chipped in: 'I am confident in the long term this is going to be a strong and successful commercial bank.'

Almost as soon as the deal was done, it turned out that nobody had realised that HBOS was a total disaster zone. By March 2009, after repeated bailout attempts had failed, the government was forced to take majority ownership of the merged bank in return for insuring it against future losses on £260 billion of toxic loans, more than 80 per cent of which came from HBOS. If all these loans turn out to be worthless, then the government will have just blown enough money to pay for the NHS for two-and-a-half years. At the time of writing, Sir Victor Blank has resigned as chairman, but chief executive Eric Daniels is still in place.

Then we have Northern Rock where chief executive Adam Applegarth received a salary and bonus of £1.7 million in his final year, was wise enough to sell £2.6 million of shares just before the credit crunch and received a £760,000 payoff and a £2.5 million pension pot. Over at Bradford & Bingley, after its collapse the chief executive Steven Crawshaw stepped down due to ill-health having been paid £2 million in his final year and with a pension pot worth about £1.8 million.

The general conclusion must be that trashing a bank or two is not so good for the taxpayers, who have been volunteered by the government to pick up the bill, but can be excellent for bank bosses' personal financial health. Such an outcome hardly provides much of an incentive for current and up-and-coming bank chiefs to act with much care and attention in the future.

PLIABLE BUT NOT LIABLE?

As politicians and the media heap insults on some of our deservedly execrated, underperforming bankers, one group of people seems to be slipping beneath the radar of blame. These are the accountants who signed off the banks' financial accounts and confirmed they were successful, profitable concerns, sometimes just weeks before some of the audited banks imploded. There are just four accounting firms – PricewaterhouseCoopers (PwC), KPMG, Deloitte Touche Tohmatsu (Deloittes) and Ernst & Young (E&Y) – who audit 97 per cent of FTSE 350 companies. There used to be five but Arthur Andersen self-immolated after it was caught shredding incriminating evidence linked to its involvement in the Enron scam.

One key criticism of the accountants' role in the catastrophe is that they are reluctant to blow the whistle on the banks they audit because they are also earning huge amounts selling consultancy services to the very same banks. To quote Professor Prem Sikka from Essex University: 'All distressed banks received a clean bill of health from their auditors and within days some were asking the government to bail them out. In every case, rather than acting as independent watchdogs, auditors also acted as consultants to management and raked in millions of pounds in fees. The fee dependency inevitably compromises auditor independence.'[30] Or as Austin Mitchell MP said: 'They don't want to alienate the clients: the audit becomes a market stall from which they sell other services.'[31]

The figures do seem to lend some credence to these suspicions. From 2000 to HBOS's collapse, KPMG was reported to have earned £55.8 million in audit fees and £45.1 million in other fees from the bank.[32] Also from 2000, Lloyds TSB paid PwC about £97.4 million in audit fees and £50.5 million for other work. Small-scale Northern Rock paid PwC £500,000 in 2006 for auditing and £700,000 for other services such as 'securitization transactions and the raising of wholesale funding' – precisely the things that destroyed the bank.[33] Meanwhile at RBS, Sir Fred Goodwin's former employer Deloittes were reported to have earned £31.4 million in 2007 rising to £58.8 million in 2008, the year the taxpayer had to step in to save the bank. In 2008, Deloittes were also said to have received £20.1 million for other services. It may seem incredible to the uneducated masses, who don't understand the subtleties of accounting, that at no time did Deloittes appear to raise any concerns about the financial viability of what was to become the world's biggest bank failure. Incredibly, after RBS's disastrously expensive rescue, Deloittes have been reappointed as the bank's auditors.[34]

The apparently supine behaviour of the big four accountancy firms might make some people wonder why banks bother to pay for audits in the first place if they are so clearly of such limited use. One problem seems to have been that many people had an unrealistic view of the real value, or lack of value, of these hugely expensive multi-million-pound bank audits. According to the Financial Reporting Council, the primary purpose of an audit 'is for the auditor to provide independent assurance to the shareholders that the directors have prepared the financial statements properly'. This doesn't mean that directors have to tell the truth: they only have to do their accounts according to certain accepted accounting principles. So, in spite of their huge cost, audits are essentially rather mechanical, back-covering, box-ticking exercises. In their reports, particularly with bank audits, auditors always cover themselves by stating something similar to the wording on the RBS annual accounts: 'The Listing Rules do not require us to consider whether the Board's or management's statements on internal control cover all risks and controls, or form an opinion on the effectiveness of the Group's corporate governance procedures or its risk and control procedures.' In other words, the bank may have lent billions that are completely unrecoverable or may have bought hundreds of billions of worthless bits of paper – that's not the auditors' problem. Auditors only have to ensure the correct data is presented in the correct way with all the debits and credits adding up nicely.

As was shown by the banking collapse, the audits themselves had limited value and were unreliable as a guide to any bank's real solvency. This deficiency was recognised by a House of Commons committee which therefore concluded that the auditors were not to blame for anything: 'We have received very little evidence that auditors failed to fulfil their duties as currently stipulated.'[35] It then went on to question the purpose of audits in the way they are currently provided: 'But the fact that the audit process failed to highlight developing problems in the banking sector does cause us to question how useful audit currently is.' As usual, our rulers seem to have decided that it was the 'system' which was at fault and that there was not the slightest whiff of widespread, deeply entrenched institutional greed and corruption.

One might be tempted to wonder why some banks are paying tens of millions of pounds a year to their auditors when it has now been recognised that the audit results have little real value. The high cost might have something to do with the fact that just four audit companies control the worldwide audit market. This quasi-monopoly allows the Big Four to set prices at levels which will never leave them lacking money – anyway, it's the shareholders who ultimately pay for the audits, so who cares what they cost? More worryingly, this concentration of power allows the Big Four to dominate the various committees which define accounting standards and the role and liabilities of accountants and therefore ensure that however much they earn and whatever happens to the organizations they get paid so handsomely to audit, they personally will never be legally liable.

With the banking crash, the results of years of dilution of accounting standards and the progressive reduction of auditors' responsibilities have finally been exposed. Most of us probably thought that banks had to adhere to strict codes of conduct and that regulators and auditors were acting as our watchdogs to keep bankers on the straight and narrow. Now people are beginning to realize that we were deceived and that bankers, regulators and auditors were all playing an elaborate game. In this game there were detailed and complex rules absolving any of the players of responsibility for anything, yet they all became fantastically rich from plundering our money without any meaningful hindrances or controls.

TO REGULATE OR NOT TO REGULATE

As our politicians and regulators mull over how to avoid a repeat of the recent financial crisis, there should be one underlying principle – never again should ordinary people's liabilities to any failing financial institution exceed more than 5 per cent of GDP. As for us being exposed to losses that were potentially greater than the country's GDP at just one badly run bank, this is so absurd that it hardly seems believable that our leaders allowed it to happen. Unfortunately for us, our politicians' and regulators' self-interest has become so entwined with the interests of a few bankers that our government has pursued and is continuing to pursue policies which seem to favour financiers over ordinary people. Nothing any of our politicians or regulators has said so far gives any confidence that this imbalance, where the interests of over 60 million people are so cynically subordinated to those of a small but influential elite, will ever change.

PART 4

FIGHTING BACK

CHAPTER 13

A PRODUCTIVE PUBLIC SECTOR?

HEY, BIG SPENDER!

This year our government will spend about £670 billion, while collecting around £500 billion in tax receipts. Next year it plans to up spending to £701 billion, yet is hardly likely to get more than £500 billion in tax. A similar situation is likely to extend for years into the future. Most people can see that we can't go on like this. Charles Dickens' Mr Micawber would be turning in his grave.

When the government came to power, the public sector was eating up around 38 per cent of what the country produced (our GDP); now it's heading towards 48 per cent in 2009 and maybe over 50 per cent in 2010. Various studies have shown that for every 10 percentage points increase in public spending as a proportion of GDP, total GDP will fall by around 1.5 per cent. Given that a good rate of GDP growth is about 2.5 per cent a year, the government's increase in public spending is unfortunately wiping out most of the growth in GDP we need to ever make this country's finances viable again.

Brown's reaching new heights

When Gordon Brown started on his first spending splurge in 2000, public spending as a percentage of GDP rose gracefully from about 36 per cent to 41 per cent, in spite of a large increase in GDP. But this didn't seem to satisfy Brown. Apparently he believed there was a lot more money to be wrung out of Britain's long-suffering taxpayers and hosed all over the public sector without any proper plans or controls. Unfortunately, as the government's recent second binge reached full throttle, the economy suddenly screeched to a halt, hung briefly at the edge of a precipice and then went into a stomach-churning freefall. This meant that the government, unable to control its financial incontinence, found public spending as a percentage of GDP was heading rapidly up towards a historic and shameful 50 per cent (see Figure 1).

Figure 1 The government has been on two spending sprees

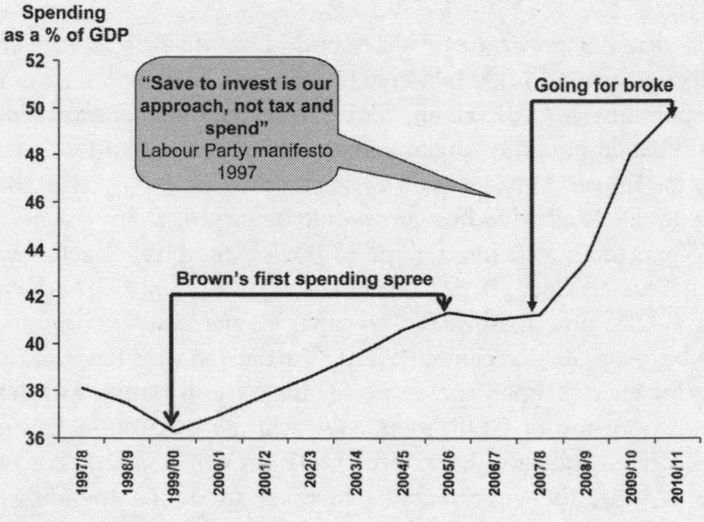

We have been here before

As a former lecturer in politics, perhaps Gordon Brown knows a little about the history of his own party. If so, he might remember how over a period of 12 years government spending as a percentage of GDP shot up from about 38 per cent in 1964 to almost 50 per cent by 1976, resulting in Britain having to go to the International Monetary Fund for a bailout, granted on condition that the then

Labour government would make significant reductions in public spending. Curiously and disturbingly, the pattern of spending increases as a percentage of GDP under our Iron Chancellor over the last 12 years almost exactly mirrors what happened back in the dark days of Labour's previous decimation of our country's finances (see Figure 2).

Figure 2 We saw a similar situation in 1964–76 when we had to be bailed out by the IMF in 1976

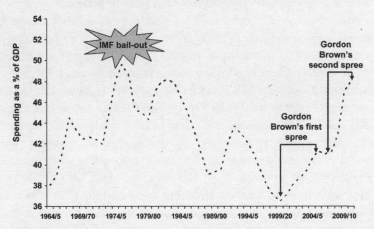

WHERE'S THE FAT?

Labour haven't a clue

If you listen to Gordon Brown's rhetoric, you'd think that the slightest attempt to rein in public spending would cause untold misery with thousands of nurses, teachers and police officers losing their jobs. One of the extraordinary number of, usually broken, pledges that Gordon Brown has given in his long political career was the following: 'Over the next few years we must seize this opportunity – by challenging ourselves to lift productivity in each and every industry towards the levels of the world's best.'[1] Totally independent of anything Chancellor Brown did, the private sector seems to have performed quite well, with productivity rising by about 20 per cent since 1997. However, in the public sector, where Gordon Brown really could influence the level of productivity, it has fallen by around 10 per cent, in spite of, or perhaps because of, the massive increase in our money being spent by the government. In health and education, the drop in productivity under this government has been nearer 15 per cent.[2] On public spending of £670 billion, this decrease in efficiency is worth about £67 billion a year in potential savings.

Another way to get a feel for the opportunities to reduce unnecessary spending is to look at how much we spend as a percentage of GDP compared with other advanced countries. Public spending in countries like Spain, Canada, Ireland, Australia, Switzerland and the US is typically somewhere between 34 per cent and 39 per cent of their GDP. The OECD average is about 39.8 per cent. Moreover, there has been a study which suggests that once a country goes over 35 per cent, it starts hitting the law of diminishing returns where further spending gives limited benefits.[3] If we could just get Britain's spending back to 39 per cent, we'd have to knock something approaching £80 billion to £100 billion off the government's spending plans. This large gap between what we spend and what many other OECD countries spend suggests there is quite a lot of room for improving how public services are delivered – something our government claims it has been vigorously doing since it first came to power in 1997.

A third indicator that the public sector might be slightly obese is the fact that in 2008, the first full turbulent year of recession, the private sector lost several hundred thousand jobs and average pay fell by 1.1 per cent. However, in the calm tranquil world of public service over 30,000 new (and possibly not terribly useful) jobs were created and average pay went up by 3.7 per cent.

Repeated surveys have suggested that the majority of the people have understood that they cannot continue spending more than they earn, but our government hasn't quite cottoned on to this basic fact of economics.

The Tories seem confused

Labour are in a state of complete denial about the need to reduce spending because they want to go into the next election lambasting the Conservatives as cruel cost-cutters. But while the Tories are trying to sound realistic and businesslike, their approach to the problem of excessive spending can appear to be severely underwhelming. In one recent Conservative publication, *It's your money. A new plan for disciplined spending in government*, they seemed to be proposing employing more accountants in the public sector when they wrote: 'The critically important Finance function in government is understaffed' and 'There is a shortage of financial expertise at senior management levels.'[4] This is not so smart, as in the short term increasing the number of finance staff in the public sector would probably increase costs rather than reduce them and we need radical action fast, not hundreds or even thousands of additional beancounters to carry out the Tories' plan to 'review every spending programme to see if it is necessary and justifiable in the new economic circumstances'.

However, there might be some reasonably simple explanations for the Tories taking this approach. Few, if any, of the influential figures in the Conservative ranks have ever experienced making major cost reductions in a large organization – few have ever had real jobs. Furthermore, several of the large accountancies are rushing to get into bed with the Tories as they see huge business opportunities available from a new government committed to improving financial control and cutting costs in the public sector. The accountancies want to sell the Tories the idea that costs can be cut by giving the accountancies huge quantities of taxpayers' money to send armies of usually junior accountants into government departments, charging each person out at £5,000 or more a week while only paying them about £600 a week. Having made billions flattering the egos of Labour ministers in building up massive, inefficient and prodigiously wasteful public-sector empires, the very same accountancies now see further mouth-watering opportunities from cutting down the bureaucratic monstrosities that they helped build in the first place.

In mid May 2009, co-author David Craig managed to arrange a meeting in Westminster with an assistant and adviser to Shadow Chancellor George Osborne. The purpose of the meeting was for Craig to try to explain to our probable future political masters a few ideas about how to go about cutting public spending without harming service levels. Amongst various proposals, Craig had one absolutely key message he wanted to put across. This was that the Tories would make themselves vulnerable to smear attacks from Labour if they let themselves be tarred as being about to cut vital services. The way to avoid this, Craig suggested, was to constantly repeat that the Tories would 'ring-fence' frontline services and workers – teachers, doctors, nurses, police, social workers and so on – but that they would hack away ruthlessly at unnecessary bureaucracy and waste.

As he was being ushered out of Portcullis House so that Osborne's adviser could go to her next meeting, Craig kept repeating that the Tories had no need to say – and in fact must never say – something like 'we will ring-fence health spending' or 'we will ring-fence education' i.e. sparing them from any cuts. Instead, Craig proposed, the Tories should say something like: 'We will ring-fence frontline services in health and education, but we will put unnecessary bureaucracy to the sword.' After all, many people are realizing that much of the extra money spent on health and education has been wasted. Sure enough, just a week or so after Craig's meeting, the Tory shadow health minister announced that the next Conservative government would 'ring-fence' the NHS, implying that the bureaucratic waste would be allowed to continue, which proves the old adage that you can take a horse to water, you can explain in great detail the joys of drinking water, you can show pictures of happy horses drinking water, you can even give the horse a huge kick up the arse so it falls into the water, but if the horse is particularly stubborn or extraordinarily stupid, no amount of effort will ever make it drink.

The shadow minister's apparent failure to understand that huge amounts of useless bureaucracy can and should be reduced, even in the normally sacrosanct NHS, might have had something to do with the fact that, according to his official CV, the main 'real' job he'd had before going into a lucrative career in politics was when he was employed at the notoriously useless, bureaucratic and unproductive Department of Trade and Industry, otherwise known by *Private Eye* magazine as the Department of Timidity and Inaction or by others as just the Department for Total Incompetence.

TIME TO LOSE WEIGHT – AT LEAST 60 BILLION POUNDS

Britain's finances are in a more than parlous state. Lacking both courage and any real work experience, most of our politicians either don't want to or don't know how to do much about the situation. So here we'd like to propose an approach which we believe could reduce public spending by up to £70 billion within 12 months, without having any negative effect on the level of services provided. As we have said previously, we think they would actually improve. But before we propose what should be done in the first 12 months of the public sector's new crash diet, we'd just like to briefly outline a few key principles that have guided our thinking.

You look like you're clinically obese

The numbers we use are estimates. There are plenty of think tanks busily producing largely indigestible reports analysing the country's finances which they will unveil to a disinterested public probably in September 2009, just in time for the political party conferences. Here we prefer to base our findings on an educated and experienced reasoning of typical departmental inefficiencies.

Anyway, there's a wonderfully useful work-saving theory called the Inertia of Large Numbers. Basically it means that if you look at any government department, wander round for a couple of days, attend a few pointless meetings, assess the poor quality of decision-making and smell the level of inactivity, you can usually make a swag about the level of savings which can be made. Thirty per cent is often not short of the mark. Our intention here is not to be absolutely precise to the nearest pound about how much weight the public sector needs to shed; rather we want to show the kind of diet which has to be imposed and the approximate levels of weight loss that we should expect from our clinically obese public services.

Preserving vital organs while getting rid of the fat

Once any organization has built up layer upon layer of unnecessary and wasteful bureaucracy in true Cyril Northcote Parkinson style, it can be incredibly difficult to cut costs without severely reducing the vital services supplied. What normally happens when you try to slim an organization down is that the many levels of management cannot see that it is actually they who are both wasteful and superfluous. So the only way they can think of to reduce operating costs is by cutting away at usually lower-paid, frontline staff – the people who do the real work. We are already seeing this in the police where the numbers of frontline officers is being reduced at the same time as middle and senior managers are being granted huge bonuses.

To avoid this happening throughout our public services, the first and most basic principle of this cost-reduction proposal is that all frontline staff positions in the public sector should be ring-fenced. As the rest of us tighten our belts to cope with the recession, it seems the public sector is still piling on the pounds. Although the government claims all the people it has hired are crucial to providing public services, there are indications that 500,000 or more of the 800,000 new posts have little to do with providing direct services to the public. Had these non-frontline people not been hired, our public spending would now be at least £20 billion less than it actually is and the public-sector pensions liability would also be significantly lower.

It's not a tough decision

As the politicians survey the disastrous state of our public finances, we're beginning to hear the expressions 'tough decisions' and 'difficult choices'. Over the coming months, these will be repeated many times as our leaders try to make us understand how hard it will be to reverse their uncontained, managerially inept profligacy of the last 12 years or so. Yet most of the actions we're proposing won't be tough at all – at least not for the vast majority of us. In fact, they will make our lives better by bringing this country back from the brink of insolvency. However, we have to admit that some of our suggestions could be painful for the ruling elite of politicians, bureaucrats and bankers who have been so freely plundering our taxes for at least the last decade in order to line their own pockets.

No need to hire a weight-loss expert

A final point is that there is no need to give tens of millions of pounds of taxpayers' money to pay expensive accountants and consultants to advise on where public spending should be cut. This just wastes money and delays the obvious decisions that have to be taken. The accountants and consultants are frantically lobbying to be given a piece of the cost-cutting action. Our government needs to have the courage to push through the necessary cuts without being conned once again by people who sometimes appear to be fee-hungry parasites.

FAT BRITAIN'S CRASH DIET

We've split the 12-month crash diet plan into six main parts:

1. Immediate reduction in the costs of bureaucracy – £7 billion
2. Improving public-sector management – £11 billion
3. Liberating frontline workers to help – £5 billion
4. Better buying – £5 billion
5. Grabbing low-hanging fruit – one-off £23 billion plus £4 billion per year
6. Taking action for longer-term savings – £8 billion

1. Immediate reduction in the costs of bureaucracy – £7 billion

Redundancy, bonuses, recruiting and salary freeze

We saw in Chapter 5 (*Self-Service in Public Service*) that at least £1 billion of our money has been flushed away by giving overly generous redundancy payments to civil-service staff while the departments handing out this cash were just hiring replacements, using consultants to do the work or in a few instances hiring back as consultants the same people who had been given large redundancy packages to leave. So the first step in making savings is to stop any payments for early retirement or redundancy anywhere in the public sector. If people want to leave, let them go, but there's no need for them to take huge piles of our money with them.

Moreover, hundreds of millions get handed out in public-sector bonuses each year without it being obvious that the lucky recipients have done anything to deserve them. So another necessary step is to stop all bonuses – public-sector managers already get good salaries and extraordinary pensions so there's no need to pay them even more just for doing their jobs.

The third step is to have a hiring freeze throughout the public sector except for frontline jobs such as police officers, nurses, doctors, other proper medical staff, teachers and a few categories of manual workers such as refuse collectors, cleaners and maintenance staff. In addition, there should be a three-year pay freeze for all public-sector employees earning over perhaps £40,000 a year.

These actions should save more than £1 billion a year. Not a lot compared with spending of £670 billion, but a start.

The three-day week

A few of us might remember Edward Heath's three-day week in the early 1970s. That was brought in at a time of national emergency – a lack of power due to the coalminers' strike. Well, we now have a new national emergency – a lack of money caused by the government's profligacy. So it's time for some drastic measures. Declaring a national emergency, the government should immediately implement a four-day week for all public-sector managerial and administrative staff who are not directly delivering services to the public. This would include all council executives and managers; all NHS executives and managers; all executives, managers and most administrative staff in the main government departments like health, education, the Cabinet Office, business enterprise and regulatory reform (or whatever it's called this week), environment and many others; and almost all staff working for regulators and quangos. Administrative staff processing things like driving licences, passports, benefits, pensions and so on should be exempted, but their managers should be put on the four-day week. Probably the least disruptive solution would be to make them take every Friday off. Partly due to flexi-time but mainly as a result of a general lack of discipline, many probably already slope off early on Fridays, but still get paid for five days. Private-sector companies have used reduced numbers of shifts and shorter working weeks to save money while protecting jobs, so there's no reason for the public sector not to be using similar techniques for anyone who is not directly delivering essential frontline services.

Moving to a four-day week will immediately bring with it a reduction in salaries and pension contributions of 20 per cent for those involved. We will probably find to our amazement (or maybe most of us won't be so amazed) that frontline workers actually succeed in continuing to deliver the same if not better services while the multitudes of policy advisers, executives, managers, communications professionals, diversity officers, community relations specialists, involvement officers, diet advisers, racial awareness specialists, equality experts and administrators take every Friday off. A quick calculation suggests that moving a few hundred thousand people to a four-day week will save taxpayers close to £100 million a week, giving about £4.5 billion a year. In the NHS alone, this will mean about 40,000 managers saving us £8 million a week, worth about £360 million a year. Over at the BBC, the four-day week for anyone not directly involved in making programmes should give us over £9 million a year

After six months of adapting to a four-day week, at least half these people should be put on a three-day week. That'll give us another £50 million a week. Total first-year savings should be in the region of £5.6 billion a year. Each full year after that will give another £6.8 billion. All of these savings would be real cash savings for the taxpayer without any costly redundancy packages or any early retirement payments.

Many of those affected might feel that their standing in the community or at work has been diminished as it's shown they are not quite as necessary as they have always believed or would have us believe. Or else they may be upset at the loss of income and pension benefits. Well, if they are unhappy, let them go voluntarily. Hopefully they will then get productive jobs in the private sector where they can produce wealth for the country rather than living well off the backs of those people who do produce wealth or do provide essential services. However, it is probable that by imposing a four-day or even three-day week under emergency legislation, the government will call most of the public-sector non-frontline workers' bluff – their working lives would still be so preferable to the stress, uncertainty and inadequate pension provision of the private sector that they'll desperately hang on to their public-sector jobs as long as they can.

In addition to saving about £100 million a week from the very moment it's implemented, this policy would give other benefits. For a start, there would be absolutely no need to pay tens of millions of pounds to the many firms of accountants and consultants hovering like vultures in the hope of juicy contracts helping the next government cut costs. It would also send a clear message throughout public-sector management and administrators that the taxpaying public has had enough of their wastefulness, incompetence and greed. It would thus help instil a new awareness that the public expects value for money rather than departments hunting around for ways to spend their budgets as is currently the case.

In a recent newspaper article, one journalist wrote that: 'David Cameron's first priority must be job cuts in the public sector.' Others have written about scrapping quangos. But by cutting jobs the taxpayer would be left with massive costs for accountants, consultants, redundancies and court cases against unfair dismissal, so we would disagree with this approach, at least in the short term. Cutting jobs is old-fashioned thinking, takes too long and often ends up costing more that it saves. We need savings and we need them fast. That's why imposing a four-day week and then a three-day week is the only viable way of making the economies we need. Then, in a year or two, the government could look a reducing the number of departments and employees.

Our leaders should show leadership
When this government came to power, about 40 per cent of our laws were made in Brussels. Now the figure is somewhere between 75 and 85 per cent. Yet in spite of this massive decrease in their workload, our MPs employ more staff, take home higher salaries and claim more in expenses than ever before. Moreover,

they have so little to do that many have two, three or even four other jobs. If anyone can go down to a four-day week, it's our MPs. We suggest that Parliament should be open for a maximum of three days a week, leaving MPs one day a week to work in their constituencies and one day a week for relaxing or working at their other jobs. The only exception should be a small core of seven or eight government ministers necessary to run the country. This would allow MPs' salaries to be reduced to nearer £50,000 a year, saving the taxpayer about £6 million a year. Another benefit would be that with MPs only needing to be at Westminster for three days a week at most, the controversial second-homes allowance could be completely scrapped and MPs could stay in hotels when in London with a price limit of say £120 a night payable on MPs showing valid receipts. This would reduce the cost of MPs' accommodation from about £12 million a year to less than £6 million – this is surely a sacrifice that MPs would be willing to make given that most of them claim to have gone into politics because of a desire to serve the public. If we could further reduce Parliament's sittings to two days a week, there would be even less justification for the second-homes allowance and we could save a few million more.

MPs constantly claim that they aren't being paid enough, but we now have too many MPs: we don't need 646 any more. After all, the number was largely decided at a time when we, not the EU, ruled our own country, when people travelled by horse and cart and when they communicated by letter. Given that most of our laws now come from Brussels, that on a good day our railways are faster than horse and cart and that we have email and the internet, we could and should reduce the number of MPs to about 300 at most, saving us over £150 million a year. So any MPs who feel that they are paid less than they are worth should be encouraged to resign as quickly as possible and find someone to employ them at what they consider their real value. Each time an MP resigns, their constituency should be merged into nearby constituencies until we have halved the number. These principles should also apply to the 297 politicians in the Scottish, Welsh and Northern Irish parliaments and assemblies, giving us millions more in easily bankable savings for no additional cost.

The recruitment and pay freeze, abandonment of bonuses and redundancy payments and move towards four- and three-day weeks are simple to implement, don't require any complex financial analysis and should give us about £7 billion a year in savings without costing us a penny. But there's plenty more to go yet.

2. Improving public-sector management – £11 billion

Managers should start managing

Management in the public sector is unfortunately too often abysmal. One problem is that the whole ethos of government departments is to ensure you spend your annual budget otherwise it might be reduced the following year. Recently David Craig was sitting in the office of a public-sector financial director when a department manager came in and told her that there was money left at the end of the financial year. A decision was made to spend it quickly by sending staff on a training course in order to justify getting a requested increase in their next year's budget. We have to change the attitude of 'how can we spend all our budget?' to 'how can we get value for money from our budget?'

Every executive, manager and supervisor in both the private and public sectors should have a double function – to run their areas as efficiently and cost-effectively as they can and to continually look for and implement improvements to their operations. So a first step we can take to improve management performance is to remove all the transformation managers, business improvement managers, operations improvement managers and all others of their ilk who are not directly managing something providing value to taxpayers. After all, if each line manager is responsible for continuous improvements, then there can be no need for a further level of transformers and improvers. These people should not be fired or made redundant as that is both costly and can take too long. Instead, they should all be moved to line-management positions – if they're so expert at improving things, think of all that they could achieve for us taxpayers by actually doing something which delivers real services rather than just sitting in meetings and writing procedures telling other people what to do.

The next step is for every manager and supervisor to be given clear deliverable improvement goals by their immediate line manager all the way up to department head honchos. They should then be assessed every few months on whether they are achieving these goals. The first time they miss their goals, they should get help from their immediate superior. On the second time, they should get a written warning. If they continue to underachieve, they should be disciplined and then fired. The thought of losing their relaxed lifestyles and fabulous pensions would concentrate these managers' minds wonderfully. Just a 2 per cent improvement in performance on the £500 billion that is spent on public services (excluding the £170 billion or so spent on buying things) would give us £10 billion saved every year. If these managers then saved a measly 1 per cent more in the second year and another 1 per cent in the third year, we'd be cashing in £20 billion of savings a year after three years.

One area in particular that needs some effective management is incapacity benefits where an estimated £4 billion of the £12 billion paid out is lost to fraud each year. Cutting this by only a quarter would give another £1 billion.

Spending 'your own' money
Another way of ensuring money is well spent is by pushing spending decisions away from central government to a more local level. The further away money is from ordinary taxpayers, the more they will see it as what is called a 'common resource' – money that's just there to be spent. However, if people have real influence over how money is spent and see that they are directly

losing something by someone wasting that money, then they will often act to stop that waste.

Here are two quick examples. If a school is given its own budget and parents see part of this being wasted on employing a diversity officer, a community relations officer, a communications and cohesion coordinator or suchlike at a cost of £30,000 or more a year, then some parents might think that the money would be better spent on more computers, books or an extra teacher. They'd soon form an action group, send the unnecessary bureaucrat packing and ensure the money was used for something more constructive. Similarly, if all the costs of law enforcement including paying for courts and prison places for the local criminal fraternity came directly out of council-taxpayers' pockets and we had elected local police chiefs, there would soon be plenty of local pressure on police bosses to pull their collective fingers out, cut down useless middle management, get their officers back out preventing crime rather than filling in government forms and bring down the cost of crime. The thought of being voted out of their hitherto untouchable sinecures would help focus our police chiefs' minds on doing the job we pay them to do rather than thinking up new schemes to get bonuses for demonstrating political correctness above and beyond the call of duty.

This localization of spending may not save a lot of money in the short term, but it would ensure that most of the money which was spent was used effectively, rather than being wasted on massively expensive, centrally controlled initiatives and so would lead to billions in longer-term savings.

3. Liberating frontline workers to help – £5 billion

Frontline workers already know what needs to be done
The people who know how to deliver much better public services for less money are, of course, frontline workers. Yet they are too often prevented from making any changes or from even

suggesting any improvements. As we saw with nurse Margaret Haywood, with staff at the Mid Staffordshire NHS Trust and throughout our public services, frontline staff risk their careers by daring to suggest ways to stop wasting money or to improve levels of service. The barriers to frontline workers' proposals are layer upon layer of managers all keen to protect their often badly run empires from prying eyes. We have to find a way of unblocking this logjam.

One option is to split the lumbering, politically subservient, conflict-shy National Audit Office (NAO) into two parts. Responsibility for auditing the accounts of government departments should stay with a greatly slimmed-down NAO. However, a separate group focusing on value for money should be moved from the NAO to the Treasury. There should be a communication channel available for frontline workers to report opportunities to improve services or save money in confidence to this Value for Money (VfM) unit. In addition, there should be a statutory obligation on the VfM unit to investigate all reported opportunities within four weeks. If the reported opportunity is found to be genuine, there should be a legal obligation on the relevant line managers to implement the suggested improvements within a defined time – weeks or months, not years. Failure to implement should be a disciplinary offence and, if repeated, result in the manager being given the appropriate written warnings. If these have no effect the manager should be demoted or sacked without compensation.

Any frontline workers reporting opportunities should be entitled to tax-free payments of perhaps 5 per cent of any savings achieved up to a maximum of £100,000. These payments should not be available to managers, as it is their job to identify and make continuous improvements. An almost trivial 1 per cent saving in direct spending would give another £5 billion a year.

4. Better buying – £5 billion

From theory to action

It is standard practice for many companies selling to the public sector to push their prices up by 10 to 20 per cent because, as one major supplier to the public sector explained to great guffaws of knowing laughter at a conference, public-sector buyers are 'inexperienced, inconsistent and incompetent'.[5] To help departments buy better, we have the Office of Government Commerce (OGC) with 375 people costing us about £33 million a year. Although the OGC produces loads of reports, best-practice documents and procedures and other blurb about how to buy properly, the public sector still gets taken to the cleaners time and time again by its suppliers. We should disband the OGC – if anyone wants to find out about correct buying procedures there are several professional bodies which issue quite helpful advice, usually for free or at little cost. So there's no need for a bunch of bureaucrats to spend tens of millions every year rewriting in bureaucratese something that has often already been written in plain English. Instead of hiding in their comfy offices bashing away at their computers, all the OGC's staff should be assigned to assist public-sector buyers in their daily work. They should be given clear cost-reduction targets. First time a target is missed, they should get help; second time, they get a written warning; continual failure and they should be fired so they can take their talents elsewhere without getting big, undeserved redundancy packages.

The public sector spends over £170 billion a year purchasing things for us. An easily achievable 2 per cent improvement (4 to 5 per cent is quite common in procurement improvement initiatives in the private sector) would reduce purchasing costs by £3.4 billion.

The False Claims Act

Since the American Civil War the US has had a law, rejuvenated by Congress in 1986, called the False Claims Act. This allows ordinary citizens with evidence of fraud or corruption against government contracts or programmes to sue, on the government's behalf, in order to recover any money taken illegally. As a reward for their efforts, whistleblowers are given somewhere between 15 and 25 per cent of the money recovered or saved. Just one partner in a US consultancy, which also works extensively throughout Britain's public sector, stood to gain $10 million for revealing how his employer had been cheating various US government departments over travel expenses.

The False Claims Act protects taxpayers' money in two ways. Firstly, it encourages whistleblowers to take action. Secondly, and perhaps much more importantly, it has an incredibly strong deterrent effect – it discourages individuals and companies from overcharging or defrauding government departments because they will always know that they run a serious and real risk of being sued by any concerned or even disgruntled employee who knows what they are up to. If any British government really was serious about ensuring value for taxpayers' money, it would introduce a version of the False Claims Act whereby whistleblowers supported, if they wished, by no-win-no-fee lawyers would be able to launch prosecutions on behalf of the taxpayer and take a share of the money that was saved.

While the Act only leads to the recovery of about $1.4 billion a year from suppliers in the US, it is generally accepted that it dissuades companies from trying to overcharge and defraud the government of many hundreds of billions more. Just a 1 per cent reduction in purchasing costs from a False Claims Act would net another £1.7 billion a year.

5. Grabbing low-hanging fruit – one-off £23 billion plus £4 billion each year

In addition to the ongoing repeating annual savings of about £28 billion in the first year and much more in subsequent years, there are some big, fat, juicy, almost over-ripe bits of low-hanging fruit that are crying out for someone to pick them.

Kill Connecting for Health

The most obvious target is the worthless NHS Connecting for Health computer system. This project should be abandoned, the organization running it disbanded and all hospitals, doctors' surgeries and other health bodies should be free to buy whatever computer systems they wished providing two conditions are met. One: all systems should be based on what are called 'common interoperability standards'. This would make different systems compatible. Two: no system should be bought unless a minimum of ten other users were also willing to buy the system. This would provide a control mechanism to ensure that no single hospital was lured by smart salespeople into buying worthless systems. Not only would this decision save us up to £10 billion, but it would also stimulate a rebirth in the British healthcare computing industry, which was almost destroyed by the incompetent and ill-conceived, monolithic Connecting for Health monster, and thus could help the country earn many tens of millions in exports.

Austerity Olympics

Someone needs to tell the olympocrats and the International Olympics Committee (IOC) that we can no longer afford their grandiose plans for glorifying and enriching themselves at our expense. We should inform the IOC that the 2012 Games budget will be fixed at about £6 billion – already 50 per cent above the £4 billion price agreed at the time the Games were won.

The new austerity Olympics will be achieved by using existing venues, cutting out all the unnecessary pomp and ceremony, getting rid of all the consultants and other hangers-on, providing modest rather than luxury accommodation for IOC officials and through ruthless cost control. If the IOC is unhappy with this, we should call its bluff and give it a couple of billion to take its worthless Games back. Then it can see if, in a time of a worldwide economic slowdown, any other country wants to spend billions of their taxpayers' money staging the Games. In future all Olympics should be held in Athens – they have the facilities (they're still paying for them) and they've hosted the event before. The IOC has conned ambitious but gullible governments into sacrificing taxpayers' billions for too long. It's time to face them down. This would save another £8 billion.

Cut consultants

The public sector's £2.8 billion annual consultancy budget should be slashed to less than £800 million. All consultancy projects costing more than £20,000 should be personally signed off by the chancellor who then takes responsibility to ensure they provide value. To prevent consultancies cutting their projects into small pieces to avoid this control, no department should be allowed to spend more than 0.1 per cent of its annual budget on consultants, interim managers and all other such questionable appointments. Moreover, all consultancy projects should publish details such as costs, goals, financial benefits planned and financial benefits achieved every three months on the Treasury website. Cutting consultants will give another £2 billion a year.

Additional savings

Scrap the identity cards scheme and save £5 billion. At the moment we've got the worst of all worlds. The government is going ahead and yet few people will have to get one, so we're getting all the costs of the scheme without any of the supposed benefits. Similarly scrap the Contact Point children's database and computer system.

We've already paid over £200 million to build it, but at least we can avoid the £44 million a year cost of running it.

Cancel all government advertising, especially job advertising. The probable saving would be at least £500 million a year. All available government jobs should be listed on a website. If people can't be bothered to look at the website, then they don't deserve to get a job paid for by the taxpayer.

In the education sector, abolish the Schools Food Trust to save another £6 million and scrap financial inducements to graduates to go into teaching – with a recession on, graduates are heading towards the job security of the public sector in an uncontrolled stampede, so there's no need to pay them extra. The government should also get a grip on the Building Schools for the Future Programme – or better still abandon it. Rather than squandering billions on badly designed new buildings, focus should be placed upon decent teaching without bureaucratic interference; the ability of schools to discipline disruptive pupils and introduce sanctions against their parents; worthwhile exams; better sports facilities and the encouragement of competition and achievement.

Close the Regional Development Agencies and the Regional Assemblies, saving over £1 billion – their 3,100 staff cost us almost £500 million a year and they probably waste around a third of the £2 billion they spend.

Consider whether our armed forces are really serving our best interests by being bogged down in a pointless and unwinnable war in Afghanistan where they are increasingly seen by locals as an occupying army supporting a corrupt, drug-smuggling government. Then review whether our soldiers would be of much more use to us helping out in our schools, youth centres and even prisons to try to sort out some of the problems our government's benefits-dependent generation have caused. If our troops were brought home and employed to help repair our fractured society, this should save hundreds of millions and bring further benefits from reducing social breakdown. Moreover, youth offenders should be given an option of serving their sentences in a correctional institution or else going into the military where they can get paid to learn a useful trade.

Scrap the Private Finance Initiative. Had our civil servants been competent, PFI could theoretically have delivered essential hospitals and roads and other projects for a lower cost than the public sector could have done. Unfortunately, PFI suppliers, their bankers and their lawyers were much too smart for public-sector buyers and the Office of Government Commerce, so most schemes have turned out to be disastrous for the country's finances.

The number of local councillors should be halved, there should be a maximum allowance of £5,000 per year and they should not be allowed to join the local government pension scheme. Passenger Focus costs us £5 million a year and achieves nothing – it should be scrapped.

There are many more things that could be done. But at least this short list shows a few of the opportunities. These actions would give about £23 billion in one-off savings and another almost £4 billion in ongoing savings. They would also show we had a government that represented ordinary people rather than powerful business and social interest groups who view taxpayers' money as an unlimited sea of cash to be siphoned off at will.

6. Taking action for longer-term savings – £8 billion

At the moment, our government's attempts to portray itself as investing in public services in comparison with Tory cuts are causing dismay in international financial circles. Our spending is out of control, our borrowing is shooting through the roof and our government has lost all semblance of any fiscal rectitude. Unless the government is seen to be taking action to bring public spending firmly under control, we risk an investors' strike – there will be nobody willing to buy British government debt. If this happens, the only option left to us will be to beg the International

Monetary Fund for help. Even if we don't have to go to the IMF, our government's incompetence and continued excessive spending put us in danger of being downgraded by the credit-rating agencies which were previously so compliant in helping get us into this mess in the first place. A downgrading will increase our cost of borrowing, further worsening our economic problems.

In the earlier parts of this chapter, we have outlined measures that we believe could be simple first steps to convincing the international financial community that we have a government which is serious about putting the country's finances back in order. However, our leaders also need to take a series of actions to ensure that we never get into this mess again.

Control public-sector pensions

We need to tackle the rapidly mounting costs of public-sector pensions. The government should explore whether emergency legislation could be introduced to base the pensions of all government employees earning over £50,000 on their average rather than their final salary. Also the retirement age for anyone in the public sector earning over £50,000 should immediately be raised to 65. In addition, all lump-sum payments to government employees should be subject to full income tax. Moreover, the Lifetime Earnings Limit of £1.8 million, whereby any private-sector worker's pension paid on money above this limit is subject to a special tax, should be imposed on public-sector employees. Although public-sector workers don't have pension savings because their pensions are paid from our taxes, it is relatively straightforward to calculate what is called the Equivalent Transfer Value of their pensions and it would therefore be easy to apply the LEL tax to them.

All people joining the public sector in future should either have their own pension contributions substantially increased or else be put in defined-contribution, rather than defined-benefit, schemes. In the short term, moving all public-sector management to a four-day or in some cases three-day week would considerably reduce the final salaries on which their pensions are based and so should start generating savings within a year or two of being implemented. Moreover, any public-sector worker receiving a pension of £25,000 a year or more should be disqualified from also getting the basic state pension. They are already pocketing enough money from taxpayers. Just this small measure should save about £400 million a year as soon as it is introduced. As a first step towards bringing the cost of public-sector pensions under control, we should be looking at cutting public-sector pension payments by about £2 billion to £3 billion a year.

Prosecute the bankers

The government should take legal action for offences such as false accounting, negligence, breach of fiduciary duties, publishing misleading information and anything else that might be relevant against the senior figures in all the banks which had to be bailed out by the taxpayer. We could probably only recover about £50 million to £100 million for taxpayers, but at least this would send a message to those who have abused their positions to enrich themselves while dumping the results of their greed on to taxpayers, that this behaviour brings punishment rather than massive rewards.

Bring the benefits culture under control

When daring to talk about Britain's benefits culture, one risks being branded as right-wing and callous. However, with French politicians complaining constantly about how our benefits culture is causing a mass migration of people from around the world trying to sneak into Britain via the French Channel ports, it may be that we are being overgenerous to the fickle and feckless and that we should ask more from them before handing over large amounts of our money. This year, we will probably pay more out in benefits than the government will get from income tax. Areas which could be looked at in order to reduce the unsustainable costs of benefits and encourage a new age of responsibility and self-sufficiency might include the following.

The provision of council housing and payment of housing benefits could be restricted to people over 21 years old – if people choose to have children before that age without being able to earn the money to house and look after them, then they should stay with their parents wherever possible. Moreover, perhaps cash benefits should be restricted to people holding British passports who are permanently resident in the UK – foreign workers who leave Britain should not receive any British taxpayers' money after they have gone and no child benefit should be paid unless their children are permanently resident in Britain. Moreover, if foreign nationals want our help, this could be restricted to food vouchers and limited accommodation support.

Of the £140 billion we pay in benefits a year, we should be looking for a decrease of at least 4 to 5 per cent through tighter, more targeted payments, saving more than £5 billion a year.

Put Britain's interests first
We should welcome people who will contribute to our society and should discourage those who see us as an easy target to rip off. Nobody should be given a British passport unless they can demonstrate that they have worked full-time and supported themselves without any recourse to benefits for five years prior to their passport application or else can prove that they are married to someone who has worked for a minimum of five years without recourse to benefits. Moreover we, like Australia, should have an immigration policy based on what this country needs rather than on who wishes to come here. Perhaps we should also stop spending hundreds of millions each year on translation. Great Britain has three main languages – English, Welsh and Gaelic. We should provide free indigenous language lessons for those who wish to become part of our society, but not encourage isolationism amongst those who wish to take our wealth and receive public services without making any effort to contribute anything. Total savings would be another few hundred million a year.

Educate for the skills we need

It has become clear that the government's obsession with increasing the number of young people going to university has resulted in an explosion in the number of people getting into hopeless debt. The government's policy has also resulted in a desperate shortage of people with practical vocational skills like builders, painters, plumbers, electricians and so on. We should provide free further education for the skills the country needs – at university this might include engineering, physics, medicine, mathematics, chemistry, computer sciences and maybe even languages. At colleges this would cover a whole range of practical skills where we currently have shortages. However, fees should be retained for courses for which we have less need.

Savings through simplicity

Having never managed a proper organization, politicians don't understand that complexity drives costs up and simplification allows costs to fall. The result is that governments are continually issuing edicts and laws which look straightforward on paper but actually impose massive costs on society. For example, by insisting that councils have an inclusion policy, suddenly the government creates a need to employ at least another 500 bureaucrats which will probably cost us about £40 million a year. Alistair Darling's small cut in VAT was another typical example – this imposed a huge amount of largely unnecessary work on hundreds of thousands of businesses across the country. Similarly Gordon Brown's complexification of the benefits system costs hundreds of millions, and possibly even several billion, a year in extra administration, increased mistakes and higher levels of fraud.

To drive down unnecessary administrative burdens, the government needs to simplify its administrative demands. For example, the TV licence could be scrapped and the BBC paid from general taxation – it's ludicrous to have a massive administrative and enforcement machine just to collect about £140 from each family. A more ambitious idea might be to get rid of corporation tax altogether and replace it by withholding a certain percentage of VAT. Corporation tax is just a game where larger international companies can use transfer pricing to move their tax liabilities to low-tax countries, leaving smaller businesses to pay more than their fair share. Over the boom decade, corporation tax paid by small businesses went up by 132 per cent, while tax paid by large companies only increased by 4.7 per cent. By just using one tax, VAT, hundreds of millions could be saved in administration and billions in lost tax could be collected.

NOT IN A BILLION YEARS

Here we have proposed a simple approach that could take tens of billions off our public spending without costing us anything and without harming public services. Moreover, under our proposals all the frontline, usually lower-paid public-sector workers would be spared from any cuts. Only department bosses, executives, managers and back-office administrators would be affected. However, some of our proposals attack the vested interests of the politicians, bureaucrats and bankers who have been creaming off our money for so long, so perhaps we should expect that everything we suggest will be ignored by those in power. Moreover, should any of the ruling elite respond to our proposals, we imagine they will seek to attack us by trying to prove that our figures are wrong. To this we would answer that the absolute accuracy of the figures is not consequential: if the ruling elite were to just start implementing what we propose, they might actually find that the financial benefits far exceed our modest guesstimates.

Anyway, by showing what could be done, we at least provide a background for people to judge our politicians when Labour

claim that making serious cuts means making 'tough choices'
and reducing frontline services; and when the Conservatives
maintain that the only way to make cuts is to give their friends in
the accounting and consulting industries enormous amounts of
our money to find out where cuts could be made.

CHAPTER 14

POWER TO THE PEOPLE

THE DECLINE OF DEMOCRACY

> 'The death of democracy is not likely to be an assassination from ambush. It will be a slow extinction from apathy, indifference, and undernourishment.' Robert M. Hutchins (American educator and writer)

It is becoming increasingly clear to many people that those who are meant to represent our interests have drifted away from us and now form part of an elite ruling caste that is uninterested in, and even contemptuous of, their responsibilities to ordinary people. In Labour's 1997 election manifesto, the now multimillionaire international statesman and possibly future EU president Tony Blair promised us:

> I want to renew faith in politics through a government that will govern in the interests of the many, the broad majority of people who work hard, play by the rules, pay their dues and feel let down by a political system that gives the breaks to the few, to an elite at the top increasingly out of touch with the rest of us.

However, rather than freeing us from the control of a small self-interested elite, he could hardly have better described precisely the kind of government he, his successor and all their cronies have given us.

The House of Commons has become a powerless and empty talking shop, where actually very little of substance goes on any more. It seldom sits for more than two days a week, few MPs attend debates, when they do they don't listen to each other and they hardly ever perform their main duty of holding the government to account. With 75 to 85 per cent of our laws coming from Brussels and most of the rest bypassing the Commons as more and more power is handed over to politically subservient quangos and other bureaucracies, it's hardly surprising that our MPs choose to fill their days thinking up ever more creative ways of claiming our money on their generous expenses. And on the few occasions when there are votes in Parliament, these are decided by pressure from government whips, so MPs are voting more with their careers than their consciences. Anyway, too often when our government does get around to forcing through new laws in the limited number of areas where it still legislates, its efforts are made a mockery of by judgments made by the European Court of Human Rights and the extraordinarily inappropriately named European Court of Justice. These leave our authorities stuck with unenforceable laws, for example making them unable to deal with serious threats to our country because their proposed actions might conceivably harm the rights of potentially dangerous foreign nationals.

The House of Commons' attempts to avoid revealing MPs' expenses were just the latest in a long series of examples of our elected rulers' disdain for those who pay for their luxury lifestyles. That this should have happened when the speaker was a former sheet-metal worker raised in a poorer part of Glasgow says much about the mental metamorphosis which takes place when people are strong enough to push, elbow, jostle and shove their way onto the ruling-caste gravy train. Meanwhile, over at the House of Lords, their lordships turn up daily in their masses to claim their allowances which can mount up to tens of thousands of pounds each year, yet the debating chamber and committee rooms are too often eerily empty. We rightly accuse the European

Parliament for its SOSO (sign on sod off) culture, but our noble lords could probably teach our MEPs a few lessons about the art of emptying the public purse for their own benefit without giving anything back in return. And now the Lords want to spend hundreds of millions of pounds building new offices for themselves with excellent taxpayer-subsidized restaurants and a huge wine cellar. The public already understand the pointlessness, greed and arrogance of our politicians: only 6 per cent of eligible voters bothered to vote for Labour in the June 2009 European Union elections.

Trade unions also seem to have deserted us to look after their own interests. In the last 30 years, trade union membership has more than halved from over 13 million to around 6 million. Moreover, there has been a huge shift in trade-union power from the private to the public sector. While around 15 per cent of the 23 million private-sector workforce are unionised, a more impressive 58 per cent of 6 million public-sector employees are members. So, even though only a fifth of those with jobs work in the public sector, they make up more than half of trade-union members. Public-sector workers should, of course, have the protection of trade-union membership. But at a time when public spending is heading towards 50 per cent of GDP – a sustainable level would be nearer 38 to 39 per cent – the power of public-sector unions to decide the government's agenda does possibly act as a barrier to ever bringing Britain's finances back under control. We've already seen this union power successfully exercised when the unions routed government plans to start raising the retirement age in the public sector to the levels of the private sector as part of its efforts to try to control the growing burden of public-sector pensions. As the recession leads to further falls in tax revenues, we can expect bitter resistance from the public-sector unions to any attempts to limit public-spending growth. Yet the cost-cutting proposals we've proposed don't really affect useful frontline public-sector employees.

As for our regulators, whether in financial services, electricity, water, gas, transport, healthcare or social care, there seem to have been huge increases in the numbers of regulatory organizations, regulators' budgets, numbers of staff and their salaries. Yet it is far from clear that increasing costs have given us better regulation. In fact, the performance of most of our regulators has been almost without exception a disgrace, with regulators looking after their own interests rather than those of the people they were meant to be safeguarding. This failure was clearest, of course, in the way the growth in dubious financial products was allowed first to lose contact with and then to seriously damage the 'real economy', while massively enriching a few, usually undeserving insiders in the process.

Journalists have mortgages, too

With our democratic institutions failing to represent our interests, one might have hoped that our free press would serve as our voice against the ruling elites. Here, too, we have been let down. For the first ten years or so of New Labour, the government brilliantly managed the lobby of Westminster journalists, offering scoops and privileged access to ministers for those journalists who toed the line and pushing any over-critical members of the press out into the cold. Some even lost their jobs after alleged government pressure on their employers. The most famous was probably former BBC journalist Andrew Gilligan who so correctly reported some of the deceit used in the lead-up to the invasion of Iraq.

Journalists, like the rest of us, have mortgages to pay, children to send to school and a lifestyle to maintain. No good stories meant no work, so a few were content to fawn at the government's feet, reporting what they were told to report and glossing over any 'bad news'. Now that the government is weakened and has lost control of the press, we're beginning to learn how appallingly we have been governed for the last 12 or so years. But for almost a decade some of the press failed to report how the government had thrown gargantuan sums of our money at public services without achieving much noticeable value for that money.

Moreover, the tendency for journalism to move from information to 'infotainment' – where the aim is to gather and keep an audience, rather then keep them properly informed – has led to a dumbing down of news reporting. With so much news now going out through fawningly obsequious and usually incredibly shallow non-interviews with ministers on breakfast TV instead of serious and intelligent interrogation, we too often get served what the government wants us to hear rather than anything approximating to the truth. Moreover, the government's clinically effective gelding of the BBC after the Gilligan affair has also reduced credible news coverage, leaving Channel Four News as one of the few opportunities for the majority of people to see effective questioning of people in authority at a mass-viewing time of the day. Thomas Jefferson wrote that: 'A democratic society depends on an informed and educated citizenry.' It is not obvious that our government has been overly interested in giving us either of these two preconditions for a functioning democracy.

GUERRILLA WARFARE

Starting the fightback

Faced with the growing power of a wasteful, self-serving, parasitic and undemocratic ruling caste of politicians, bureaucrats and bankers, most people cannot find a voice for their concerns and so feel themselves being increasingly impoverished, under-served and exploited. In Britain, we have given birth to powerful international campaigning organizations like Oxfam and Amnesty International, but because until recently we've had a functioning democracy, we've tended not to have a tradition of strong campaign groups focused on domestic political issues. Instead, we've been possibly over-endowed with think tanks, producing often indigestible reports, but not really focused on producing much action. Now that our democracy is so obviously letting us down, we need to become much better at organizing effective campaigning to protect our interests against those who are so grossly taking advantage of us. This failure of our democratic processes also has important implications for those wealthy individuals who donate to our political parties. If they are just in the selfish business of trying to buy influence and maybe a peerage or other honours, they should carry on donating to the main parties. But if they are genuinely motivated by a desire to improve other people's lives, giving money to our kleptocratic and self-serving politicians is completely pointless. Instead, they should be supporting campaign groups and individuals who actually do defend the rights of ordinary people.

In this section, we'd like to touch on some of the ways in which individuals and campaigning organizations have successfully fought back against our rulers and propose some other methods which can be used to derail the selfish plans of those who have so demonstrably failed to represent us. We'll frequently be focusing on the kinds of legal action that can be taken against the authorities. This is not because we want Britain to become a lawyers' paradise like the US. Rather, it's because now we have been increasingly deprived of the possibility of expressing our interests through democratic institutions, one of the few ways left to us to preserve our remaining freedoms is to use some of our government's laws against it and its agencies.

Indecent exposure – Freedom of Information laws

The most effective and recently newsworthy weapon that can be used by the largely powerless majority against the small ruling minority has been the Freedom of Information Act. The main reason given by New Labour for introducing the FoI concerned the supply of military hardware to Saddam Hussein during the previous Tory administration. As Labour explained: 'The

Scott Report on arms to Iraq revealed Conservative abuses of power.' Anyone still wondering about the exact whereabouts of Iraq's many weapons of mass destruction which Blair told us could be deployed in just 45 minutes – apparently the reason we invaded that country – might find this statement more than slightly ironic.

After being elected in May 1997, New Labour moved forward fairly swiftly with its opening up of government. In December 1997 the government issued a White Paper entitled *Your Right to Know*, seeking views for a Freedom of Information (FoI) Act by February 1998. A draft bill was published in May 1999 and the Freedom of Information Act received Royal Assent in November 2000. However, despite this rush to legislation, there are indications that the government might have been slowly losing its appetite for openness. Although the Act was passed in late 2000, it didn't become effective until 1 January 2005, giving government departments just over four years to prepare for the Act's implementation – almost the longest time given to any new law within living memory. In these four intervening years, there were constant stories of government departments cleaning up their archives and removing information ostensibly in the interests of efficiency and proper record-keeping.

The most effective and entertaining use of the FoI Act has clearly been by campaigner and journalist Heather Brooke, Ben Leapman of the *Sunday Telegraph* and Jonathan Ungoed-Thomas from the *Sunday Times* in their campaign to force the House of Commons authorities to reveal details of MPs' expenses. However, had the *Telegraph* not got hold of the original electronic files, much of the cheating and fraud would have remained hidden thanks to liberal 'redacting'. Gordon Brown declared himself a supporter of FoI: 'I am convinced that we need a new kind of politics . . . And that means more change . . . Change to strengthen our liberties to uphold the freedom of speech, freedom of information and the freedom to protest.'[1] Yet not only did he conspicuously fail to oppose MPs' attempts to block publication of their expenses, he actually led the government's January 2009 last-ditch attempt to stop publication.

The single lesson which should be taken from this sorry saga is the need for openness. MPs and peers behaved the way they did because they thought they would get away with it. If every claim was published online, they would only claim what they think their voters would tolerate. The smarter MPs might even realize there is some political mileage in reducing their claims for legitimate items, like office and transport costs, so that their constituents think they are getting value for money. Transparency is the ultimate disinfectant and if MPs have to publish their claims in full we will never slip back into the expenses mire. The challenge now is to push the same level of openness and transparency on to other areas of the public sector, tackling abuses that cost billions rather than just millions.

The TaxPayers' Alliance has successfully used FoI legislation to discover the surprisingly high salaries being paid to tens of thousands of local authority executives and managers. Other campaigners have worked with FoI to expose waste and lavish expenses at the pampered and protected BBC. However, while there has been some success using FoI legislation in Britain, the big challenge ahead is the hugely profligate, viscerally corrupt and congenitally secretive European Union. Now that our European politicians and bureaucrats have seen the devastation wreaked on the British political class from campaigners' energetic application of FoI, they'll be pulling up the drawbridge and aggressively resisting any attempt by taxpayers to pry into what the euro-elite consider is their private business: how they spend, waste and steal our money. Moreover, while the FoI should allow us to find out how the government uses our money, there are hundreds of public bodies such as city academies, regional development bodies, the nationalized banks, quangos of all sorts and fake charities which are funded by the taxpayer but are exempt from FoI requests.[2] The FoI Act needs to be extended to these bodies if we are ever to see the much-promised but seldom-delivered transparency our leaders keep proclaiming.

While FoI is the most obvious way of prising power out of the tightly clenched fists of the ruling caste, there are other perhaps more forceful ways of making our largely unaccountable masters serve us rather than the other way round.

Killing me softly – corporate manslaughter laws

At Maidstone and Tunbridge Wells NHS Trust in 2005–6 two outbreaks of Clostridium difficile killed at least 90 patients and infected another 1,100 because of what one of the many NHS regulators, the Healthcare Commission, called 'significant failings' in care including a lack of isolation units, beds being squeezed too close together, unwashed bedpans and some patients with diarrhoea being told by nurses to 'go in their beds'. An additional 255 patients died with the infection, though the trust claimed this was not the main cause of death. At the time, the trust reported that it was compliant with national government standards for hygiene and infection. Speaking about this disaster, the chief executive of the Healthcare Commission said that the lack of infection control at the trust had been 'unacceptable', that 'what happened to the patients at this trust was a tragedy' and that NHS needed to ensure 'that the same mistakes are never made again'.[3]

Spool forward about a year and move north to the Mid Staffordshire NHS Trust. In one of the greatest scandals in the history of the NHS, between 400 and 1,200 patients died unnecessarily between 2005 and 2008 in what the then Health Secretary Alan Johnson called 'a totally unacceptable failure to treat emergency patients safely' and 'a complete failure of management to address serious problems and monitor performance'.[4]

While the government, Monitor (the NHS trust regulator which awarded the trust the coveted foundation status which netted the trust's chief executive a huge pay rise in the middle of

the whole miserable affair) and the hospital's new management
puffed and posed and pretended to be doing their jobs, the families
of dead patients desperately campaigned to have the situation at
the hospital improved. Months after all the head honchos had
briefed the press on the many important 'lessons that had been
learnt' and changes that were now being made, families bereaved
by the trust's negligence were still reporting widespread problems
at the hospital:

> We have continued to hear of more cases of neglect from
> some of the wards. What has changed is that we are hearing
> of cases much earlier with some people on the wards still
> suffering. This has helped because at least they are still alive
> and we can try to help. We have now found a new channel
> for complaints. Sadly though in most of the cases the
> damage has already been done and most haven't returned
> to their homes.[5]

These two appalling cases bring us to the Corporate Manslaughter
and Corporate Homicide Bill which received Royal Assent in July
2007 and became law in April 2008. Previous legislation around
corporate manslaughter was found to be difficult to use because
of the necessity to link gross negligence to one specific individual.
Under the new law an organization can be found guilty of
corporate manslaughter (corporate homicide in Scotland) if the
way in which its activities are managed or organized by its senior
management amounts to a gross breach of the duty of care it
owes to its employees, the public or other individuals and those
failings cause a person's death.

The slaughter at Maidstone and Tunbridge Wells NHS
Trust occurred before the corporate manslaughter law was
strengthened, although there are good grounds for supposing
that the chief executive and possibly other managers could have
been charged under the previous legislation. While the story was
front-page news the police claimed they were looking at whether

charges should be brought against the hospital's management. But as soon as the furore died down, we heard no more from our politically compliant police.

However, it seems much more likely that charges could and should have been brought against the chief executive and management team at the Mid Staffordshire NHS Trust using the new updated legislation. At the time, many police services were running an expensive advertising campaign about how they were listening to the public, so David Craig wrote to the chief constable at Staffordshire Police Headquarters asking him to open an investigation into allegations of corporate manslaughter by the Mid Staffordshire management team leading to the deaths of hundreds of patients following gross breaches of the duty of care owed to those patients exposed by the Healthcare Commission's recent report. Craig also reported the chief executive of the Mid Staffordshire NHS Trust, Martin Yeates, whom we discussed in Chapter 6, for 'continued and multiple serious breaches of duty of care leading to many people's deaths' which gave rise to the possibility that he could be 'guilty of the common law offence of gross negligence manslaughter'.[6] As part of his complaint Craig requested that the chief constable: 'Open up a Crime Number and start an investigation of both the Trust and of Mr Martin Yeates'.

Although the police are obliged to respond to such a request, David Craig hasn't even received an acknowledgement and nothing seems to have happened. However, in spite of the inaction in these two shocking cases by the regulators, the government, the police and the NHS, both the old and the new corporate manslaughter laws could have been used to send a message once and for all to NHS management that the self-serving, bureaucratic disregard for patients' safety that we see in some hospitals will no longer be tolerated. We can only hope that the next time a similar event happens in one of our hospitals, those whose lives are affected will have the time, money and courage to conduct a successful prosecution for corporate manslaughter as this will force NHS managers to finally understand that they are in their £150,000 plus a year jobs and get their huge pensions for serving their patients and not just themselves. Also, it may make our police realize that they are paid to protect ordinary people and not just their political and bureaucratic masters.

What about our rights? – Human rights legislation

A less drastic weapon than trying to bring a corporate manslaughter prosecution is to use human rights laws against the ruling caste. The Human Rights Act (HRA) 1998 received Royal Assent in November 1998 and mostly came into force in October 2000 – considerably faster than the four years that the FoI Act took. The Act makes it unlawful for any public body to act in a way which is incompatible with the European Convention on Human Rights (ECHR). Perhaps the most worrying thing about the HRA is that it gives rights without suggesting any corresponding responsibilities. For example, it confers the right to 'education and to have access to vocational and continuing training', but it doesn't dare propose that people have any responsibility for ensuring they and their children get the best education they can so they can contribute to society. We all have the 'freedom to choose an occupation and the right to engage in work', but, of course, there is no hint of the possibility that we have a duty to society to work rather than live off the taxes of those who can be bothered to get out of bed in the morning. And we all have the 'right to marry and found a family'. It is never proposed that when deciding how many children we want to produce we should think about whether we, rather than the state, can afford to support them and give them a good upbringing.

Like so many laws introduced by this government, it can seem as if the HRA has been mainly hijacked by the feckless, idle, greedy and criminal rather than serving the interests of the huge majority of the population. A serial killer tried to use the HRA when a prison governor refused him access to hardcore pornography. A schoolboy arsonist used it to get compensation when he was prevented from attending the school he tried to burn down and two men photographed by a speed camera claimed that admitting which of them was driving was an infringement of their human rights. More serious was the ruling by an immigration tribunal that nine Afghan hijackers escaping the Taliban could remain in Britain even after the Taliban had been pushed from power.

Perhaps the most controversial problem with the HRA is the potential danger posed to European citizens by their governments' inability to deport people believed to pose a threat to European citizens. A European Court of Human Rights judgment stated that: 'Whenever substantial grounds have been shown for believing that an individual would face a real risk of being subjected to treatment that was inhuman or degrading, it is unlawful to remove him.' The court also ruled that: 'The activities of that individual, however undesirable or dangerous, could not be a material consideration.' This put the right to dignity of foreign nationals above the right to life of EU citizens. This issue was most clearly demonstrated in June 2005 when the European Commissioner for Human Rights visited London to express his view to the British government that new anti-terror legislation risked breaching the HRA. A month after the commissioner had scuttled back to the well-paid safety of his Brussels office, there was a synchronized series of suicide bombings in London killing 52 people and injuring about 700 others.

The people who seem to have done best out of human rights law are of course lawyers, especially the Matrix group where former prime minister Tony Blair's wife Cherie Booth has worked. Matrix claim that: 'Human rights law occupies a central position in the collective expertise offered by Matrix', and seem proud to be 'the strongest human rights practice in the country'.[7] Moreover, these lawyers appear to be looking towards a rosy, well-rewarded future when writing about the coming business opportunities for their human rights practice: 'The promise of the new legislation has been increasingly borne out in a wide range of areas of domestic legal practice – in criminal justice and the regulatory process, in public law, in commercial and employment law.' In fact, Matrix lists no fewer than 11 major areas of law to show how human rights legislation will affect (lucratively for the lawyers) almost every aspect of Britain's legal system.

Thankfully, ordinary people are beginning to realize that the HRA can be used by those who want to obey the law rather than just those who are intent either on breaking it or getting rich from practising it. In 2008, a judge ruled that families of soldiers killed in war zones because of faulty equipment could sue the Ministry of Defence under Article 2 of the ECHR which safeguards the right to life. And now the mother of a soldier killed in Afghanistan has won the right to force the government to review the use of 'snatch' Land Rovers which are particularly vulnerable to roadside bombs. But this is just scratching the surface of the potential of the HRA to protect us against the mismanagement of politicians and bureaucrats. Any relative of someone who has died unnecessarily in hospital, for example from a hospital-acquired infection, should be considering suing the hospital and NHS for breaching the deceased's right to life. Similarly, any relative of someone murdered by a known criminal or following a failure of policing or the probation service in their area should investigate taking the police or probation service to court for breaching Article 2. Moreover, anyone who is the victim of a crime should look at possibly suing our police for failing under Article 1 – our right to dignity.

Another possibly productive human right is covered in Article 41 of the ECHR. This gives us the Right to Good Administration: 'Every person has the right to have his or her affairs handled impartially, fairly and within a reasonable time by the institutions, bodies, offices and agencies of the Union.' Moreover, 'Every person has the right to have the Union make good any damage caused by its institutions or by its servants in the performance of their duties.' With the EU's wasteful and corrupt spending of our money having been repeatedly criticized by the auditors who have now refused to sign off the EU's accounts for 14 years, there seems to be the potential for a member country or a group of citizens to take the European Commission to the European Court of Human Rights for breaching our right to good administration and for not solving the problem 'within a reasonable time'. At the moment it's not clear whether the British Parliament would be included under the need for EU institutions to provide good administration. Perhaps after the Lisbon Treaty is forced through, it could be argued that Parliament is an agency of the EU and therefore the theft of our money by our MPs is also a breach of our right to good administration. Perhaps the squandering of billions of pounds on the NHS computer system and many other hopelessly-managed government projects are also a breach of taxpayers' right to good administration.

With a bit of creative thinking, somewhere in the ECHR's 54 verbose articles many people will find some reason why their leaders are possibly breaching their human rights – and when they find it, they should attack with all guns blazing. In fact, the ECHR is a goldmine of opportunities for ordinary people to fight back against the incompetence, mismanagement, profligacy and avarice of our ruling elites. Readers should try testing their rights – for example Article 42 concerns the Right of Access to Documents: 'Any citizens of the Union, and any natural or legal person residing or having its registered office in a Member State, has a right of access to documents of the institutions, bodies, offices, offices and agencies of the Union whatever their medium.' So why not email Robert Galvin, auditor of the European Parliament at robert.galvin@europarl.europa.eu and ask for a copy of Internal Audit Report no. 06/02 about how our MEPs have been stealing much of the €204,000 a year they each get to pay for assistants and request the names of the MEPs whose theft of our money was investigated by Robert Galvin's team? You can point out that failure to provide this report and the names of those implicated would be a breach of your human rights and you could threaten to take Mr Galvin to the European Court of Human Rights if he fails to provide access to the information you have requested.

Bring the bankers to book – prosecuting financiers

In one of his many perceptive articles, Professor Prem Sikka explained the possibilities for taking action against some of the bankers whose excesses have lost taxpayers so many billions as well as leading to hundreds of thousands of people losing their jobs and homes. To quote Professor Sikka:

> Section 171 of the Companies Act 2006 states that a director must act in good faith, promote the success of the company for the benefit of its members [shareholders] as a whole and in doing so have regard (among other matters) to '(a) the likely consequences of any decision in the long term, (b) the interests of the company's employees, (c) the need to foster the company's business relationships with suppliers, customers and others, (d) the impact of the company's operations on the community and the environment, (e) the desirability of the company maintaining a reputation for high standards of business conduct, and (f) the need to act fairly as between members of the company'.[8]

Professor Sikka pointed out that: 'Lawyers could use this law to argue that directors have been negligent and harmed the interests' of shareholders. However, according to British law, directors do not owe a 'duty of care' to any individual shareholder, employee, depositor or any other stakeholder. Shareholders may bring class actions to sue directors for negligence, but the law does not empower employees, pension scheme members or depositors to do the same. As for auditors, they only owe a duty of care to the company, as a legal person. So they cannot be sued by any of a company's stakeholders however incompetent and self-serving their work. As we saw with RBS, not only was no action taken against auditors Deloittes, but they were actually reappointed as auditors after the bank crashed, taking tens of billions of pounds of our money with it.

Many of our unit trusts and pension funds were significant shareholders in banks like RBS, Lloyds TSB, Northern Rock, HBOS and Bradford & Bingley. Yet none seem to have shown any appetite for taking legal action against the banks and their well-rewarded executives. Moreover, the Bank of England, the Treasury and even the ever supine FSA should be considering launching civil lawsuits against such characters as Adam Applegarth, Sir Fred Goodwin, Sir Tom McKillop, Andy Hornby, Lord Stevenson, Peter Cummings, Sir James Crosby and many others for negligence, breach of fiduciary duty or violation of investment regulations by publishing potentially misleading information about the financial condition of the banks over which they presided. Even though some charges might be difficult to prove, faced by years of potentially ruinous litigation, many of our great financiers might be prepared to settle out of court. Given the vast wealth that these people have accumulated over the years, this action could rake in tens of millions for taxpayers and send a message to other people that the public, through their representatives, will not tolerate the kinds of behaviour that we have seen over the last few years.

Predictably but disappointingly, the politicians and the bureaucrats who are paid so generously by us seem unwilling to turn on their friends in banking. Once again this inaction might reinforce many people's impression that the political/ bureaucratic/banking triumvirate is admirably united in its determination to guard its own privileges while showing nothing but utter contempt for those whose interests it should be representing.

Taking the law into our own hands – private prosecutions

Repeatedly, we have seen that our masters shy away from taking any legal action against any members of their own charmed circle. There always seem to be excellent excuses why our corrupt politicians, negligent public-sector bosses and dishonest bankers are seldom properly investigated and almost never prosecuted for their misdeeds while ordinary members of the public are groaning under the weight of the thousands of new laws introduced by this government.

One remedy open to members of the public is to launch private prosecutions against individual public-sector employees – politicians, civil servants, hospital managers, local council bosses, police chiefs and so on. Unfortunately, this can be a risky and expensive course of action. However, the advantage is that the burden of proof in a private prosecution is lower than in a criminal trial. Perhaps wealthy philanthropists thinking of giving money to our politicians would achieve much more by helping individuals bring private prosecutions against corrupt politicians and incompetent public-sector managers. Just a couple of successful cases would make our masters realize that they are actually paid to be our servants and thus force a revolution in the way the ruling caste behaves.

Some taxpayers are less equal than others – discrimination laws

Then we have our discrimination laws. These are less potent than some other ways of protecting ourselves against our masters, but are still worth considering.

In October 2007, the new Equality and Human Rights Commission (EHRC) took over from three previous quangos: the Commission for Racial Equality, the Disability Rights Commission and the Equal Opportunities Commission. We contacted the EHRC to ask just two simple questions – what its annual budget was and how many employees it had. Although it is a taxpayer-funded public body, it refused to give us the information and told us that we would have to submit a Freedom of Information request. We did so and consequently learnt that the EHRC costs us an incredible £60 million a year and employs 482 people excluding agency and seconded staff.

The role of this organization for which we pay so much and which is meant to represent us is: 'To protect, enforce and promote equality across the seven "protected" grounds – age, disability, gender, race, religion and belief, sexual orientation and gender reassignment' and its aim is to 'build a fairer Britain'.[9] Most of us only hear about the EHRC's work when the media reports cases which might seem ludicrously trivial or look like they have been brought by feckless chancers eager to get some easy cash or to appear on TV as victims of 'appalling persecution'. We've had schoolgirls refusing to obey their school's dress code against no jewellery by claiming they were wearing important religious symbols. After wasting many thousands of pounds of taxpayers' money on her legal challenge to her school's dress code, one described her extraordinary sacrifice and suffering to protect the freedoms that most of us probably didn't realize were threatened by her particular school's dress code: 'I am so happy to know that no one will ever have to go through what me and my family have gone through.'

A Muslim catering manager claimed he was being discriminated against when he refused to cook sausages and bacon: 'The reason for this refusal is because of the fact it is well known that if you are cooking bacon or sausages which I was asked to do, I was exposed to splash and contact with pork which I object to.' One might think that it is the job of a catering manager to provide the food customers want: if his personal beliefs prevent this, he should go and get a different job.

Perhaps because of the disrepute such cases risk causing to our discrimination laws, their potential to protect the interests of more responsible members of our society are often overlooked. However, discrimination laws can be useful weapons as they're strongly biased in favour of the person bringing the claim because they have overturned the basic principle of British law that a person is innocent until proved guilty and have replaced this with a situation where a person or organization accused of discrimination must prove their innocence. As one website advising people how to bring claims for discrimination explained: 'If the facts from which discrimination could be inferred have been proved, it is for the respondent to show that s/he did not discriminate.'[10]

There are many areas where an enterprising taxpayer could use discrimination laws to put a spoke in the wheels of our lumbering and increasingly oppressive state. For example, if you're waiting for a council house and a family of immigrants is placed ahead of you in the queue, you could claim that you are being discriminated against for being British. You could do likewise if your children miss out on a school place because travellers' children are given priority. All the government's 'positive discrimination' policies such as giving travellers priority at doctors' surgeries and hospitals and promoting women and ethnic minorities in the public sector are potentially discriminatory. If you complain against any of these, then it's up to the government to prove that it has not discriminated against you, rather than you having to prove you have been discriminated against.

If a person hasn't got a serious complaint about discrimination, they could just have some fun by drowning the costly bureaucrats at the EHRC in pointless investigations to show up that they waste many millions on political correctness gone mad. After all, isn't there a risk that companies like Club 18-30, Saga and Sheila's Wheels are discriminatory? Club 18-30: 'We know about 18 to 30 year olds. Over 80,000 of them spend the most important weeks of their year with us. We know what's hot. We know what's not. And we know that it could all change again tomorrow. We have long been the voice of this generation.' Couldn't this be seen to be discriminating against miserable grumpy old people who have long since forgotten what it was like to be young?[11] Saga 'offer a wide range of options to the over 50's, from Car and Home Insurance to World Cruises and Package Holidays'. Isn't that also age discrimination?[12] And Sheila's Wheels' 'Cheaper car insurance, home insurance, travel insurance and pet insurance online for women' – isn't that blatant gender discrimination against men, not to mention an appalling example of the worst kind of insensitive transgender discrimination against those whose exact sex is not immutable?[13]

But this is just a start; imaginative members of the public could easily have the laughable EHRC chasing its own tail for many happy years to come by deluging it with completely valid but evidently ridiculous complaints.

DEFENDING DEMOCRACY

The post-democratic age

While making entertaining reading, the MPs' expenses scandal was just a symptom of a deeper malaise. Our democracy is probably in terminal decline because most of Parliament's power has been handed over to the EU, quangos and other unaccountable administrative bodies. Some people have referred to this as the 'post-democratic age', the idea being that power has been taken away from the ignorant masses and given to a small enlightened administrative elite in Brussels and London. Now that they have almost unlimited power over us, our politicians, bureaucrats and bankers no longer care what we think or what we want. However, we have seen the result of this – massive greed, widespread corruption, monumental waste and financial collapse leading to impoverishment of the majority and enrichment of the small inner circle of politicians, bureaucrats and bankers.

Voters have understood that in this glorious new post-democratic, bureaucratic age, their votes don't count for much and so ever fewer of us are bothering to vote. Politicians have repeatedly accused us of apathy, but will never admit that people are giving up on electoral politics because they can see it doesn't matter who they vote for as nothing much ever changes. Voters in most constituencies are wasting their time going out to vote. Of the 646 seats in the House of Commons, about 405 are 'safe' seats and will always be won by the party which has held them for years. MPs in these safe seats can pretty much do whatever they want as they can hardly lose their jobs. This leaves just 241 constituencies where individual voters can actually influence the result. But even here, the electoral swing has to be pretty large to worry most of these MPs. Furthermore, the first-past-the-post system ensures that it is virtually impossible for an independent candidate to unseat an incumbent from one of the main three political parties. Moreover, in Brussels, most of our laws are now made by 27 unelected European commissioners, supported by over 45,000 unelected bureaucrats and 100,000 unelected part-time advisers. As for the European Parliament, in spite of the huge amounts of money its members pocket, it actually has very little power to change what the commissioners decide and can only make small amendments to about half of the legislation brought in by the commissioners supported by their huge empires of bureaucrats.

Is this the death of democracy?

Various proposals have been suggested over the years for trying to breathe some life back into our dying democracy. One is proportional representation (PR). The advantage of PR is that it means the proportion of MPs from each party in the Commons will represent the proportion of the vote received by each party. However, as the lists of candidates for each party and their positions on each party's lists are chosen by a few party insiders, there would no longer be any real link between the MP and the constituency.

There are other ideas aimed at strengthening the relation between MPs and their constituents so that MPs become more answerable for their behaviour. These include having 'primaries' where local people rather than a few party stalwarts choose the candidate. It has also been suggested that constituents should have the power of 'recall' whereby 25 per cent of voters in a constituency could demand a new election if their MP had behaved in a particularly reprehensible manner. This system might have avoided Derek Conway's constituents having to put up with him representing them and continuing to fill his own pockets with our money for two years after he was disgraced and lost his party's whip. But while these ideas are worthy, they will do little to breathe new life into our democratic processes and they are unlikely to be adopted by a political and bureaucratic establishment whose power could be threatened by them.

It can sometimes seem as if the democratic political process has now passed the point of no return. So the only way we can defend the rights and interests of the majority against the greed, arrogance, waste and incompetence of the small ruling elite of politicians, bureaucrats and bankers is by active campaigning and using their laws against them. It will be interesting to see whether we can ever successfully fight back to defend our interests against the rapacious, self-serving, new ruling caste.

NOTES TO CHAPTERS

CHAPTER 1: WHERE HAS OUR £3 TRILLION GONE?

1. *The Times*, *New York Times* and *Guardian*, 11 May 2007
2. This extra £150 billion includes things like off-balance-sheet PFI costs, Network Rail's debts (£22.3bn) and the costs of nuclear decommissioning
3. Gordon Brown budget speech, April 2007
4. Speech to the World Bank Joint Annual Discussion, September 1997
5. www.burningourmoney.blogspot.com, April 2009
6. *Madoff Corruption, Deceit and the Making of the World's Most Notorious Ponzi Scheme* by Peter Sander (Lyons Press, 2009)
7. *David Copperfield* by Charles Dickens
8. Gordon Brown's New Year message, 30 December 2007
9. Sky News, 15 April 2008

CHAPTER 2: MONEY MAKES THE WORLD GO ROUND

1. *Turner Review*, March 2009
2. Ibid
3. Moody's website, June 2009
4. Standard and Poor's website, June 2009

CHAPTER 3: SAVING OUR SAVINGS

1. *Sunday Times*, 15 February 2009
2. UBS Global Asset Management and Datastream
3. *Sunday Times*, 8 February 2009, and www.housepricecrash.co.uk/newsblog/2009/05/blog-history-says-fill-your-boots-sell-your-wife-dive-in-23293.php
4. *Challenge to Judgement* by Paul Samuelson, 1974, and *The Loser's Game* by Charles Ellis, 1975
5. *Sunday Times*, 8 February 2009
6. *Sunday Times*, 29 March 2009
7. *Sunday Times*, 15 February 2009
8. *Sunday Times*, 8 March 2009
9. Ibid
10. *Sunday Times*, 3 May 2009
11. Based on a 2 per cent asset increase on the £5+ trillion balance sheets of British banks
12. BBC news, 4 June 2009
13. www.thisismoney.co.uk, 3 June 2009 and *Daily Mail*, 22 July 2009
14. Ibid

CHAPTER 4: PROTECTING OUR PENSIONS

1. *Pension Facts*, Pensions Policy Institute, June 2009
2. Pensions Minister Angela Eagle, quoted in the *Daily Mail*, 24 June 2009
3. *A Bankruptcy Foretold* by Nick Silver, IAE Discussion Paper No. 22, November 2008
4. *Daily Mail*, 24 June 2009
5. *The Times*, 3 June 2009
6. www.thisismoney.co.uk, 11 October 2007
7. Pension Review Associates website, June 2009
8. BBC news, 14 April 2008
9. Ibid
10. 'A long-term perspective on pension fund investment', UBS Pension Fund Indicators 2009
11. Ibid

12. *Money Management* magazine, March 2009

13. *Cityboy* by Geraint Anderson (Headline, 2008)

14. *Pension Facts*, Pension Policy Institute, June 2009

CHAPTER 5: SELF-SERVICE IN PUBLIC SERVICE

1. Public and Commercial Services website, June 2009

2. *Paying for the Credit Crunch*, William Norton (The TaxPayers' Alliance)

3. www.fda.org.uk, June 2009

4. *Guardian*, 15 January 2009

5. Economic Research Council Quango database

6. *Community, Opportunity, Prosperity: Annual Report 2008*, Department for Communities and Local Government

7. *Plundering the Public Sector*, David Craig with Richard Brooks (Constable, 2006), pp. 84–5

8. *Guardian*, 15 January 2009

9. *Defence Management Journal*, 22 May 2009

10. *The Efficiency Programme: A second review of progress*, Public Accounts Committee HC 349

11. Ibid

12. PCS website, June 2009

13. BBC news, 24 April 2009

14. Review Board on Senior Salaries report 2009

15. *Public Sector Rich List*, TaxPayers' Alliance, November 2008

16. Ibid

17. *Financial Times*, 17 April 2009

18. BBC news, 20 May 2009

19. Ibid

20. *Public Sector Rich List*, TaxPayers' Alliance, November 2008

21. Based on a salary rise of £50,000 to £100,000, retirement at 60 and not paying the Lifetime Earnings Limit tax which private-sector workers have to pay

22. Mark Thompson's speech to the Changing Media Summit, London, 2009

23. *Daily Mail*, 21 March 2008

24. *On-screen and on-air talent*, BBC Trust, May 2008

CHAPTER 6: THE WASTERS AND WRECKERS

1. European Health Consumer Index 2008
2. *Measuring the Health of Nations: Updating an Earlier Analysis*; *Health Affairs* by Ellen Nolte and C. Martin McKee, Jan–Feb 2008
3. *The Times*, 9 December 2007
4. Government website, www.communities.gov.uk, 30 June 2008
5. BBC news, 14 August 2008
6. *The Times*, 27 March 2009
7. *Wasting Lives*, TaxPayers' Alliance, 2009
8. Patient Safety Report, NHS website, 2007
9. *Daily Mail*, 19 March 2009
10. *Daily Telegraph*, 23 May 2009
11. BBC news, 26 September 2000, *Independent*, 14 April 2000, and www.number10.gov.uk/Page5399, 24 February 2004
12. www.direct.gov.uk, 10 March 2009
13. *Transformational Government Annual Report*, 2008
14. *The Gods that Failed* by Larry Elliott and Dan Atkinson (Vintage, 2009), p.179
15. *Transforming the Organization* by Kelly and Grouillart (McGraw-Hill, 1995)
16. *The Economist*, 6–12 May 1995
17. www.uk.capgemini.com/aspire/
18. *Public Sector Efficiency: an international comparison*, European Central Bank working paper 242

CHAPTER 7: THE TRIUMPH OF INCOMPETENCE

1. Public Accounts Committee: Uncorrected oral evidence Department of Justice C-Nomis system
2. *Public Sector Rich List*, TaxPayers' Alliance
3. *Plundering the Public Sector*, David Craig with Richard Brooks (Constable, 2006), pp. 183–226
4. *Department of Health: The National Programme for IT in the NHS*, Public Accounts Committee, March 2007

5. *Ministry of Defence Major Projects Report*, Public Accounts Committee, 2008

6. *The Times*, 21 July 2006

7. Ibid

8. *Independent*, 13 June 2006

9. *Independent*, 21 September 2007

10. TaxPayers' Alliance website, 13 May 2009

CHAPTER 8: THE TIMID AND THE TOOTHLESS

1. *Daily Mail*, 13 February 2009

2. www.24dash.com/news/Central-Government, 17 March 2009

3. *Daily Telegraph*, 19 June 2008

4. BBC news, 1 October 2007

5. *Sunday Times*, 31 May 2009

6. *Daily Mail*, 29 April 2009, and *Sunday Times*, 31 May 2009

7. *The Times*, 16 October 2008

8. Gordon Brown speech, 13 October 2008

9. *Independent*, 23 September 2008

10. *Independent*, 1 July 1999

11. *Seattle Times*, 22 May 2002

12. SEC Press release 2003–32

13. FINRA news release, 19 December 2005, and www.consumeraffairs.com, 15 March 2005

14. *Dividend Tax Abuse*, United States Senate, 11 September 2008

15. *The Times*, 22 January 2009

16. SEC Press release 2003–87

17. FSA Press release, 28 June 2005

18. SEC Press release 2008-290

19. *Dividend Tax Abuse*, United States Senate, 11 September 2008

20. *Guardian*, June 2009

21. *Financial Services Global Competitiveness Group Report*, p.8

22. Ibid, p.10

23. *Financial Times*, 7 May 2009

24. *Daily Mail*, 5 August 2009

CHAPTER 9: LOCAL MISGOVERNMENT

1. These figures are the most accurate that we could obtain. Some may just be salaries while others may include benefits, bonuses, profit share and possibly some expenses. However, they do give a reasonable indication of the amounts of our money council chiefs receive
2. *Daily Mail*, 6 April 2009
3. *Sunday Times*, 4 January 2009
4. Email from Leader of the Council Nigel Ashton
5. 'Thinking of Joining', Local Government Pension Scheme, May 2008
6. The full list can be found at www.taxpayersalliance.com/CSU2-pensions.pdf
7. Job ad for a 'Consultation and Community Engagement Officer' in Merton

CHAPTER 10: OUR PLUNDERING POLITICIANS

1. Speech at the Campaign for Freedom of Information's annual awards in March 1996
2. *Guardian*, 17 May 2008
3. *Daily Telegraph*, 'The Complete Expenses Files 2009'
4. Freedom of Information (Amendment) Bill debate, House of Commons, 7 February 2007
5. Ibid
6. Mark Fisher, 18 May 2007, Hansard column 918
7. David Winnick, 18 May 2007, Hansard column 939
8. Mark Fisher, 18 May 2007, Hansard column 924
9. BBC news, 18 May 2007
10. The full list of the 172 MPs who voted to block expenses reform can be found at www.guardian.co.uk/politics/2008/jul/04/houseofcommons1
11. Harry Cohen MP website, printed out on 5 July 2009
12. *Daily Telegraph*, 'The Complete Expenses Files 2009'
13. Ibid
14. BBC World Service interview, reported on www.labourlist.org
15. *Birmingham Mail*, 27 May 2009

16. www.timesonline.co.uk/tol/comment/columnists/guest_contributors/
    article6374856.ece

17. *Daily Mail*, 17 May 2009

18. *Daily Telegraph*, 'The Complete Expenses Files 2009'

19. Ibid

20. *Daily Telegraph*, 2 June 2008

21. *The Times*, 21 January 2009

22. *Guardian*, 21 January 2009

23. Ibid

24. *Metro*, 12 May 2009

25. *Daily Mail*, 31 May 2009

26. *The Times*, 11 June 2009

27. www.youtube.com/watch?v=y6xO4xEebNU

28. www.labour.org.uk/we_will_uphold_the_highest_standards_of_integrity_
    gordon_brown

CHAPTER 11:   SNOUTS IN THE TROUGH

1. *Daily Mail*, 14 February 2009

2. *Daily Mail*, 8 February 2009

3. *Daily Mail*, 14 February 2009

4. *Daily Mail*, 8 February 2009

5. *The Green Book* guide to MPs' expenses claims

6. *Daily Mail*, 22 March 2009

7. Ibid

8. The maximum claimable from 1 April 2009 under the Personal Additional
   Accommodation Expenditure category www.parliament.uk/documents/
   upload/M05.pdf+mp+resettlement+allowance+2009&hl=en

9. In 2007 the Liberal Democrats estimated that the government spent only
   £16 million of a necessary £50 million in preceding year to upgrade army
   accommodation, branding it a 'national disgrace'

10. For further details, see www.commonsleader.gov.uk/files/pdf/House%20
    of%20Commons%20Calendar%200809.pdf

11. The *Mail on Sunday* investigated this story, 27 May 2007

12. One senior accountant publicly queried this, explaining how HMRC doesn't accept voluntary contributions and may simply return her cheque. Brian Fieldman, *Daily Telegraph*, 28 May 2009

13. *Daily Telegraph*, 30 May 2009

14. A video of the stunt is set to the theme music of the BBC 'Groundforce' series and is available on YouTube

15. For further discussion of this point, 'Moats, Mortgages and Mayhem', BBC R4, 28 June 2009

16. For a more detailed account of the background to the case, see www. telegraph.co.uk/news/newstopics/mps-expenses/5340349/Ben-Chapman-overclaimed-15000-on-mortgage-MPs-expenses.html

17. *Daily Mail*, 10 May 2009

18. Some other criticisms are given in the 'Analysis' column of the *Daily Mail*, 31 March 2009

19. Further details of these investigations and the circumstances leading to Elizabeth Filkin leaving her post can be found in Peter Oborne's book, *The Triumph of the Political Class* (Simon & Schuster, 2007)

20. *Sunday Times*, 25 January 2009

21. *Evening Standard*, 30 January 2009

22. *Sunday Times*, 31 May 2009

23. Ibid

24. Ibid

25. *Guardian*, 9 May 2009

26. Ibid

CHAPTER 12: THE BANK ROBBERS

1. Article by Gordon Brown in *The Times*, 18 February 2009

2. *Daily Mail*, 16 February 2009

3. Ibid

4. *Daily Telegraph*, 18 February 2009

5. *Independent on Sunday*, 15 February 2009

6. *The Times*, 22 June 2009

7. *Independent on Sunday*, 15 February 2009

8. *Daily Mail*, 13 February 2009
9. *Daily Mail*, 16 January 2009
10. Professor Miles Robbins, writing in *Compass* magazine
11. Speech by Hector Sants, chief executive of the FSA, Reuters Newsmakers event, 12 March 2009
12. blogs.thisismoney.co.uk, 13 March 2009
13. FSA statement re: HBOS, 11 February 2009
14. *The Times*, 20 January 2009
15. Professor Miles Robbins, writing in *Compass* magazine
16. 'CNN Money', 9 December 2008
17. *New York Daily News*, 22 January 2009
18. *RBS Group Annual Report and Accounts 2007*
19. Ibid
20. Ibid
21. RBS first quarter 2009 results update
22. HBOS Annual Results 2007 press release
23. *Observer*, 29 June 2008
24. *The Times*, 14 February 2009
25. *Evening Standard*, 17 February 2009
26. *Sunday Times*, 8 March 2009
27. *Lloyds TSB Annual Report and Accounts 2007*, 21 February 2008
28. *Daily Mail*, 16 February 2009
29. Ibid
30. *Guardian*, 14 December 2008
31. *Guardian*, 30 September 2007
32. *Sunday Times*, 25 January 2009
33. *Accountancy Age*, 1 October 2007
34. *Accountancy Age*, 10 March 2009
35. *Banking Crisis: reforming corporate governance and pay in the City*, Treasury Select Committee, September 2008

CHAPTER 13: A PRODUCTIVE PUBLIC SECTOR?

1. Gordon Brown, Budget Speech, 1998
2. *Public sector productivity – Education* and *Public sector productivity – Health*, Office for National Statistics 2005 and 2006
3. *Public spending in the 20th century: a global perspective* by V. Tanzi and L. Schuknecht (Cambridge University Press, 2000)
4. *It's your money. A new plan for disciplined spending in government*, Conservative Party publication, 2009
5. Conference for IT systems suppliers. Contact authors for more details

CHAPTER 14: POWER TO THE PEOPLE

1. Gordon Brown's first speech as Prime Minister to the Labour Party conference, Bournemouth 2007
2. www.fakecharities.org
3. *Daily Telegraph*, 11 October 2007
4. www.dash24.com, 17 March 2009
5. Email from Cure the NHS campaign group, June 2009
6. Excerpt from David Craig's letter of 31 March 2009
7. Matrix website, July 2009
8. *Guardian*, 25 October 2008
9. EHRC website, July 2009
10. www.yourrights.org.uk, July 2009
11. Club 18–30 website, July 2009
12. Googling Saga, July 2009
13. Sheila's Wheels website, July 2009